The Politics of Race and Ethnicity in the United States

The Politics of Race and Ethnicity in the United States

Americanization, De-Americanization, and Racialized Ethnic Groups

Sherrow O. Pinder

palgrave
macmillan

GN
560
.U6
P56
2010

First published in 2010 by PALGRAVE MACMILLAN® in the United
States—a division of St. Martin's Press LLC, 175 Fifth Avenue, New York,
NY 10010.

Where this book is distributed in the UK, Europe, and the rest of the
world, this is by Palgrave Macmillan, a division of Macmillan Publishers
Limited, registered in England, company number 785998, of Houndmills,
Basingstoke, Hampshire RG21 6XS.

Palgrave Macmillan is the global academic imprint of the above companies
and has companies and representatives throughout the world.

Palgrave® and Macmillan® are registered trademarks in the United States,
the United Kingdom, Europe and other countries.

ISBN: 978-0-230-61356-0

Library of Congress Cataloging-in-Publication Data

Pinder, Sherrow O.
   The politics of race and ethnicity in the United States : Americanization,
de-Americanization, and racialized ethnic groups / Sherrow O. Pinder.
      p. cm.
   Includes bibliographical references.
   ISBN 978-0-230-61356-0 (alk. paper)
   1. Ethnicity—United States. 2. Ethnic groups—United States. 3.
Whites—Race identity—United States. 4. Multiculturalism—United States.
5. United States—Ethnic relations. I. Title.

GN560.U6P56 2010
305.800973—dc22   2009035111

A catalogue record of the book is available from the British Library.

Design by Scribe Inc.

First edition: April 2010

10 9 8 7 6 5 4 3 2 1

Printed in the United States of America.

For Amber Chambers
And Anthony and Alyssa Greaves

With Love

Contents

Acknowledgments

The idea for this book grew out of a class that I teach on race and ethnicity at California State University, Chico. Based on this, I submitted a proposal on race and ethnicity at the Midwest Political Science Association annual meeting and presented the paper there in April 2007. After a meeting with Anthony Wahl, who was then a senior editor with Palgrave Macmillan, about expanding my paper into a book, I started to think seriously about America's cultural identity and the question of where and how racialized ethnic groups fit into such an identity. In this respect, I would like to sincerely thank Anthony Wahl for supporting my book project.

At California State University, Chico, I was given a course release to work on my book, for which I was very appreciative to have received. While I had initially started to think about what I would write in my book during this time, it was not until my time spent during the summer of 2008 at the W. E. B. Du Bois Institute for African and African American Research, at Harvard University, that I truly started to focus on and solidify my ideas for this book. I learned a great deal about blacks' endless struggles in the United States for racial equality. In this respect, I would like to thank my colleague, Robert Stanley in the Department of Political Science at California State University, Chico, for his support.

Also, I would like to thank the National Endowment for the Humanities for their financial support. I also benefited enormously from my participation in the Multiculturalism and Beyond Conference at Bielefeld University, Germany, in 2009 and the Re-orienting Whiteness Conference at the University of Melbourne, Australia, in 2008. Thanks to my colleagues at the conferences for all their feedback on my papers. I would particularly like to thank Demetrius L. Eudell in the Department of History and the Center for African American Studies, Wesleyan University; Juergen Heinricks, Department of Art History, Seton Hall University; and Mariangela Orabona, University of Naples, Naples Italy.

I am especially grateful to my friend and colleague, Cynthia Bynoe, for reading and commenting on the book proposal and the first draft of the book. I particularly wish to thank my dear friend Nadia Louar, who teaches in the French and Francophone Department at the University of Wisconsin,

Oshkosh, for reading, rereading, and editing the first draft of my book. Her constant feedback kept me grounded and focused. My thanks, in addition, to the artist Carrie Mae Weems for allowing me to use her work for my book cover. For this, I am truly delighted.

During the time I was working on this book, I was motivated by the love and support of my family and friends. I would like to thank my sisters Allison Greaves, Pauline Matthews, and Lorna Pinder-Jackson and my uncle Bruce Wendell Richmond. Also, I would like to thank my nephews Anthony, Cory, Jordan, Loxley, and Kirk Matthews who kept me sane with his goodwill and humor and my nieces Amber and Alyssa. My warm thanks to my friends George Joseph, James-Henry Holland, and Thelma Pinto of Hobart and William Smith Colleges; Teresa Cotner who teaches in the Art Department at California State University, Chico; Jim Cotner, a graduate student in the MFA program at California State University, Los Angeles; Kevin Johnson and Jennifer Asenas, the Department of Communication at California State University, Long Beach; Monica Ciobanu, the Department of Sociology, State University of New York, Plattsburgh; my friends in Canada, the Landaus—Ariel, Daniel, Enoch, Remy, and Sophie for their steadfast love; and Sheryl Thompson and Michele Ball. Last but not least, I would like to thank Claire Martin, Nancy Shealy, and Elena Tzelepis for their love and support for which I am incessantly grateful.

In the white man's world the [person] of color encounters difficulties in the development of his [or her] bodily schema.

—Frantz Fanon, *Black Skin White Masks*

The history of American [colored] is the history of this strife.

—W. E. B. Du Bois, *The Souls of Black Folk*

Introduction

The Brevity of the Argument

From the very beginning of America's formation, there has been a witting attempt to forge a single American cultural identity in spite of the presence of culturally and physically diverse groups of people in America.[1] First Nations[2] were already in America before the arrival of Europeans; blacks were, by force, transported to America; Chinese came during the gold rush; Mexicans were, in the beginning, enclosed by America's expanding border.[3] Racialized ethnic groups including First Nations, blacks, Chinese, and Mexicans, viewed as unlike whites, were looked on as racially and culturally inferior. Nonwhites' presumed inferiority served as a basis for their exclusion from an American cultural identity, which justified the discriminatory practices toward them. This I openly dub as the Americanization of America's cultural identity. Accordingly, the quest to construct a homogeneous American cultural identity was paramount.

Multiculturalism has been developed to recognize and celebrate America's cultural manyness (cultural heterogeneity), which conflicts with America's cultural oneness (cultural homogeneity). For the antimulticulturalists, multiculturalism represents a threat to America's cultural homogeneity. The presumed threat, I maintain, is another way to reclaim America's cultural identity as white. Even though nonwhites have been in America since the very beginning of America's founding, nonwhites are always viewed as foreigners, alien to America's cultural oneness/homogeneity. This is what I call the de-Americanization of racialized ethnic groups. What are some of the implications of de-Americanization for racialized ethnic groups and America's society as whole? Is multiculturalism as a racially charged strategy equipped to deal with the underlying consequences of the all-encompassing de-Americanization? What is at stake in the very discourse of multiculturalism seeking to recognize "otherness" and retain the normative thinking that "otherness" is celebrated as un-Americanness? Is multiculturalism contributing to de-Americanization? Is there a need to transcend multiculturalism and move in the direction of "postmulticulturalism"? In other words, can postmulticulturalism recognize "otherness" as Americanness? Even though there are no simple answers to these questions, they will serve as the foundation on which to frame the discussion that I present in this book.

The purpose of this book is to examine and analyze Americanization, de-Americanization, and racialized ethnic groups in America. More specifically, it will show the distinctive effectualness that Americanization and de-Americanization serve in harboring and maintaining the racial status quo where "whiteness" as fundamental to an American cultural identity is established and maintained. I take on a more practical investigation of Americanization and de-Americanization as I attempt to reconcile the reality that America's cultural identity based on the notion and persistent affirmation of whiteness has been instrumental in denying racialized ethnic groups their American identity. This has important consequences for nonwhites in America. At the heart of this study, who is an American becomes overriding. Although racialized ethnic groups remain unassimilated into America's cultural oneness, the celebration and recognition of cultural manyness in the face of an oppressive cultural oneness is an important element of multiculturalism. Yet multiculturalism is flawed because of its emphasis on the recognition of cultural "otherness" where "otherness" is looked on as un-Americanness. For this reason, there is a need to move beyond multiculturalism. Postmulticulturalism, then, would be the new possibility.

From the foregoing analysis, various indications of well-being—social status including cultural differences—are tied to the racialized bodies, bringing to the surface the substantial racial inequality that operates in the United States of America. "It is like a plague," to use the much cited words of the political activist and professor Angela Y. Davis. "It infects every joint, muscle, and tissue of social life in this country."[4] This is not to say that all racialized groups in America are monolithic or reductively compartmentalized. The range and complexity of gender distinctions, for example, are played out in different and important ways due to a dominating and belligerent masculine ethos. This is essential because, to borrow the words of Kalpana Seshadri-Crooks, an English professor, "everyday life regularly contests gender's 'essential' meanings."[5] Women, because of their embodied social status, are situated differently from men. The oppressive sex/gender system that is in place, in many ways, interacts with other systems of oppression including racism, classism, and homophobia to extensively make invisible and marginalize women of color. Women's experiences, to a great extent, are linguistically contained, socially constructed by relations of cultural ascendancy, and discursively mediated.[6] Their experience continues to be defined in accordance to the white hegemonic discourse that has made nonwhite groups inferior. Particularly exemplary in regard to nonwhites' position is the work of the postcolonial francophone scholar Frantz Fanon on racism and culture in the book *Towards the African Revolution*.[7] Fanon's work, which is by far one of the most rife and systematic attempts to reveal how power works within the paradigm of the colonized/oppressed and colonizer/oppressor dichotomy, is important for understanding the doctrine of "cultural hierarchy" and how this hierarchy is manifested in the United States. Cultural hierarchy is established so as to socially and culturally protect and privilege the very dominance of those in power.

In the United States, all major institutions are intended to support those who have habitually been in power, or the groups that are perceived to be dominant. It is no coincidence that the French philosopher Michel Foucault's notion that power is dispersed and it is everywhere is developed by feminist theorist and scholar Elizabeth Spelman. She indicates, with unmitigated certainty, that within the United States, every avenue of power is mostly in the hands of heterosexual, white males, a fact that is likely to prevail. For the first time in America, a black man, Barack Obama, has been elected to the highest position of power. Does having a black man as president disrupt the power structure that is already in place? In an attempt to answer this question, we need to understand fully how power works. I will come back to this topic in the course of this book but for now, the straightforward observation is that concession, as a marker of a civilized society, is necessary to keep the power structure in place. This is a good example of what Professor Louis F. Mirón calls the "moral exercise of power."[8] Nonetheless, in the United States, whites continue to disproportionately occupy positions of power.

Power produces certain forms of epistemology that are consequential, and it legitimizes and extends the interests of those served by the effects of such operative power.[9] In other words, power is despotic. It fastens the marginalized to the effigy of the inferiors, an image that imprisons and determines them, especially their social position in society. On the other hand, it can be generative, in the sense that the oppression experienced by marginalized groups can be transformed into unmitigated action. In order to appease the antagonized and maintain stability within the system, some concessions (i.e., antidiscrimination laws) as a set of stratagems are proposed, at least in theory, to appease these groups through visible representations.[10] Yet, as we understand from Foucault's theory of power, power must remain indeterminate since it is this indeterminacy that is the very state of its existence. Critical Race Studies, a new school of legal thought that developed within the auspices of African American Studies, uses a method that is especially helpful and effective in documenting the dynamics of such unrestrained and undeniable power.[11] The many ways in which crime, for example, is defined benefits those in power. It is not surprising, then, that a large percentage of men in prisons are blacks and Mexicans.

Because, for the most part, "power is somehow always invisible," in the sense of what the postcolonial theorist Homi K. Bhabha conceptualizes as "a tyranny of the transparent,"[12] the question, then, on how to relinquish power becomes a necessary one. Power cannot be separated from the complexity of power itself or the "polymorphous techniques of power," as Foucault puts it.[13] Foucault further tells us that "there are no relations of power without resistance."[14] Even though resistance to power is inevitable, and it does make a difference since it can reallocate the temperament of power, it is constantly regulated and policed. If Foucault is correct, then, according to the feminist philosopher Judith Butler, power must be understood "as forming the subject as well, as providing the very condition on its existence and the trajectory of its desire."[15] Power, then, is not merely what whiteness goes up against—in this case nonwhiteness—but also, in a real sense, it is what whiteness depends on for its daily maintenance and existence. Any resistance on the part of whiteness to power is in itself a cherished part of that power, because power is not "given up," it is just transformed into another form of domination. "Whiteness" is maintained and privileged greatly by institutionalized power. While there are different meanings of "whiteness" that are espoused by many whiteness scholars,[16] I am inclined in this discussion to analyze whiteness, as the anthropologist John Hartigan Jr. explains it, as a normalized, unmarked structural position maintaining white privilege and authorizing systematic power.[17]

Instead of privileging whiteness, the African American poet and historian Maya Angelou's important insight, as cited by political scientist Samuel P. Huntington, sees it "as evil threats to the well-being and real identities of people within their sub-national groups,"[18] because, for the most part, whiteness is internalized and is reproduced in conflicting ways between and within nonwhite groups. Professor Keith Osajima, drawing on Fanon's formulation of how the colonizers imposed their depreciating image of inferiority onto the colonized, explains it best when he writes, "The oppressed internalize an identity that mirrors or echoes the images put forth by the dominant group."[19] For this reason, many racialized groups have presented an unconcealed predilection toward whiteness and have expressed their ambivalence toward their "blackness," "First Nationness," "Chineseness," or "Mexicanness." Consequently, for the most part, they have alienated themselves from developing significant interaction with members of their own groups.[20] On the other hand, others endlessly have challenged the dominant representations through the use and practices of resistance in their everyday lives, which can become a site for agency. The Ghost Dance was employed by First Nations in their effort to uphold an oppositional culture. Also, blacks have developed a culture of resistance based on music and religion.[21]

In terms of histories, situatedness, and cultural distinctiveness, racialized ethnic groups are separate and distinctive from the dominant group. It is true that all racialized ethnic groups have faced and continue to undergo gross discrimination and hardships in America. First Nations, who were already present in America before the arrival of Europeans, were looked on as uncivilized and lacking in "culture" and religion by the European newcomers. Blacks who were imported from Africa were also looked on as "different." The fact that the inferior status of First Nations and blacks was already embedded in the Europeans' cultural psyches at the very beginning of America's existence as a nation is not without signification. Blacks' inferiority, which would later on become institutionalized through slavery and the Jim Crow South, is vastly important. It stood as the model for the harsh treatment of all other racialized groups in the United States.

The struggle of racialized groups to be incorporated into America's politics and political life was recognized through civil rights. This was the first step in a historical process whose present phase is the complex interchange of identity politics and multiculturalism.[22] Because identity categories are normative, they are exclusionary. Given a certain ineluctability and directionality of multiculturalism's locational dimensions—in the sense that it is directly situated in oppositional relations to Americanness or whiteness—the projection of the specificity of cultural otherness is appropriated and reappropriated, and is eventually alienated from cultural oneness or Americanness. While some individuals within their designated group identity deviate from regulatory group norms and form separate identities within these collective identities, the individuation from group authenticity, it is quite clear, can inevitably lead to "misrecognition." Yet the apparent conundrum is not a communitarian cultural and racial formation that unites a diasporic community of ethnocultural purity or authenticity—"blackness," "Chineseness," or "First Nationness," for example—it is the capacity of racialized ethnic groups in America to generate opposition to an oppressive and repressive status quo. Hence, I argue that the task of multiculturalism, which is to recognize and celebrate cultural differences, does not resolve assumptions about identities that are formulated from racialized differences, and thus it remains limited as a racially charged strategy equipped to deal with the underlying consequences of America's cultural identity as white. For the most part, the celebration of cultural differences is restricted to the private sphere, a point that I want to return to later. The Labor Day parade in New York City is an example of how the public sphere is transformed into a private sphere.

In an effort to emancipate multiculturalism from the racialist ontology from which it has evolved, then, a sound and realistic option to multiculturalism must first be guided by the recognition of multiculturalism's divorce from the long-standing and broader struggles for racial/cultural inclusiveness that had, to a large degree, produced it in the first place. Instead of the recognition and celebration of cultural "otherness" as the discursive condition for exchange and acknowledgment of the politicized subject position as "other," an important goal of multiculturalism must be to celebrate cultural inclusiveness. But first, the monocultural United States has to be transformed into a multicultural United States where the social and political institutions no longer identify with America's single cultural tradition that is based on whiteness.

This transformation, in part, would permit or require a new form of multiculturalism, one that does not buy into the racial script of America, where racialized groups, especially blacks, are the ones responsible for America's "race" problem. The sociologist Eduardo Bonilla-Silva understands this too well. He points out that "many whites insist that minorities (especially blacks) are responsible for [America's] racial problems."[23] Postmulticulturalism, then, is the new possibility. It is not a leaving behind the past, or an erasure of past and present aesthetic practices that maintain whiteness as the status quo. Postmulticulturalism will capture fully the vexed history of whiteness that self-evidently works incongruent to nonwhiteness and maintains an American cultural identity as white. Postmulticulturalism would embark on a racialized ethnic identity as an American identity that would permanently dislocate the association with "otherness" as un-Americanness. This undertaking, for good reasons, is, routinely, an entirely complicated one. The monocultural state would have to be transformed to a multicultural state. Also, whiteness would have to be denormalized in order for postmulticulturalism to be effective. Is "whiteness studies" a form of denormalizing whiteness? I will return to this question later.

The Extent and Organization of the Book

Chapter 1 conceptualizes the politics of Americanization, de-Americanization, and racialized ethnic groups in the United States. While in this discussion's contextual reflection, even though I have no training as a historian, a historical perspective is taken into consideration. And a sociopolitical approach is particularly helpful, that is, the need to reflect on Fanon's classic formulation of "cultural hierarchy," where the dominant culture as white, which remains unmarked and invisible, is fundamental. Any thoroughgoing and fundamental analysis, then, that is not structural or systemic and does not focus on the complex experiences of racialized groups in America by employing a racialized discourse runs the risk of being limited.

The intersectionality of gender, class, race, and ethnicity as a primary and organizing principle of America society, which locates and positions nonwhite women, is an important factor. Although difference is the very momentum of such categorization, at the same time, it intrinsically brings to the forefront the foundation of these identity categories, that is, race, class, gender, and ethnicity. Since these identity categories are homogenizing and universalizing, those who do not fit these categories would be "misrecognized." Because of the homogenization and universalization of women in terms of identity politics and the politics of recognition, intersectionality situates women of color differently from white women.[24] Its aim is not to set up a "series of equivalences between race, gender, and class"[25] or to privilege a particular facet of experience.

Nonwhite women's experiences cut across gender, race, ethnicity, class, age, sexuality, religion, and nationality lines, and these identity categories are experienced in rather complex ways. In fact, Spelman's "popbead metaphysics" is relevant here because women experience themselves in multiple fashions that are not detachable from one another.[26] At the same time, the interesectionality of race with other kinds of identities, such as ethnicity, gender, and/or sexuality, for example, is disadvantageous for nonwhite women. Race as an identity category, however, is not a unified and exclusionary category. A black, lesbian, single mother welfare recipient, living in the Bronx in New York City, for example, will, for the most part, experience race differently than will a heterosexual, black, male lawyer on Wall Street. Nonetheless, the saliency of race in determining one's position cannot be readily discarded.

Chapter 2 demonstrates how whiteness functioned as an ontologically nonaligned social category that advanced and promoted whiteness as the norm, raceless, and invisible. Looking back at America's history, racialized ethnic groups were considered to be racially inferior and were denied an American cultural identity, which justified the discriminatory practices toward nonwhites. Besides, nonwhites' inferiority, especially blacks', was codified into law in slavery and the Jim Crow South, which no doubt was one of the fiercest acts of racial discrimination. The treatment of blacks served as a template for the treatment of all racialized groups. Whiteness, even though it was a part of everyday discourse, eventually became institutionalized. It functioned as a rationale for whites to sharply distinguish themselves from all nonwhite groups. The "them" and "us" scenarios and their binary logic operated in conjunction with each other and created hallow, racial boundaries between the relational white self and the nonwhite "other." The self, nonetheless, can only be socially and intersubjectively constituted; it is implicit in the social and cultural context that gives it its meaning.

For racialized ethnic groups, racial inequality is compounded with ethnic inequality. It is for this precise reason that it is necessary to problematize and expose the binding constraints of the ethnicity paradigm where the emphasis is based entirely on an assimilation that means "becoming the same." As a matter of fact, the utilization of the European experience and its extension to nonwhites in America lay bare, indeed, "an American dilemma." In interrogating the compelling evidence that, unlike European whites, for whom assimilation is possible, for racialized ethnic groups—First Nations, blacks, Chinese, Mexicans,[27] and other racialized groups—assimilation is, for the most part, impossible, because these individuals are always viewed as non-Americans, and in many cases as *new immigrants*, a racially inflected term that characterizes the newcomers as belonging to an inferior culture. This characterization has been employed in everyday social relations shaping the very ways in which nonwhites are wittingly viewed in America.

Who is an American? This is the crucial question. A careful scrutiny of American identity confirms that American identity is based on whiteness. In fact, it has been complicit with the prevailing conditions of the domination of blacks and other nonwhite minority groups. It is not a secret from anyone that nonwhites are consistently denied an American identity. It officially started with the Naturalization Act of 1790, granting citizenship and incorporation into the body politic only to white men. Blacks, First Nations, other racialized groups, as well as women, were excluded from democratic citizenship and thus did not benefit from the evolution of modern civil society. Racial classification, an obvious and complex occurrence, has always functioned as an opprobrious device for the construction of an American identity as white. Chapter 3 examines how whiteness continues to shape and determine today an American cultural identity. It shows the clear interlink between whiteness and Americanness, and how it continues to discursively determine who is an American.

Given that multiculturalism has developed, shaped, and conditioned the binary cultural domination and marginalization, it apparently carries the inevitable marks of that oppression and subordination. Chapter 4 examines the pitfalls of multiculturalism. It demonstrates that the main task of multiculturalism is to celebrate cultural "otherness" instead of cultural oneness. Cultural "otherness" is viewed as un-Americanness, and it goes up against whiteness. Nonetheless, if one willingly ignores and disguises the various strata of its conceptual complexities, surely multiculturalism is one of the most significant political achievements in America in recent years. In fact, its emphasis on cultural recognition and differences is at the forefront of America's race and ethnic relations. The important point here is that the integration of racialized groups into America's political life has taken place without confronting the very basic structures of cultural domination and marginalization. Even though marginalized groups are struggling for inclusion and recognition by reclaiming their so-called blackness, Asianness, or Mexicanness, for example, it is in fact tempting to conclude that multiculturalism masks accountability for the problematic of whiteness as a structure that is solidly in place.

The emphasis on multiculturalism, with its emphasis on cultural pluralism, has been, for many observers, a threat to an American cultural identity. A clear reason for this unnecessary concern is that cultural pluralism has come to signify cultural "multiplicity in a unity," in the phrase of its official source, Horace Kallen, who wrote an article titled, "Democracy versus the Melting Pot: A Study of American Nationality," in 1915. This seeming threat to America's cultural identity, I argue, is another attempt to egregiously reclaim an American identity as white. Since whiteness must be contextualized in an analysis of power, domination and its specificity cannot go unnoticed.

It is necessary to rethink and reframe multiculturalism. Chapter 5 serves this purpose. It calls for another form of multiculturalism, post-multiculturalism, which is not a signal of sequentiality. Postmulticulturalism serves as an important backdrop for recontextualizing and analyzing the history of whiteness that works incongruent to nonwhiteness in order to address the exclusion of nonwhite people from America's cultural oneness (cultural homogeneity). Instead of celebrating cultural otherness as un-Americanness, as does the focus on multiculturalism, postmulticulturalism would embrace America's cultural manyness (cultural heterogeneity) as Americanness. It would open up a liberatory space to challenge America's cultural oneness and truly embrace America's cultural manyness. However, political theorist Wendy Brown's concern that "it is possible as well that this ostensible tool of emancipation carries its own techniques of subjugation—that it converges with unemancipatory tendencies in contemporary culture, establishes regulatory norms, coincides with the disciplinary power of ubiquitous confessional practices; in short, feeds the powers it meant to starve,"[28] raises important and unavoidable questions. Emancipation is, without a doubt, inextricably linked to liberation. In the end, in order for postmulticulturalism to be realized, two things have to take place. One, America's monocultural state has to be transformed into a multicultural state; two, whiteness has to be denormalized in order to produce a postwhite subject. Since the historical legacy of "otherness" binds all racialized groups in America, even though racial meanings are challenged both within and between groups, as a part of my preliminary conclusion, I think the first task at hand is for all racialized groups to be ready and willing to engage in discursive practices that would promote and celebrate cultural differences in the name of "respect," as opposed to "disrespect," as the direct indicator for the recent social crises among African Americans, Mexicans, and Koreans in California, especially in south-central Los Angeles, for example.[29] However, articles such as "Black vs. Brown: African Americans and Latinos," published in the *Atlantic Monthly*, in which Jack Miles contends that Latinos are taking jobs from African Americans, do not help.[30]

Even though some marginalized groups are driven by the willful intention to conceive of themselves as the "model minority," and imagine that they are "different" from the other marginalized groups, as Stuart Hall puts it, it is "the kind of difference that doesn't make a difference of any kind," especially when juxtapositioned against the majority.[31] Indeed, the discrimination that any racialized group experiences, for the most part, has direct consequences for the other racialized groups.[32] Accordingly, there is a need for a shared sense of purpose among racialized groups. The "model minority" espoused by those in power has to be recognized for what it is; it is a way of keeping racialized minorities tied to a false sense that they are accepted by the majority. Racialized groups, if they are willing to shed such colonized thinking, can open up a space for reflecting and thinking about what the postcolonial and feminist scholar Chandra Talpade Mohanty defines as the egalitarian "political community."[33] It will refocus and call into question the seemingly paradoxical liberal principles of equality, individual rights, privacy, and autonomy, which are positioned within relations of power that reinforce the interests of the most privileged. This is not to say that power remains static. By extracting from a Foucauldian conceptualization of power, we can clearly see that power of various types circulates throughout society and cannot be viewed as originating within a particular milieu.

Even though a fully inclusive cultural community is indeed impossible given that, as Chantal Mouffe reminds us, "there will always be a 'constitutive outside,' an exterior to the community that is the very condition of its existence."[34] Iris M. Young's concerns that the very term *community* relies on sameness "and on the desire for social wholeness and identification" is significant.[35] "Once it is accepted that there cannot be a "we" without a "them" and that all forms of consensus are of necessity based on acts of exclusion, the issue can no longer be the creation of a fully inclusive community where antagonism, division, and conflict will have disappeared."[36] Even so, it provides an analytic framework for the revisiting and recontextualizing of the relationship between the histories of racialized groups and how it gets played out in today's society.

The complicated history of racialized ethnic groups in America is, in many melancholic ways, about America's past and present, where nonwhites have been relegated to the margins of society because, for many ill-conceived reasons, they have been categorized as non-Americans and inferiors. This history is a pretty ominous and often daunting one. Can "we" undo this long, vexed history of substantial Americanization? Multiculturalism is a good starting point for the recognition of multiethnic identities, but it has to move beyond the politics of recognition and confront the all-encompassing dominance of whiteness if we are to choose a "politics of every day resistance"[37] in an effort to reprove racist, cultural formation, especially when such a formation becomes commonsensical. Whether America would meaningfully embrace nonwhites as Americans is not a pseudo-question but a familiar one that should concern all of us. Given the recent racist hysteria as an unwarranted response that nonwhite groups are threatening America's cultural identity, the nature of race relations in America is justifiably worrisome.

As an understandable opposition to the collective consequences of Americanization, de-Americanization, and their manifest impact on both racialized ethnic groups and the American society as a whole, in this book, I am faced with a rather sobering and inspiring task of critically elaborating such a rather complicated but necessary perception. It is only then, I hope, that we can accurately begin to explore the true meaning of a multicultural society. This book remains a privilege and safe space for these issues to be discussed and reflected on.

I

Conceptual Framework

In the context of my discussion, a historical perspective is taken into consideration and a sociopolitical understanding is necessary. However, I make use of Frantz Fanon's remarkable insight of "cultural hierarchy," which shows how the dominant group dictates the norms, values, and ethic of society to the masses. "The doctrine of cultural hierarchy," as Fanon puts it, "is thus but one aspect of a systematized hierarchization implacably pursued."[1] To a greater extent, it organizes and strengthens the configuration of the normal (dominant) and the abnormal (subordinate) cultural practice, which is then locked in immutable conflict and structurally irresolvable differences; the main one being racialized difference as a preapproved allegory for culture and its signification.[2]

Even though there is a need to transcend the dichotomy between normal and abnormal, good and evil, civilized and uncivilized, which has revitalized itself after 9/11, this very dichotomization of dominant and subordinate relations is at the point where ethnocentrism and its glaring desire to privilege the normal (dominant) over the abnormal (subordinate) continues its propagation and preservation. In post-9/11 America, ethnocentrism has been revamped and made shamelessly discernible. I am attempting here to explain and define ethnocentrism as the cultural practices and values that are viewed as natural and as a result are normalized. The fundamental process of normalization is explained accurately by John Caputo and Mark Yount in their article "Institutions, Normalization, and Power."

> Normalization does imposes homogeneity, but at the same time makes it possible to individualize, to measure gaps to differentiate according to the norm whose function it is to make differences intelligible as such. The norm has tolerances for a vast range of individuals, ample enough to promote diversity even as it constrains all deviations by its standard measures. Normalization keeps watch over the excessive and the exceptional, delimiting the outcasts who threaten the order of normalcy.[3]

While the veneer of naturalness/normalness, in itself, defends power/ knowledge[4] as a form of cultural practice, which is always hedged in by the cognitive process of metonymy and projection, it brings into play the comparison and measurement of the countercultures against the dominant culture. The cultural theorist Stuart Hall, with palpable dejection, reflected at length on this depiction in "The Spectacle of the 'Other,'" in which he hauntingly writes,

> There is the powerful opposition between "civilization" [white] and "savagery" [nonwhite]. There is the opposition between the biological or bodily characteristics of the ["nonwhite"] and "white" "races," polarized into their extreme opposites—each the signifiers of an absolute difference between human "types" or species. There are the rich distinction which cluster around the supposed link, on the one hand, between the white "races" and intellectual development—refinement, learning and knowledge, a belief in reason, the presence of developed institutions, formal government and law, and a civilized restraint in their emotional, sexual and civil life, all of which are associated with "culture"; and on the other hand, the link between the [nonwhite] "races" and whatever is instinctual—the open expression of emotion and feeling rather than intellect, a lack of "civilized refinement" in sexual and social life, a reliance on custom and ritual, and the lack of developed civil institutions, all of which are linked to "Nature."[5]

This is truly a good description of the "us" and "them" scenario that functions to classify whites (usual) as superior and nonwhites (unusual) as inferior. However, does the white/nonwhite framework oversimplify how racial categories are positioned in the United States? Should there be rather a multidimensional representation? Even though there is the "other" within the "them," in post-9/11 America, the "us" and "them" paradigm seems to be fixed.

In this new discourse—new in the sense that culture is reconfigured as a substitute for race—a nonnegotiable space is created so as to maintain and propagate highly politicized cultural categories and stereotypes, or "controlling images" of the "them" as separate from the "us." The "us" and "them" model has continued to be a "signifying practice," where Muslim Americans and people who "look" Middle Eastern are among other things viewed and treated as the "them." The "them" and "us" model is far from being redundant. More importantly, this model remains crucial for one's exclusion and inclusion into the dominant culture. Since the "them" is perceived as culturally different from the "us," it is in this instant of differentiation that domination in the form of cultural supremacy is produced and propagated.

Does racial hybridization complicate the white–nonwhite model? In other words, does it create an autonomous space for the neither white nor nonwhite, not fully one or the other? Is racial hibridization another way of claiming whiteness? It was not so long ago that the one-drop rule was imposed on an individual through law as well as practice. Nowadays, racial in-betweenness, neither white nor nonwhite—unless he or she passes for white—has become a site for identity self-definition, that is, an alternative way of thinking about oneself. Identity formation, in this sense, is not self-determined, and works autonomously from the racial ordering of society. The racial hybrids have to transgress the boundaries between whites and nonwhites and reach a space in which racial signification remains at the forefront. Yet the signification of race, for good reasons, continues to be deeply contested and remains a bothersome term causing a tremendous amount of apprehension. It is toward this dilemma that I now turn. But first I will draw on Hall's careful reading and problematization of race as is modeled on Claude Lévi-Strauss's "floating signifier."[6] "Signifiers," as Hall explains in his canonical text, "refer to the system and concepts of a classification of a culture to its making meaning practices. And those things gain their meaning not because of what they contain in their essence but in the shifting relations of difference which they establish with other concepts and ideas in a signifying field. Their meaning because it is relational and not essential can never be finally fixed, but is subject to the constant process of redefinition and appropriation."[7]

In fact, the media never-ending enthusiasm for racial image and account is essential to its yearning to signify. A plethora of research and studies have shown how racialized images circulating in the media can alter the nuance and complexity of human identities and social issues into one-dimensional stereotypes.[8] As I have argued elsewhere "the media have chosen the idealized images of full-faced pictures of welfare cheats as the 'others' to make the headlines in the newspapers and the six o'clock news."[9]

The Legacy of Race and Its Consequences

John Hartigan Jr. draws on the historical legacies of race in America: "The middle passage, slavery, and the experience of racial terror produce a race of African Americans out of subjects drawn from different cultures. Genocide, forced removal to reservations, and the experience of racial terror make Native American subjects drawn from different linguistic and tribal affiliations: a race. War relocation camps, legal exclusion, and the experience of discrimination make Asian American subjects drawn from different cultural and linguistic backgrounds: a race. The process of forming the southwestern states of the United States through conquest and subjugation and the continued subordination of Puerto Rico constitutes Chicanos and Puerto Ricans as races."[10]

In addition, there are a number of ways in which race thinking unfolded and was, and still is, reflected in America. Thomas Jefferson in his *Notes on the State of Virginia* referred to blacks, whites, and First Nations as distinct races. As a matter of fact, it was fixed in Jefferson's mind that blacks and whites could never coexist in the United States of America because the difference between these two races "is fixed in nature. . . . And is this difference of no importance," Jefferson reasoned in *Notes on the State of Virginia*.[11] For Jefferson, then, "blacks whether originally a distinct race, or made distinct by time and circumstances, are inferior to whites in the endowments both of body and mind."[12] Jefferson's ontological claim that blacks are inferior helped him to reconcile with the idea that whites are superior to blacks. In the end, Jefferson, in order to cure America from the presence of blacks, proposed a form of "ethnic cleansing." Blacks should be shipped to an "all black state."

Richard J. Herrnstein and Charles Murray's *The Bell Curve: Intelligence and Class Structure in American Life*, published in 1994, provides an illustration of the assumed inferiority of blacks and other nonwhites. Using statistical evidence, they claimed, quite unabashedly, that when compared with blacks, whites achieve higher test scores.[13] Three years later, Lino Graglia, a law professor at the University of Texas, following in the footsteps of Herrnstein and Murray, points to the bell curve's rendition that "blacks and Mexican-Americans are not academically competitive with whites in selective institutions."[14]

For some scholars, the concept of race has been discredited. In fact, race as a category seems basically hard to define because of the new emphasis on multiracialism. Given that race is the determinant of social relations in the United States, I think that race requires some serious contemplation. Race is not understood in secure or abiding terms, but its workings are manifested in the tangible cultural milieu in which it exists. The uniqueness of race, its historical litheness and immediacy in daily experience and social conflict in America is hard to dismiss. First Nations' battles, slave riots, lynching, and race riots are some illustrations of racial strife.[15] If we dismiss the significance of race in America's past, we fail to comprehend the specter of racism and how it has shaped America's present perspective on race relations. Professor Cornel West's warning is taken quite seriously when he writes that in order "to engage in a serious discussion of race in America" it is not fruitful to start with people of color "but with the flaws of American society—flaws rooted in historical inequalities and longstanding cultural stereotypes,"[16] and, I would add, social practices and relations. Race has always been, and continues to be contentious. It is this contention that I will now briefly examine.

The Debate about Race

Recently, Paul Gilroy in his book *Between Camps: Nations, Culture and the Allure of Race*, sincerely begs us to move in the direction of a color-blind position on race, transcend race thinking, and get rid of what he describes as "raciology."[17] On the other hand, West's work *Race Matters* (2001) suggests that race indeed matters in America and is a concern that remains fundamental.[18] "Race matters," West tells us, because "race is the most explosive issue in American life precisely" because it is central to contemporary relations. "It forces us to confront the tragic facts of poverty and paranoia, despair, and distrust."[19] In fact, "it matters so much that it has become almost impossible for one to think outside of 'racial' categories"[20] and decontextualize or ahistoricize the conception of race. Since race matters, as Professors Robert Miles and Rodolfo D. Torres explain, then, truly "races," as categories originating from racial classification, must exist.[21] And since races exist, even though an article in the *Chronicle of Higher Education* titled "A Growing Number of Scientists Reject the Concept of Race" denies their existence, there needs to be a concept of race.[22] Race in the United States is far from over, and David R. Roediger, in *Colored White: Transcending the Racial Past*, draws our attention to that fact.[23] Race and its historical specificities continue to shape the disreputable presence of race and racial meanings in America. In other words, race is just as active in America's present as it has been in America's past. In 2007 the fact that six black students at Jena High School in central Louisiana were sentenced to prison without parole after a school fight, in which a white student was brutally beaten, is also illustrative. In addition, on April 21, 2009, "The U.S. Supreme Court Tackles Race" appears as a headline in *USA Today*. Indeed, race thinking, race as an aesthetic idea, a social phenomenon, does exist. One of the consequences is racial difference.

Racial difference is the groundwork for racism.[24] It is a structure that is in place, benefiting all whites. Limiting our understanding of racism as ideological would only amount to an unwarranted and disingenuous oversimplification of racism. [25] More so, it does not explain, in full, the persistence of institutionalized power in disadvantaging and subordinating nonwhites. It is challenging for blacks and other nonwhites, for the most part, to acquire resources including education, housing, and high income on an equal footing with whites. In this sense, an adequate analysis of racism has to consider the working of power. Power's tendency to subordinate nonwhites shapes the very conditions of nonwhites' daily existence and makes room for whites to extend into spaces that have already taken their shape, spaces in which nonwhites stand out, stand apart from whites, "unless they pass, which means passing through space by passing as white."[26] Those that pass as whites are able, usually, to transgress boundaries and cross cultural borders.[27] As Ruth Frankenberg, the British-born sociologist, reminds us, "to be white means to have some sort of advantage or privilege."[28] Given the concrete advantages of white privilege, it is not unreasonable that the "passers" are tempted to go over to the white race so they, too, can reap the benefits of whiteness.[29]

To conceal the discriminatory practices in the United States, a few individuals from subordinate groups must be incorporated into high-profile positions so long as society retains its essential goals of maintaining, reinforcing, and finding new ways to secure whiteness.[30] In other words, the few who have gained positions of power, as they must (concession, as a marker of a civilized society, is necessary to keep the power structure in place), are sometimes removed from a genuine critique of the racist, sexist, classist, and homophobic structures that are solidly in place. It is not in their best interest to threaten or challenge the very structures/systems that have co-opted them. However, they are not suddenly immune to, or separated from, the laws and discourses that subordinate and inferiorize them despite their efforts to assimilate. So in order to keep their subordination intact, they are constantly surrounded by the materialism that permits entry into the so-called honorary whiteness.

In America, like in colonial Hispanic America, is it likely for a person in spite of his or her phenotype (physical appearance) to become an honorary white by acquiring a certificate of whiteness? Does this indicate that "money whitens"?[31] If the answer to this question is a simple yes, we are then faced with the illusion and therefore a false consciousness that there is a "declining significance of race."[32] If, then, all that matters is class, has class then become a metonymy for race? Can we talk about class in America without talking about race while we know perfectly well that its class system is decidedly racialized? The social historian Eric Lott reminds us that "race is the modality in which class is lived."[33] On the other hand, Andrew Hartman, also a historian, asserts the primacy of class over race.[34] The African American sociologist William Julius Wilson has attempted to explicate "the declining significance of race."[35] The important question remains: How does gender and sexuality play into the "it-is-not-race-but-class" debate, or vice versa? The race and class dialectic surely must be challenged. Furthermore, the need to recognize the complex interconnectedness of race, gender, class, and sexuality is important in order to avoid simple dialectic relations. Gender, for instance, no longer relies on two sexes, male and female. Anne Fausto-Sterling, in *Sexing the Body: Gender Politics and the Construction of Sexuality*, identifies five sexes.[36] Queer, bisexually, transgendered, transsexual, and sexually fluid individuals have challenged the dichotomy of homosexuality and heterosexuality.

Institutionalized power relegates blacks and other marginalized groups to a lower class and excludes many of them from accessing power through various forms of social control.[37] Power imposes itself on those on the margins of society in order to augment and replicate its cultural practices of discrimination and prejudice. Besides, access to that power is based on, to use the terms of Teun A. van Dijk whose work is centered on critical discourse analysis, "privileged access to socially valued resources such as wealth, income, position, status, force, group membership, education or knowledge."[38] While all whites are not the actual perpetrators of racist laws and policies, whites have bona fide membership in a class-society that benefits from white ascendancy, the foremost structuring force in society that underpins and perpetuates white skin privileges.[39] The theory of white ascendancy implies that what matters is a white skin, and it guarantees all whites, even those who occupy the lower echelons of the social class, privileges that no nonwhite person has. It is not surprising, then, that "class markers have often been read as inborn racial characteristics."[40] For blacks and other racialized groups, class position is readily assumed as lower.

Nonwhites who are striving to maintain "middle class" status continue to be bombarded by what Vijay Prashad brilliantly brands as "the inevitable chatter of benevolence racism."[41] "You're not like the rest of them," "You act so different," "You speak so well for a Chinese person" are these types of well-rehearsed discourses and conversational practices, which are continuous pestilences in nonwhites' daily lives. What it really means is that "You" are not like "them," which, in turn, makes you less threatening to "us." Whiteness, "a socially constructed category of racial and cultural identity maintains and reproduces its hegemony."[42] I am not arguing that white is an essentialist category—since the meaning of who is white differs from context to context; also the context, after all, is unsaturated and unclosed.[43] Nonetheless, whites were never assigned as a biological category on the basis of the one-drop-of-blood that was applied to African Americans. The one-drop rule as a racial project emerged and functioned as an uncodified societal norm in the slave society, and continued to be present in America for a long time. Until the 1970s, in some states the one-drop-of-black-blood rule still existed. In 1982, Susie Guillory Phipps, a descendent of a white planter and a black slave, unsuccessfully sued the Louisiana Bureau of Vital Records to rework her racial categorization from black to white.[44] Phipps tried to deny and erase her black ancestry. For Adrian Piper, in her article "Passing for White: Passing for Black," denying one's black ancestry "is a really authentically shameful thing to do."[45] However, this is a good example of how the dynamics of the cultural production of whiteness work. It is nothing but white self-racialization or what the social theorist Ghassan Hage calls "identity fetishism."[46] White self-racialization is the

symptom of understanding too well how whiteness works. Thus, to understand its psychological ramification, as Kalpana Seshadri-Crooks argues,
whiteness must be positioned at the heart of "Freudian theories of subjectivities."[47] The "psychological wages of whiteness" emphasizes whiteness as
an enormous benefit in itself, which many whites adhere to by expressing
their preeminence over nonwhites.[48]

The concept of "passing," in spite of its racial essentialism, is important as a cultural production of whiteness. Passing means veiling your
blackness; for example, resigning from the race that is nonwhite.[49] Harryette Mullen, a poet and literary scholar, explains this very well when she
reminds us that passing "requires an active denial of [nonwhite] identity
[by] the individuals who pass for white."[50] Today, passing is about getting
a license for entry into honorary whiteness. It is no longer about looking
white. But, it does, unfortunately, require freeing oneself from the labels
associated with nonwhiteness; adopting a lifestyle that allows for the association of white images; presenting oneself, or being presented to a white
society in a manner that make whites feel safe and unsusceptible. It is like
joining a private club. Once you have become a member you must put up
with the rule. A black person who stands out is O. J. Simpson. Once, he was
permitted into the white world, well, so it seemed, but now he is despised
by many whites. One can enter "the white world," as the African American
law professor Cheryl I. Harris cogently puts it, "albeit [it is] a false passport,
not merely passing but trespassing."[51] It is not surprising, then, that if honorary whiteness can be bestowed, it can also be withdrawn. More recently,
there has been a shift from passing to claiming a multiracial (African and
European) identity. Does claiming a multiracial identity raise any threat,
for example, to blacks' racial unity? Is claiming a multiracial identity about
the impact of internalized racism and its damaging effects on the psyche?
For the most part, is it a way of revolving toward whiteness? In the United
States whiteness does matter; and it is complicit with the domination of
blacks and other nonwhite minority groups. For sure, a person with a multiracial identity is subject to the same stigma and penalties as a black person. Probably the person with the multiracial identity thinks that he or she
should be spared that stigmatization because he or she is not "truly black."
The African American historian Barbara J. Fields points to "the anguish
of the Jean Toomer or the Anatole Broyard, [which] rests, ultimately, on
a thwarted hope to be excused, on grounds of mixed ancestry, from a fate
deemed entirely appropriate for persons of unambiguous African ancestry."[52] This is a good illustration of how whiteness works.

Racial thinking in America justified slavery, the Jim Crow South, First
Nations' allocation to Indian reservations, and the Chinese Exclusion Act
of 1882. Race and its historical legacies continue to shape the unrelenting

structural position that is intact, maintaining, protecting, and privileging whiteness. It is against whiteness that nonwhiteness is constructed, judged, and reduced to "otherness." And, to borrow the words of the American sociologists Michael Omi and Howard Winant, there is "nothing inherently white about racism."[53] It is a "kind of macro-agent with its own agenda, operating separately from white people."[54] It is exactly for this reason that bell hooks is fed up with constructed narratives based on a shared victimhood of whites with racialized groups where whiteness is recentered and masks specific ways in which racist domination impacts the lives of racialized groups.[55] Whites are not capable of experiencing racism as intrinsically incorporated within a racist system based on white privilege. For this reason, as Roediger admits, racism "just made no sense to [white people]."[56]

I am not arguing that nonwhites are the victims of racism and whites are the perpetrators. This dichotomization is far too reductionistic given that racism is viewed as a social and historical phenomenon that has produced racially structured social relations.[57] As Fields points out, "the targets of racism do not 'make' racism, nor are they free to 'negotiate' it, though they may challenge it or its perpetrators and try to navigate the obstacles it places in their lives."[58] First Nations, blacks, Chinese, Mexicans, and other racialized groups "have often been systematically excluded from residential areas, occupations, and organizations, and even sometimes denied equal rights under the law."[59] Even though the British sociologist Avtar Brah is suspicious of any interpretation of racism through what she calls "simple bipolarities of negativity and positivity, superiority and inferiority, inclusion or exclusion [because there is] the changing forms of a plurality of racisms,"[60] it is sad to say that even in the twenty-first century the underlying asymmetry of power between those on the margins and those located within the center of privilege is far from anachronistic and is solidly in place in America.[61] The countless examples at hand take a complex structure such as racism and render its outcomes as rather straightforward. When a police officer, acting on racial intelligence based on common sense, kills an innocent, black or Mexican person on the spot, and he is not punished for such outrageous behavior, it tells us how institutionalized power works. The old process of the oppressor and oppressed model is still at work as if nothing has changed.[62] The pervasiveness of racial profiling,[63] the curtailing of welfare for the poor (the poor are mostly blacks and other racial minorities), increasing police brutality directed at blacks and Mexicans, the curtailing of racial justice, the rising incarceration of blacks and Mexicans, and the violence perpetrated against women, gays, and lesbians—assigning people to an inferior group as a determinant of their social, economic, civic, and human standing,[64] all point to the system of domination and subordination, and how the manifold axes of power work. Power is an anchorage point for reorienting toward the "new racism" clothed in its old ways. It leaves a noticeably enduring mark on the subordinate subjects who have inhabited the margins of society.

In the wake of desegregation in military, transportation, and schools, the Civil Rights Act of 1964, and the implementation of various antidiscrimination laws, the more modernizing modes of expression of racism are increasingly associated with issues that include urban renewal and poor public schools and neighborhoods. Racial groups are located in different neighborhoods than are whites. In addition, lack of employment mobility for nonwhites, hyperunemployment and poverty among nonwhite groups, a large percentage of nonwhites' high school dropouts, and lack of federal funding for the expansion of programs beneficial to racial minorities (Medicaid and welfare), have all proliferated. Ample evidence of welfare racism, for example, has been provided by many contemporary scholars.[65] These scholars accurately show how racism was a large factor in the decision of the federal government under the Clinton administration in 1996 to reform the welfare state and to move poor people from welfare to mandatory work programs. This is what the African American historian Evelyn Brooks Higginbotham calls "metaphoric and metonymic identifications"[66] of welfare with racialized groups, especially blacks and Mexicans. The association of welfare with blacks and Mexicans has, in part, encouraged policymakers to come up with commonsensical formulas such as welfare equals dependency and the lack of the Weber work ethic. Work equals independence and the end of poverty. According to President Clinton, in his apodictic statement on signing the 1996 Welfare Reform Act, "no one who works full time and has children at home should be poor anymore."[67]

The specific need to view race as a social construction that has no biological or genetic basis is now commonplace because it is necessary in order to attack whiteness "as a destructive ideology" and makes it visible.[68] The "invisibility of whiteness as a racial position in white (which is to say dominant) discourse" is a part of its "ubiquity." [69] Because race is the underlying marker for the maintenance of the great classificatory of difference between whites and nonwhites, it is not a metonym for ethnicity. Ethnicity, which is constructed through a focus on difference, in fact, becomes decisive in passing judgments against individuals and communities; it is the culture of people and their beliefs, customs, and practices, which are manifested through such signals, including language, race, and religion. Ethnicity is not only a cultural occurrence; it is a political one as well. The 1790 Naturalization Act denied citizenship to all racialized ethnicities as well as to women.

Race and Ethnicity

In terms of the discursive foundation of racialization or the development of racial subjects that draws on physical differences to construct and provide meaning to racial groups and the hierarchy in which they are entrenched, race and ethnicity "balance each other and respond to each other in an extraordinary reciprocal homogeneity."[70] Professor Cynthia Hamilton's work, "Multiculturalism as Political Strategy," draws our attention to the problematic of treating race and ethnicity as synonymous.[71] It is also for the political scientist Victoria Hattam, in her book *In the Shadow of Race: Jews, Latinos, and Immigrant Politics in the United States*, to capture quite well "the paradoxical sense of proximity and difference between ethnicity and race."[72] For this exact reason, I think, we have to interrogate race and ethnicity separately as well as together to meaningfully demonstrate how race is invariably defined and shaped, and how ethnicity is experienced and determined as racial subjects are formed. When we interrogate race and ethnicity in this manner, the propensity to reduce race to a simple appearance of ethnicity becomes problematic. What we have here is the racialization of ethnicity which reinscribes rather than confronts the formidable inequalities that accompany racial difference. First Nations, blacks, Chinese, Mexicans, and other racialized groups have been and, to a large extent, still are subject to the inescapability of American racism. I am not arguing that racism itself is inevitable and natural. The ontological claim that racialized ethnic groups were inferior, and are still perceived as inferior, is a direct marker for the acute discrimination against these groups.

Racialization

The need to critically analyze the "natural" veneer of racialization as an ongoing and dynamic process is not without signification for three reasons.[73] One, groups such as the Irish, Italians, Greeks, and Jews[74] were designated as nonwhite at various historical stages in America.[75] To trace this process, Matthew F. Jacobson, in *Whiteness of a Different Color: European Immigrants and the Alchemy of Race*, suggests that race be recognized as an "ideological, political deployment rather than as a neutral, biologically determined element of nature."[76] As I have already mentioned, race, as a social construct, rather than a biologically determined one, is now commonplace as well as axiomatic. Two, racial meaning is ascribed to social relations, practices, and groups' situatedness. Three, whiteness determines how the process of racialization works. It carries with it "the oppressive inscriptions of power that are structurally determined, politically organized, and ideologically inflected . . . within positions of domination and power,"[77] which, for the most, is devoid of interrogation. I am using the term *racialization* "to signify the extension of racial meaning to a previously racially unclassified relationship, social practice, or group,"[78] and as "an activity that has the power to deconstruct racial categories and reveal their historical making."[79] Yet it is the emergence of race that was, and still is, the direct marker for the fluid and multifaceted process of the racialization of ethnicity—the representation and definition of the "other" based on constructed differences.

The racialization of Chinese Americans, for example, "involved the muting of profound cultural and linguistic differences"[80] as a way of reinforcing and maintaining domination based on racial characterization, a specificity that is fashioned out of its socially entrenched milieu. Racial characterization reverberates in racially conceived terms. When white labor was too expensive, Chinese were hired at low wages. And even though Chinese were employed to build the railroads, they were enormously discriminated against. As Ronald Takaki points out, what enabled the Chinese to "be degraded into a subservient laboring caste was the dominant ideology that defined America as a racially homogenous society and America as white."[81] Replacing the predictable signifiers of racial difference (phenotype and skin color) with a completely relativistic one (language) simply exposes racialization as a problematic and ideological as well as structural process that decidedly operates in the United States. Racialization of blacks, for example, involves institutional arrangements that accompanied slavery, the Jim Crow South, black ghetto, and, more recently, the hyperghetto and prisons.[82]

These are good examples of what Loïc Wacquant refers to as "racemaking," which works to strengthen and maintain the idea that race is the underlining indicator highlighting genuine, resilient differences between whites and nonwhites.[83] Racialization and its sociohistorical processes, in its diverse articulations, are very well linked to the discourses and practices of gender, sexuality, and class configurations. In fact, these essential discourses and practices do not just independently coexist. The complex interrelation of these identities permits a complicated and sophisticated interchange that "strengthens each other's grip on popular consciousness and cements social relations across a range of axes."[84] Hence, any alternative discourse or practice that would denaturalize the hegemonic discourse has to be suppressed.

Racialization of Gender

Ideas about race are subject to substantial disparities from one culture to another and one period to another, and have also defined gender, sexuality, and class constructions in important ways. Attempts to theorize the racialization of gender is important because gender processes, in many conspicuous ways, relate to those of race. Black feminists and other feminists of color have correctly pointed to the ethnocentric nature of white feminism, especially second-wave feminism, because of its focus on gender inequality and its failing to examine race and class.[85] According to Floya Anthias and Nira Yuval-Davis, in *Racialized Boundaries: Race, Nation, Gender, Colour and Class and the Anti-racist Struggle,* "White feminists have begun to pay attention to their own ethnocentrism to explore the links with feminism and racism."[86] These links must be established because a feminist discourse is essential for the promotion of antiracist projects, pedagogy, and political activities. Such a project would require the kind of critical space that the post-Gramscian concept of the subaltern puts forward, as it is expanded by Gayatri C. Spivak, in her 1988 seminal essay, "Can the Subaltern Speak?"

Race is not simply an additive to, or an offshoot of, gender difference. The relationship between race and gender is multidimensional, and the need to understand both race and gender in terms of their theoretical discursive differences as well as their synchronizing tendencies within America's social relation is in order, as black feminists and other feminists of color have demonstrated. However we conceive of race, it has a power effect on gender construction and representation in America, and has been "the ultimate trope of difference, arbitrarily conceived to produce and maintain relations of power and subordination"[87] within the patriarchal capitalist structure. For instance, the racialization of gender has left black women and other women of color at the bottom of the economic and social ladder. Higginbotham, in her penetrating discussion of the metalanguage of race, points to the fact that black women, for example, were never fully identifiable with their gender and were invariably associated with their race. She remarks that in America "where racial demarcation is endemic to [its] sociocultural fabric and heritage—to [its] laws and economy, to [its] epistemologies and everyday customs—gender identity is inextricably linked to and even determined by racial identity. . . . In Jim Crow South prior to the 1960s . . . little black girls learned to use the bathroom for blacks instead of the bathroom for women."[88] Even though race is a category by which women of color systematize their identities within discourses and practices that are specific to the sociocultural contexts in which they live is important, the symbiotic relationship between race and gender does exist.

Besides, what constitutes this identity as a "woman" and how differences within the category "woman" are deemed as significant has been given a tremendous amount of analysis. It was an unrelenting attempt by those in power to give context and legitimacy to the category "woman" and its programmed set of normative idealizations. In societal emblematic order in which the reading of a "woman" is accessible, it is no coincidence that the professor of African and African American Studies Evelynn M. Hammonds asserted that "white is what woman is; not white (and the stereotypes not white gathers in) is what she better not be."[89] In other words, gender identity, in terms of nonwhite women, is reconstituted and defined in a predominantly physical way, in that one's identity as a woman is rooted in one's embodiment as a racialized body. The racial body bears the imprint of history creating identity and refracting recognition through the terror of a fixed regime of visibility and performativity. "Performativity," as Judith Butler explains, "must be understood not as a singular or deliberate 'act,' but rather as the reiterative and citational practice by which discourse produces the effects that it names."[90] Hence, a nonwhite woman does not become a woman, in the Beauvoirian sense, because she is born female. As Chandra Talpade Mohanty, the postcolonial feminist theorist, explains, "It is the intersection of the various systemic networks of class, race, (hetero) sexuality and nation . . . that position [nonwhite] women."[91] For nonwhite women, the language of intersectionality becomes important. It impels "new ways of thinking about complexity and multiplicity in power relations."[92] Yet it is necessary to interrogate and recognize the degrees of differences among women of color in factors that range from ethnicity, class, sexuality, and age to abilities and disabilities. The desire here is not to focus on the differences that identity politics and politics of recognition lamely permit, it is to draw analytically on these crosscutting cleavages and to recognize how different forms of subordination and marginalization operate in a society where the multidimensional systems of oppression operate and produce specific outcomes. The inevitable contradictions within these fixed identity categories become paramount.

Having explored some of the characteristic features of racialization, I now turn to "differential racialization" where, for some scholars, the process of racialization may make racial minorities more powerful in certain areas (popular culture) and less powerful in others (the law);[93] and, in turn, these contradictory arenas would aid in the construction of what Michel Foucault conceives as "a plurality of resistances"[94] to hostility and exclusions based on whiteness. However, in any discussion of racialization can we do away with an analysis that encompasses race and racism as separate? For sure, the "new racism," or what Fanon in *Toward the African Revolution* labeled "cultural racism,"[95] does not depend on racial categorization. In fact, with the "new racism" coded within a cultural logic, culture is substituted for race. Migrants and refugees are constructed as inferiors and undesirables, and, in some cases, where assimilation into the hegemonic culture and structure is unreachable, these groups are openly despised and excluded from normative Americanness. Xenophobic sentiments toward these groups, especially those that are the naturalized racial "other," are readily displayed with an unsuppressed enthusiasm. In other cases, racism is demonstrated as deeming an entire group of people as having a deficit culture. After 9/11, all Muslims are viewed as terrorists, and, to legitimize its racism, the U.S. government must implement "homeland security," which is hidden within such rhetoric as "preventing another 9/11"; "keeping America protected from terrorists." Racism, in these instances, does not rely on racialization that produced racial apartheid in America, including the allocation of First Nations to Indian reservations, the Jim Crow South, Asian exclusion, and Japanese American internment. In fact, the racist practice is always imbedded in the theory of racism, and it is for this reason that John Derbyshire, in his essay "Thinking about Internment," did not think that the Japanese internment "was a very deplorable thing to do. . . . The camps were rather comfortable—they contained beauty parlors," for example.[96] For mainstream Americans, after 9/11, Muslim Americans are seen as the "problem," and singling out Muslims for "extra security" is not a bad thing after all, even though it openly infringes on people's hard won civil rights and liberties.

Racialization is analogous to, and intimately linked to the concepts of race and racism. Field's analysis of the difference between the two is significant. She argues that substituting race for racism "transforms the act of a subject into an attribute of the object."[97] In this regard, what Fields recognizes, with the same profoundness, that "not all racializers do the same things when they racialize,"[98] is just as important.[99] The racializers have to familiarize themselves with the modifications in the laws, policies, and public attitudes, assuming different appearances as the circumstances demand. Racialization, to borrow from Robert Miles's *Racism*, "has to be redefined to refer to a wider range of phenomena."[100] Race, seemingly a signifier, is further complicated by how the classification systems—including ethnicity, gender, sexuality, class, and physical and mental abilities—organize, reinforce, and maintain differences, which is further implicated by nationality and religiosity, although in some cases nonwhites are able to negotiate differences in gender, race, sexuality, and class. Yet we have to be careful about negotiation because identities are made, they are not given.[101] Nonwhites are forever confronted with the difficulty of negotiation, not with a single set of oppositions that position them in the same relation to others, but with a series of diverse positionalities and situated subjectivities.

Another Look at Racialization

Recently we have witnessed an explosion of new thought and practices in race and ethnicity in spheres of literature, music, film, and art. Recent examples of this new politics of representation can be found in American popular culture. "Popular culture carries that affirmative ring because of the prominence of the word 'popular,'"[102] as is evident, for example, in the African American literary canon. Also, rap and hip-hop music are a part of popular culture.[103] It is an alternative to the dominant tradition, which has triggered some resistance from the dominant, and has produced a racist discourse, defining "high" and "low" cultures. The works of African American novelists Richard Wright and Toni Morrison are only just now considered to be "literature" and are rewarded. But these works are measured by the degree to which they correspond to what is recognized as "high" culture.[104] Nonetheless, the boundaries of "high" and "low" cultures are not static and at the same time are never completely disconnected.[105] They sometimes change depending on locality and positionality. "Through the prism of culture," in the words of Annop Nayak in "Whites Lives," "we are now witnessing increasingly complex processes of racialization refractured in the rich and dense constellation of experimental ideas, theories, and practices."[106] In fact, literary genres or authors, for example, are positioned in a hierarchy analogous to social classes,[107] and "literary critical tradition arose from and reflects a culture created and dominated by men."[108] For some scholars, the process of racialization can be productive. Nayak, for one, asks, "Can we begin to fashion a productive notion of racialization? Can a critical use of racialization really challenge the power of white supremacy as is evident in the materialist account?"[109]

> The materialist use of racialization as an imposition of the ideologic state apparatus implies that certain groups, institutions, or organs of the state have ownership over power while others do not, and this may underplay the numerous sites and interrelationships that enable power to be effective. In particular, the role of human agency and the countless modes of resistance might be overlooked.[110]

To answer these questions, as Nayak points out, we need to look and "turn to culture" within the arts, humanities, and social sciences.[111] "It is the mark of difference inside forms of popular culture—which are by definition contradictory and which therefore appear as impure, threatened by incorporation or exclusion—that is carried by the signifier 'black' in terms of black popular culture."[112] Furthermore, the fact of the matter is that the term *popular culture*, in spite of the defiant modifier that goes before it, is always a term at risk of presuming too much. Hence, the modifier entices us to reevaluate the problematic of black popular culture.

We need to extend our analysis of the concept of racialization and include, in the words of Philip Cohen, "the hidden narratives in theories of racism."[113] Within a white-dominated society like the United States, and among white people, "whiteness," as Kalpana Seshadri-Crooks aptly remarks, "often functions as an ontologically neutral category that advances a subject as raceless and unmarked."[114] As a consequence, according to Alastair Bonnett, "most white people don't consider themselves to be part of a race that needs examining."[115] By assigning race to nonwhite people, the cultural production of whiteness and its dominance functions as, to use the words of African American activist and poet Audre Lorde, a "mythical norm."[116] Race is, for the most part, associated with nonwhiteness, and whiteness, for the most part, as "whiteness studies"[117] postulate, remains an unmentioned racial identity unless it juxtaposes itself against racialized groups.[118] In this case, Fields's conclusion, according to which race is equated with identity and attributed to white persons, that "whiteness seems to banish the troubling asymmetry that is the essence of racism,"[119] is essential. In this sense, racism, as a compulsory and authoritative assignment of race, is shrunken into racial identity. Racial identity functions as a tool for domination as well as for resistance.[120] Racialized groups have tried to create lives of their own, but in many cases they are faced with structural and cultural barriers that prevent racial equality.[121] I am referring here to discriminatory practices that are ubiquitous, in the workplace, the schools, and the criminal justice system.

The Evolution of the Ethnicity Framework

Ethnicity theory emerged in the 1920s as an apparent conundrum to the conceptualization of race as rooted in biological determinism. Simply put, whites were considered superior to nonwhites. Eventually, the argumentation for whites' superiority and nonwhites' inferiority based on the Lamarckian conceptions of heredity and biological determinism came under attack; first by the Swedish sociologist Gunnar Myrdal in his book *An American Dilemma: The Negro Problem and Modern Democracy*, and then by Horace Kallen's *Cultural Pluralism and the American Idea*, where the concept of cultural pluralism gained some importance.[122] Cultural pluralism, a highly complex and modern phenomenon, is understood "as in an orchestra, [where] every type of instrument has its specific timbre and tonality founded in its substance and forms; . . . each ethnic group is the natural instrument, its spirit and culture are its theme and melody and the harmony and dissonances and discords of them all make the symphony of civilization."[123]

Cultural pluralism was to become a key element of the ethnicity model.[124] Cultural pluralism has led to a new emphasis from the biological to the cultural/symbolic as an explanation for blacks and other nonwhites' inferiority. Its uncritical usage of commonsense racist imagery as an explanation for nonwhites' inferiority was indeed problematic. Particularly important in this regard was the influence of Nathan Glazer and Daniel P. Moynihan's work, *Beyond the Melting Pot: The Negroes, Puerto Ricans, Jews, Italians, and Irish of New York City*, which nonetheless produced and maintained its racist orientation about nonwhites' inferiority. Once this new concept of nonwhites' inferiority was introduced, within America's racial discourse, it began to take shape, and continued its negative imposition of limiting, restricting, regulating, and prohibiting equality among citizenry. In fact, Glazer and Moynihan attributed the status of inferiority to nonwhites, particularly African Americans, as the absence of middle-class principles and norms. This idea continued to flourish, and two years later, in *The Negro Family: The Case for National Action*, Moynihan concluded that the current pathology embedded within black culture is "capable of perpetuating itself without assistance from the white world." Moynihan's engagement with the dominant structure of white supremacy was uncritical; instead, he fixated on the sphere of culture. Culture became a substitute for race, which, I think, only served to obscure key factors explaining the continued salience of race and the synchronizing of race and class, for example. It makes sense, then, that for Moynihan and his contemporaries, assimilation was the answer to curb nonwhites' inferiority. "Curb" is to be understood not in the sense of ending racial oppression but as a desperate attempt to deal with the so-called increasing pathology of nonwhite people. In fact, whether blacks and other nonwhites were made inferior by the social conditions as Moynihan and his contemporaries claimed to be the case, the bottom line was, nonwhites were still viewed as inferior by the dominant class. The concept of nonwhites' inferiority is still in place today and it sets the stage for ill treatment of nonwhite groups.

Civil rights leaders, for example, have pushed for equality that has been so long denied to blacks and other marginalized groups. The aftermath of the civil rights movement has, for good reasons, increased blacks' emphasis on "black power" and a psychic need to solely differentiate and, in some extreme cases, segregate themselves from white America. There was a rise in the black Muslim movement, and some blacks decided to discard their "slave names" and replace them with Muslims' names. For example, Cassius Clay changed his name to Mohamed Ali. Many blacks were becoming Muslims[125] as a way to liberate themselves from America's oppressive system.

Robert E. Park, an American urban sociologist, introduced assimilation as a major current that was to apply to immigrants in the United States in the 1930s. Assimilation was viewed as the most logical response to the predicament imposed by racial discrimination. This strand of the ethnicity model became fashionable from the 1930s to the middle of the 1960s. Nonetheless, after 1965, the ethnicity model became the hallmark for what Omi and Winant refer to as "racial formation." Racial formation is "the sociohistorical process by which racial categories are created, inhabited, transformed, and destroyed."[126] Racial formation is important in demonstrating the limitation of the ethnicity model as a paradigm of race.[127] While the ethnicity model has transformed itself into a mere egalitarian conservatism where there is a discontent with group rights in favor of individual rights, there is an emphasis on blindness to race, gender, class, and sexuality, which has raised some important concerns. It is these concerns that I now briefly examine.

Blindness: Some Concerns

"Blindness," to use Ruth Frankenberg's expression, is a "power-evasive discursive repertoire in play."[128] Law professor Robert C. Post points out that blindness "renders forbidden characteristics invisible; it requires employers to base their judgments instead on the deeper and more fundamental ground of "individual merits" or "intrinsic worth.""[129] Blindness, then, is committed to a merit-based society, a society that looks beyond mere appearances and does not take into account race, gender, or sexuality. In this sense, it is clear that for proponents of blindness, blindness is not interrelated with policies such as affirmative action because affirmative action is not based on merits. In November 1996, in California, for example, the California Civil Rights Initiative, or Proposition 209, ended affirmative action programs in all the state agencies. The argument for Proposition 209 was propelled by a renewed emphasis on merits.[130] I must add quickly, What kind of meritocracy would exclude women, nonwhites, immigrants, gays, lesbians, and the disabled from access to resources that would enable them to compete on a somewhat similar footing with heterosexual, white men, even though this competition is already marred by connections, which count for much more than merits and industry or hard work? A concrete illustration of this point is that a university applicant is guaranteed extra points if and only if his or her grandfather graduated from the same university. [131]

Is the emphasis on blindness nothing but normative discrimination reinforcing the status quo? Is the appeal to blindness a dangerous distraction from the lingering effects of prejudice stemming from racism, sexism, and homophobia, for example? If blindness is what American society is about, why is there a need for laws to combat and prohibit discriminatory practices stemming from gender, race, and sexuality identities? To make any sense of the blindness trope, I think we have to make believe, for example, that opportunities and resources are allocated and distributed in race- or gender-blind fashion. We have to wholeheartedly buy into the notion of equality of opportunity and free choice for all, and arrive at a very problematic conclusion about the reasons why most women or blacks or Mexicans remain poor in this society. Mickey Kaus, who was a writer for the *New Republic*, has argued that blacks are poor because they lack entrepreneurial drive, and their energies are directed into gangs, drugs, and sex. Conclusions like this, I think, are at fault because of their failure to interrogate racism, sexism, classism, and homophobia as embedded within America's social, economic, and political structures. It would be unusual, then, if blindness could transcend race, gender, or sexuality as a category, which is socially created and transformed; if it could operate in a way that rendered these identities truly irrelevant. Take the case of race: Butler reminds us that "racial identities are marked and some are unmarked, which means that some stand out, such as blackness, as visible social signs, whereas whiteness, which is no less social is nevertheless part of the taken-for-granted visual field, a sign of its presumptive hegemony."[132] Hegemony is a lived system of constitutive meanings and values that is grounded in specific practice.

Because nonwhiteness is compared and measured against whiteness and is reduced to "otherness," blindness, in this sense, works both to destabilize and to rationalize identities such as race, gender, and sexuality. In fact, blindness invalidates the racial opposition by which the maxims of white supremacy and nonwhite inferiority were constructed. Consequently, blindness erases the history and institution of white, heterosexual, male supremacy; it interacts with other approaches of race, gender, and sexuality in arguments over the unquestioned legitimacy of distributive practice. Foucault, in "Questions of Method," explains how this practice works: "Not just governed by institutions, prescribed by ideologies, pragmatic circumstances—whatever roles these elements might actually play—but possesses up to a point [its] own specific regularities, logic, strategy, self-evidence and 'reason.' It is a question of analyzing a 'regime of practices'—[practice] being understood here as places where what is said and what is done, rules imposed and reasons given, the planned and the taken for granted meet and intersect."[133] The enactment of antidiscrimination laws, as an opposition to the historical patterns of segregation and racial hierarchy, has only served to strengthen white supremacy as a system that is solidly in place in America, and fails to address the entrenched unequal practices directed toward racialized peoples. More so, antidiscrimination laws mask accountability for the problematic of whiteness as a sign of its presumptive hegemony. Butler cautions us that "there is no opposition to power, which is not itself part of the very workings of power."[134] It is precisely for this reason that I will put forward a dire need for us to recognize whiteness for what it is, unmarked, "unique, a special ideological case apart from race."[135] Race, in this case, "is placed under erasure as something outside immediate consideration, at once extratextual and extraterrestrial."[136] A view of "whiteness as a relational identity constructed by whites defining themselves as unlike [racialized ethnic group]" is paramount.[137] Neil Foley draws on this analysis of whiteness as relational. For him, though, whiteness symbolizes both the "pinnacle of ethnoracial status" and the "complex social and economic matrix wherein racial power and privilege [are] shared not always equally, by those who [are] able to construct identities as Anglo-Saxons, Nordics, Caucasians, or simply whites."[138] Not all whites are "equally white" as Foley explains. For example, poor southern whites were always low-ranking members of the "whiteness club" and are viewed as inferior to the other whites.[139] However, unlike racialized ethnic groups including First Nations, blacks, Chinese, and Mexicans who are viewed as inferior by culture, the liminal whites are inferior because of their socioeconomic status. Nonetheless, poor whites accept quite readily what whiteness has to offer which is "property rights in whiteness."[140]

The binarism of whiteness and nonwhiteness is important within cultural exigencies and it deserves particular attention. It allows for a repositioning of the binary oppositionality (whiteness and nonwhiteness), which is caught in the web of conflicting interests and cultural identities. Since nonwhiteness can exist only as the immanent possibility of whiteness, "whiteness alone" as Morrison remarks, "is mute, meaningless, unfathomable, pointless, frozen, veiled, curtained, dreaded, senseless, and implacable."[141] As such, in order for whiteness to maintain its preeminence, nonwhiteness serves as the pervasive form of "otherness" and provides a serious impediment to embracing America's cultural oneness. Instead, nonwhites are fastened to cultural "otherness." This preoccupation with cultural "otherness," as we will later see, becomes the mainstay for multiculturalism's submission to racialized ethnic groups' cultural recognition.

Multiculturalism

The shift from assimilation, as the production of whiteness, to cultural pluralism, with its emphasis on multiculturalism, a fairly recent phenomenon, is important.[142] Multiculturalism was developed in the middle of the 1970s to diversify the education system.[143] Courses in Ethnic Studies, even though they continue to be on the fringes, were beginning to be a part of the school curriculum. By the 1980s, there was an emphasis on making public school education more diverse. The 1989 Report of the Task Force on Minorities: Equity and Excellence emphasized the importance of such an initiative. "African-Americans, Asian-Americans, Puerto Ricans/Latinos and Native Americans have all been the victims of an intellectual and educational oppression that has characterized the culture and institutions of the United States and the European American world for centuries."[144] For this precise reason, the report calls for curriculum reform. Arthur M. Schlesinger, in his book *The Disuniting of America: Reflections on a Multicultural Society*, with an uncustomary conservatism, expresses his unwarranted concerns that America and its institutions of knowledge production will soon disintegrate because of multiculturalism. His direct assault on multiculturalism and his stanch attempt to maintain the canon of Western civilization by focusing its majestic narratives on what defines America's history, has led him to ask quite provocatively "at what point does [multiculturalism] mutate into an ethnocentrism of its own? Is it a function of schools to teach racial pride? When does obsession with difference begin to threaten the idea of an over-arching American nationality?"[145] It is precisely this sort of unfounded logic that makes it difficult to take him seriously. Yet we have to take him seriously because he continues to sway quite a number of academics toward what they perceived as multiculturalism's threat to America's cultural homoge-neity and the cohesiveness of American society. Nathan Glazer,[146] for one, is concerned with keeping "nonsense and exaggeration and mindless eth-nic racial celebration" from being incorporated into the schools and their curriculums,[147] which, not omitted, would for Dinesh D'Souza mindfully lead to an "illiberal education."[148] The epistemological consistencies of these scholars, at its worst, promote racist discourse and stereotypes. Nonethe-less, for the antimulticulturalists, multiculturalism is seen as unnatural, literally ridiculous, and illogical in the established order of what defines America's cultural identity. It becomes this assumed threat to America's cul-tural homogeneity because it assumes emphasis on cultural heterogeneity. Schlesinger, for one, begs for "the return to the melting pot" because, as he admits, America's culture would soon be fragmented "into quarrelsome spatter of enclaves, ghettos and tribes."[149]

Multiculturalism is supposed to advance the notion that cultural dif-ferences are important, therefore each cultural group is to be recognized and celebrated. We will see the limits of multiculturalism, not only in terms of its authenticating and totaling of cultures, but in coming to terms with the incorporating of racialized groups into the dominant culture. In fact, what multiculturalism does is to celebrate and maintain "otherness" where "otherness" is viewed as un-Americanness. In this respect, there is a need to move beyond multiculturalism, "to engage in new practices, to enter new relationships, and to embrace new concepts and discourses,"[150] all of which will profoundly transform an American cultural identity and practice that is based on whiteness.

For this precise reason, there needs to be a more elaborate discourse that speaks about whiteness, analyzes its histories, and renounces whiteness as the definitive concept of America's cultural identity. However, I have no intention of providing a detailed blueprint on future race relations in the United States. Without overstating the case, in an effort to emancipate multiculturalism from the racialist ontology from which it has evolved, which besets it from promoting a politics of cultural inclusiveness, a sound and realistic alternative to multiculturalism must be envisioned. This alternative must work against the coercive sensibility of whiteness as the central plank of America's cultural homogeneity. This alternative must assert and promote heterogeneity in ethnoracial and cultural terms. However, the alternative has to be first guided by the recognition of multiculturalism's divorce from the long-standing and broader struggles for racial and cultural inclusiveness that had, to a large degree, produced multiculturalism in the first place. The alternative is postmulticulturalism.

Postmulticulturalism

Postmulticulturalism is not about sequenciality; it is not leaving behind the past, or erasing the past and present aesthetic practices that maintain America's cultural identity as white. Rather, it is to fully capture the vexed history of whiteness in the United States of America that self-evidently works incongruently to nonwhiteness. Instead of celebrating cultural "otherness" as multiculturalism does, postmulticulturalism would dislocate the association of "otherness" as un-Americanness. It would embrace a multiethnic identity as an American identity.

Given the many unsettling ways in which the power elites and scholars have projected their own deep-seated apprehensions about America becoming a multiethnic society—even though America has always been a multiethnic society—and the presumed threat this holds for America's cultural identity, it is not surprising that issues of racial and cultural diversity are intimately tied to endless attempts of mainstream society to ostracize and stigmatize racialized communities. Vijah Prashad, in *The Karma of Brown Folk*, warns us that while all nonwhite groups are affected by racism, those groups like blacks and Mexicans, for example, are seen as "the detritus of U.S. civilization."[151] The troublesome implication is that "racial and ethnic minorities are not and should try to be part of American culture."[152] Bell hooks's *Black Looks: Race and Representation* discusses the representation of race in American culture. Hooks reminds us that the visual images we see of the racialized "others" are the images that "reinforce and reinscribe white supremacy."[153] This has fundamentally proved to be the case.

Even though the term *Asian American* was coined by activists on college campuses in the 1960s, and reflects a similar racist treatment toward Chinese, Japanese, and Koreans, *Asian American* is a term that in itself is problematic. Today, Chinese, Japanese, Koreans, Vietnamese, and Indians are lumped together as Asian Americans and are viewed as the model minority.[154] For sure, some Asians are seduced by this model minority nonsense. The model minority is nothing but a myth which, as Prashad makes clear, "emerged in the wake of the Civil Rights movement to show up rebellious blacks [and Mexicans] for their attempts to redress power relations,"[155] and to discard the notion of blacks' and Mexicans' inferiority. Hence, in the process of creating a model minority there is another process at play, which is the "othering" of the "other." You are a doctor, a CEO, or a novelist, situated within a nonhegemonic racial group. Because of your social and economic status, you think of yourself as "different" from the members of the group in which you are situated. You present yourself like one of "them" from the hegemonic group. When your nonwhiteness is juxtapositioned against their whiteness, you are different from the members of the hegemonic group. Homi K. Bhabha puts it very well when he points out that "to be different from those that are different makes you the same."[156] The accuracy of Bhabha's observation shows that the model minority as an emancipatory signifier from the racialized self can never be truly accomplished.

Racialized people are dominated not only by whiteness but also by the privileges that go along with whiteness. Both germinate because of power's despotic and legitimizing practice that engenders and naturalizes a racial category, which defines itself as white, "pure, authentic, and 'naturally' dominant."[157] Whiteness invariably must exclude from that power any group that is presumed to be unlike itself.[158] The gaze is now shifted from differences to sameness—it is what Philomena Essed calls "cultural cloning." "Cultural cloning," she points out, "is a process of control, of preservation, of (constructed) sameness in view of maintaining privilege and status difference."[159]

To truly accept racialized groups as Americans, one needs to move beyond multiculturalism in an effort to promote structural changes, and carve out a new discourse. Professor Sneja Gunew envisions what she calls the future of "critical multiculturalism [that] lies in an alertness to the inherent 'hybridity' and diverse affiliations of all subjects which may be mobilized in various combinations by particular projects or events."[160] We are in that moment now, when a change is necessary. However, this change could only be possible if we move beyond multiculturalism and in the direction of postmulticulturalism. Instead of celebrating cultural "otherness," as is the emphasis of multiculturalism, postmulticulturalism would embrace cultural inclusion. But first, the transformation from a monocultural state to a multicultural state is necessary.

Second, since whiteness would provide some challenges for postmulticulturalism, there has to be the denormalization of whiteness. In other words, whiteness would have to be unveiled, broken up, and transformed. In a society, such as the United States, where structural inequality is at its core, a multicultural state cannot rid itself of such reoccurring problems of social and economic marginalization and subordination, but it can for sure break away from the homogenizing of American culture as white. It is only in a multicultural state that whiteness can be decentered.

Whiteness

The Definitive Conceptualization
of an American Identity

The emergence of an American cultural identity as white crystallized fairly early in America's history with the founders and early settlers who for the most part came from the British Isles. The separation of the colonies from British rule was important. The role First Nations and blacks were to play in the uniqueness of America's cultural identity was readily apparent. In the minds of the colonists, First Nations and blacks were both seen as cultureless savages. They never looked at them as Americans because they were unlike whites "in appearance, customs, and language."[1] Eventually, the American government had to take on the task of determining who was an American. Even though there was a social practice already in place, nothing offered a more powerful description of who was an American than the first Naturalization Act of 1790, which provided citizenship only to white men. What the American historian Alden Vaughan would later describe as the unbearable "multiethnic mix"[2] was thus legally obliterated. Citizenship was not only about the legality it entailed in terms of rights; it also signified one's equal status in society, equality that was denied to all racialized groups as well as to women. That America was "a white man's country" gained both literal and symbolic meaning.

The development and progression of whiteness as an axiological code of white supremacy was already culturally operational and started way before the Naturalization Act of 1790. Indeed, it laid down the roots for determining who were Americans and how to access normative Americanness. Access was, for the most part, determined by one's color, which dictated the rules for white ownership of America's cultural identity. From the beginning of the formation of the United States, Americans were viewed as white. Even though First Nations, or "native" Americans, and blacks were already in

America, their presence was obliterated. This forgetfulness, this self-inflated amnesia, is perfectly illustrated in the history told by historian David Ramsay, who boasts that the Scots, Swiss, Irish, Germans, New Englanders, and Dutch "have been the sources from which [America] has derived her population."[3] Equally oblivious was the French political thinker Alexis de Tocqueville who, when he visited the United States in 1830, described America and its citizens as "Anglo-Americans." All documents that defined America, including the Declaration of Independence, the Constitution, and the Bill of Rights, contributed to promote a white America.

Unfortunately, the crucial details describing the process of the Americanization of America's culture whereby First Nations, blacks, and other racialized groups were not looked on as Americans and were viewed as inferior have been rarely examined. Americanization percolated into practically every aspect of America's daily life, from political debates to literature. Dana Nelson, in *The World in Black and White: Reading "Race" in American Literature 1638–1862*, pointed to the many ways in which "white" writers from the seventeenth to the nineteenth century constructed versions of an American cultural identity by defining themselves in opposition to racialized ethnic groups.[4] Nonwhites' alleged inferiority no doubt functioned as the underlying principle for whites to piercingly differentiate themselves from nonwhites.[5] Cheryl I. Harris argues that it was not only the concept of racial inferiority that historically subordinated nonwhite people in America but "the interaction between the concepts of race and property."[6] In the same vein, the American historian Matthew Frye Jacobson frankly asserts that "who can own property and who can be property"[7] played a critical role in the oppression of nonwhite people.[8] Indeed, their inferiority carried with it a mark that would justify the discriminatory treatment of nonwhites in America, and was endorsed and daily reinforced within America's institutions, public discourses, and social settings.

In fact, at the beginning of the formation of the United States, there was an emphasis on America as a homogeneous society despite the presence of culturally and physically diverse groups of people. In this sense, I will challenge and call into question the totalizing dominance of whiteness and its ambushing of an American cultural identity as white. Racialized ethnic groups including First Nations and blacks, who were already in America, and later Chinese, were not expected to embrace this so-called cultural oneness and become Americans. More fundamentally, it was the emphasis put by the founders on cultural oneness that would asphyxiate America's cultural manyness.[9]

My purpose in this chapter is to elaborate and show how the Americanization of America's cultural identity denied racialized ethnic groups access to an America identity because nonwhiteness signified inferiority.

Nonwhites' inferiority emerged to justify a social structure organized around various forms of subjugation and mistreatment that would determine nonwhites' unequal positions in America. While all racialized groups underwent enormous subordination, nonwhite women, caught between their race and their gender, among the many identities that inextricably created and shaped them, were not immune to such subordination. They had to deal with the sordid brutality of such practices that surrounded the intersectionality of race and gender oppression.

The Roots of Whiteness: A Prelude

In order to understand fully how an American identity as white gained its roots, we must first ask these questions: Why were blacks instead of whites the direct victims of chattel slavery in America? Are we to believe that the enslavement of blacks and First Nations was not based on the concept of racial thinking even before slavery manifested itself in America? Orlando Patterson, in *Slavery and Social Death: A Comparative Study*, has demonstrated that racial thinking was "the assumption of innate differences based on real or imagined physical or other differences."[10] These differences were in turn transformed into mere deficiencies.

It will not do to assume that racial thinking and the symbolic dimensions of racial domination was not in place before chattel slavery. Why, then, were First Nations and blacks looked on by the colonists as inherently inferior to whites? Why did blacks and First Nations lack rights that were bestowed on whites even before slavery became institutionalized? I maintain that the enslavement of blacks was not accidental. For this reason, it is important to recognize that race in America took on a deeper and more disturbing meaning with the enslavement of blacks. "Black" racial identity marked who was subject to enslavement; "white" racial identity marked who was "free" or, at minimum, not a slave.[11] The material reality of slavery allowed blacks to be defined and treated as chattel, the master's property, rather than as people.[12] Later on, Thomas Jefferson would try to resolve the inconsistency between enslavement and the necessary right to freedom by interpreting slavery as a fact of blacks' inferiority.[13]

Slaves, by hurting themselves, would be destroying the master's property. In the case of the slave woman, she might commit infanticide, an act against the master's property (his surplus profits). Therefore, in an endless effort to harness and tame his anxiety over losing his property, a thing of value, "perhaps the only thing over which the master had true power,"[14] the master stripped slaves of their dignities and denied them basic human rights. The master had to continuously concoct a compendium of new ways to devalue, control, monopolize, and annihilate the slaves. It was in the best interest of the master that the slaves remain docile. Yet "even where the slaves remained completely docile, the very totality of his master's power over him made his master dependent on him."[15]

America's commitment to whiteness started at an early stage of its history. Race and racial thinking, I will maintain, was a formative factor in determining who should be masters and who should be slaves. Blacks and First Nations were viewed as inferior, marked as abnormal, and lacking in humanness. As a result, blacks' and First Nations' racial differences were automatically alleged to be a deviance from the norm. White supremacy within the ideology of racial hierarchy encouraged the expansion of chattel slavery. Also, it was during this period that the construction of race became, to use Barbara J. Fields phrase, "the self-evident truth,"[16] and it would determine the rights, liberties, and freedoms of nonwhites.[17] It was out of this construction of race and racial difference that whiteness gained its dominance.

Racial thinking strengthened and maintained whiteness as the yardstick for determining "inalienable rights" for those perceived as Americans. Whiteness, unmarked and uninterrupted, was the determining factor for denying nonwhites an American identity. The very concerns, who should be slaves and why were blacks instead of whites enslaved, are paramount. Despite various arguments presented by scholars according to which the heathenism of the Negroes and Indians and not their race served as a foundation for their enslavement,[18] racial thinking was already a socially structuring principle among the colonists. The European colonists were a product of the racial thinking that prevailed in the ancient world. Oliver C. Cox explains and elaborates this very issue by showing that even prior to the sixteenth century, Europeans "have not been content merely to accept their present social and political dominance as an established fact. Almost from the first they have attempted to rationalize the situation and to prove to themselves that their subjugation of other racial groups was natural and inevitable."[19]

How did the preference for whiteness over nonwhiteness prevail in America? Why was there not a preference for nonwhiteness over whiteness? Why did whiteness become the racial norm? In the following section I examine, in brief, the emergence of whiteness. I draw on two established arguments for chattel slavery in America to show the "official" starting point for the normalization of whiteness. Also, I will show how racial thinking was fundamental to blacks' enslavement.

The Origins of Slavery and the Inscription of Whiteness

The question of the origins of slavery is always hotly debated. In 1944, Eric Williams made a powerful contribution to this debate when he observed in his book *Capitalism and Slavery* that "slavery was not born of racism: rather, racism was the consequence of slavery."[20] Williams's contribution to the fact of slavery as an economic phenomenon that predated racism influenced Barbara Lewis Solow and Stanley L. Engerman to produce an edited volume, *British Capitalism and Caribbean Slavery: The Legacy of Eric Williams*, in 1987.[21] A similar argument was presented in Oscar Handlin and Mary Handlin's essay in 1950, "Origins of the Southern Labor System." They argued that Africans in Virginia in the seventeenth century were not at the start singled out for enslavement, and black indentured servants were treated the same as white indentured servants. However, the historian Winthrop D. Jordan, for one, reluctantly conceded that "there simply is not enough evidence to indicate with any certainty whether Negroes were treated like white servants or not."[22] Carl N. Degler, also an historian, provided countless examples of white servants being treated much better than black servants. A good example that Degler has drawn on to illustrate this difference was the treatment of three servants, two whites and one black, who ran away together in 1640. After they were caught and returned to their masters, the three men were each given thirty lashes. For the white servants, an extra three years of service to their masters was administered. The black servant had to serve his master for the rest of his life. Similarly, Negro women, free or bond, were treated differently from white women even if white women were servants.[23]

Handlin and Handlin claimed that the pressure of the New World contributed largely to the association of Africans with slavery. Even though, for Degler, it is far from proper to saddle the changes in the New World as a direct marker for the enslavement of blacks,[24] Handlin and Handlin made clear that black enslavement was not there from the start. Slavery came late in the century; racism came much later.[25] For sure the condition of the Negro was that of servant until around the 1660s.[26] Besides, Fields tells us that the rights slaves enjoyed up until 1661 were not afforded to free blacks even in the nineteenth century.[27] Yet there was a difference in treatment between black and white servants.[28]

For white indentured servants, the terms of service were decreased with a greater reliance on the labor of blacks. Yet racial lines were neither consistently nor piercingly demarcated within social groups. Activities between blacks and lower-class whites were socially communal.[29] Both black and white indentured servants joined the militia formed by Nathaniel Bacon to attack First Nations who represented a threat to white settlers. Whites joined the movement with the aim of getting free land and becoming farmers. Blacks, on the other hand, learned, as Ronald Takaki noted, that revolution was the pathway to freedom from a lifelong bond-servitude.[30] During that time there was no indication that blacks would be freed from bond-servitude.

Bacon's Rebellion of 1676 was instigated by black and white bond-laborers trying to put an end to bond-servitude.[31] Consequently, Bacon's Rebellion equipped those in power with new aims: poor whites had to be made to feel superior to blacks and other nonwhites; and women had to be viewed as subordinate to men in an effort to reaffirm patriarchal structures and interests. In the end, Bacon's Rebellion would establish not only the subordinate position of First Nations, blacks, other racialized groups, and women but, more important, what Theodore W. Allen has referred to as "the monorail of Anglo-American historical development, white [male] supremacy."[32]

In an effort to alienate blacks from white servants and promote racial hierarchy as a logical conclusion, the white servants were entitled to land at the end of their servitude, even though some unforeseen problems in allocating the land were inevitable.[33] Racial categorization, which embraced skin color, defined and shaped the unequal position between black and white servants. Yet, in assessing this claim, we must turn our attention to Degler's provocative essay, "Slavery and the Genesis of American Race Prejudice." In his essay, he reminds us that in early America, there was always contempt for Africans. For this reason he warns that any account of the origins of slavery has to pay particular attention to what is labeled "the color prejudice" of America.[34] Slavery, Handlin and Handlin remarked, materialized "from the adjustment to American conditions of traditional European institutions."[35] Whatever the cause of the materialization of slavery, when it did emerge, "it became infused with the social attitude, which had prevailed from the very beginning, namely, that Negroes were inferior," Degler writes.[36] Drawing from countless sources of evidence, "discrimination against the Negro occurred before the slave status was defined and before Negro labor became pivotal to the economic system"[37] "because it was the cheapest and best."[38] William Goodell sums it up: "The Negro race, from its introduction, was regarded with disgust."[39] Thus, by the time slavery became fixed in law, the inferiority of the blacks was an already established and recognized custom.[40] Nonetheless, in spite of the genesis of slavery and racial prejudices, the synchronizing of both, by all means, lay the groundwork for the inscribing of whiteness and white privilege into America's cultural psyche, which, later on, would be supported by America's institutions.

The debate over the conditions that laid the groundwork for slavery did not fade away. In fact, in "Modern Tensions and the Origins of American Slavery," Jordan pointed out that the racist concept of slavery was advanced after slavery was already in place in America. Blacks would not have been enslaved if there had not been any need for labor in the colonies.[41] Yet there are countless sources of evidence that refute Jordan's stipulations according to which America's racial attitudes toward blacks predated the eighteenth century, and this made it easier for whites to enslave blacks. Jordan would eventually go back on his conclusions and apologetically confess that "Modern Tension and the Origins of American Slavery" was written "at a time when (as [he] now thinks) he was far from comprehending the origins of slavery."[42] In his later book, *White Over Black: American Attitudes Towards the Negro*, he reformulated his argument pertaining to the foundation of slavery. *White Over Black*, published in 1968, earned Jordan the National Book Award, the Francis Parkman prize, and the Ralph Waldo Emerson prize.[43] In addition, it was singled out for the 1996 Seminar on "Constructing Race: Differentiating People in the Early Modern World, 1400–1700."[44]

Another Look at Racial Thinking

Race and racial thinking permeated the laws and public discourse, and embedded itself in the very core of American cultural consciousness. Degler has argued that in the colonies, a Negro, whether he or she was a servant or free, was "treated as an inferior to white men."[45] Hence, it is enough to point out that it was necessary to construct blacks as different at an early period in America's history. Race was thus constructed on the notion that blacks and other nonwhites were inferior to whites. This racial construction had to be an ongoing process that hinged on a repeated appeal to the hegemonic position of whiteness—the kind of trepidation that provided the basis for collective self-fashioning of whiteness that the African American philosopher Lucius T. Outlaw Jr. spoke about. "One of the most deeply felt and widely shared experience by the settler colonists . . . [was] the fear of being both similar to . . . and profoundly different from the supposed inferior people."[46] White supremacy must "repeat itself," as Judith Butler explains, "in order to establish the illusion of its own uniformity and identity."[47] Blacks' inferiority was so marked that, in 1630, "Hugh Davis was soundly whipped before an Assembly of Negroes and others for abusing himself to dishonor of God and the shame of Christians by defying his body by lying with a Negro."[48] To enforce racial difference and maintain racial purity, by 1691, a law was implemented to increase the punishment of any white woman who married a black or First Nations man. The seriousness of this offense was harshly punishable by a whipping, or by enslavement if a woman should marry a black man. In Virginia, for example, if a white person married a black or First Nations person, within three months of the marriage, he or she was banished or removed from the community.

In order for us to really understand how the separation of nonwhites from whites was in part accomplished, we have to turn our attention to the social historian Lerone Bennett's most graphic but necessary account of the state's role in maintaining nonwhites' subordination. Bennett recalls,

> The whole system of separation and subordination rested on official state terror. The exigencies of the situation required men to kill some white people to keep them white and to kill many blacks to keep them black. In the North and South, men and women were maimed, tortured, and murdered in a comprehensive campaign of mass conditioning. The severed heads of black and white rebels were impaled on poles along the road as warnings to black people and white people, and opponents of the status quo were starved to death in chains and roasted slowly over open fires. Some rebels were branded; others were castrated.[49]

In the end, the state served its purpose in normalizing and maintaining whiteness, which, in Bennett's words, "was an inherent part of the new system"[50] of institutionalized state violence.

In addition to keeping the races separate and maintaining the purity of the white race, mulattoes were viewed as an "abominable mixture."[51] The assumed purity of whites would eventually give rise to white supremacist groups such as the Ku Klux Klan (KKK).[52] Like First Nations and blacks, mulattoes were looked on as the "other." Later on, Chinese would also be viewed as a threat to white racial purity. John F. Miller at the 1878 California Constitutional Convention, as Takaki has observed, openly declared, "Were the Chinese to amalgamate at all with our people, it would be the lowest, most vile and degraded of our race, and the result of that amalgamation would be a hybrid of the most despicable, a mongrel of the most detestable that has ever afflicted the earth."[53]

The meaning of nonwhites' racial identity could not be understood apart from the specific way nonwhites were not white. It was important to differentiate "us" from "them." The "them" and "us" scenarios, which operated, often aggressively, in conjunction, have created boundaries, hallow, racial boundaries between the antagonistic relational white selves and the nonwhite "others." Since the white selves were unmarked, as a category for analysis, it is the nonwhite "others," to borrow from Toni Morrison, that "became the means of thinking about body, mind, chaos, kindness, and love; provided the occasion for exercises in the absence of restraint, the presence of restraint, the contemplation of freedom and of aggression; permitted opportunities for the exploration of ethics and morality, for meeting the obligations of the social contract, for bearing the cross of religion and following out the ramifications of power."[54]

Power is a major factor in the relationship between the self and the "other." The "other" is not, to use Sander L. Gilman's words, "the antithesis of the mirage of whiteness."[55] Whiteness and "otherness" are relational. White supremacy correlates with nonwhites' inferiority. Whiteness cannot stand alone; it cannot exist by itself. The nonwhite self is measured against the white self and it is reduced accordingly to the "other." The upshot is that the predatory nature of "whiteness is parasitic" on "otherness."[56] This exploitation generates ways of thinking about race, gender, sexuality, culture, and nations as categories for determining whiteness.

The unleashing of the imperialist ideology of self and "other," the dominant culture and the nondominant culture, has been nurtured through the practice of Fanon's notion of cultural hierarchy. Cultural hierarchy, or what Takaki labels the superstructure of ideology, is "an order in which a certain way of life and thought is dominant, in which one concept of reality is diffused throughout society in all its institutional and private manifestations, informing with its spirit all taste, morality, customs, religious and political principles, and all social relations particularly in their intellectual and moral connotation."[57] Cultural hierarchy was particularly important in the development of the material conditions of racialized ethnic groups in America. The treatment and conditions of blacks under slavery, as captured in slave narratives,[58] is dehumanizing, horrible, and provides the template for the harsh treatment of the other racialized groups in America.

The black–white racial model, which can be hardly underestimated, extended itself to incorporate all racialized groups. Black became the signifier for nonwhite. In this respect, any arguments that the black–white model of race relations in America excludes and marginalizes other nonwhites are, in large part, misconstrued. I will return to this point later in the discussion. In fact, the encounter of the colonists with First Nations helped to shape race relations in America. First Nations, who were perceived as different from the vantage point of religious as well as racial grounds, were already subjugated and displaced. The status of First Nations during the colonial and early antebellum period, 1679–1709, was that of servitude. *Hudgins v. Wrights* is a case in point.[59] Nonetheless, the enslavement of First Nations represented tremendous difficulties because it was easy for them to escape and retaliate.[60] Partly for this reason First Nations were viewed by the colonists as the uncivilized, primitive, and "unredeemable savages." This vision would justify the colonists' genocidal treatment of First Nations. Nonwhites would continue to be discriminated against because whites had the power and ample encouragement to do so. Later on we will see how the violence perpetrated against nonwhites in America, especially blacks, became institutionalized.

If the fundamental purpose of the slave codes was to prevent and dissuade slave rebellion, which was not common, why would free blacks, along with the slaves, have to adhere to the severity of the slave codes? These vicious slave codes, exacerbated by a desperate desire to keep blacks in their place, were more than the barbaric and convenient obligation of subjugating Negroes to laws different from the laws that pertained to whites. It was one more way to confirm whites' jurisdiction over blacks. It was the beginning of the institutionalization of whiteness.

The cue to understanding this phenomenon can be recognized when we examine the status of free Negroes. The historian Joseph Boskin notes that Negroes and slaves become homogeneous and convertible.[61] In fact, free Negroes, like slaves, were denied the rights that were enjoyed by whites. For instance, "no Negro may carry any weapon of any kind, nor leave his master's grounds without a pass, nor shall any 'negroe or other slaves . . . presume to lift his hands in opposition against any Christian,' and if a Negro runs away and resists recapture it 'shall be lawful for such persons or person to kill said negroe or slave.'"[62] Slaves who resisted the authority of any white person were whipped; parts of their bodies (hands, ears, or legs) were mutilated. They were hanged in chains publicly as a reminder of what would happen to blacks if they should resist the authority of a white person. This is a good illustration of the "operations of power" as a regime of force or symbolic violence, to use Michel Foucault's terms.[63] Foucault insightfully illustrates how this form of power works: "[It] applies itself to immediate everyday life which categorizes the individual, marks him by his own individuality, attaches him to his own identity, imposes a law of truth on him which he must recognize and which others have to recognize in him. It is a form of power which makes individuals subjects. There are two meanings of the word *subject*: subject to someone else by control and dependence, and tied to his own identity by a conscience or self-knowledge. Both meanings suggest a form of power which subjugates and make subject to."[64]

The Workings of Whiteness

As long as blacks remained slaves, the whites, even poor ones, remained superior to blacks even though their economic position was no better than that of the free blacks or the slaves. Whites were deemed more important, valued, and powerful even if they did suffer in the hands of other whites. After all, to be a poor white did not mean that he or she inhabited a space of nonwhiteness. Wilbert E. Moore and Robin M. Williams, in "Stratification in the Ante-bellum South," have demonstrated this quite well. They recognized that slavery bestowed on the poor whites "a social status higher than that of blacks. This peculiar stratification system based on whiteness acquired priority over economic and class interests."[65] In other words, slavery linked the privilege of whites to the subordination of blacks through a legal regime that attempted the conversion of blacks into objects of property. Similarly, the settlement and seizure of First Nations' land was implemented through law. In 1763, the British Crown ruled that First Nations were "sovereign nations with inalienable rights to their land." Eventually, the Indian Removal Act of 1830 and its aftermath forced First Nations to occupy Indian reservations, and by 1890, a large number of First Nations lived on Indian reservations.[66]

Whites had to control First Nations' land and had to control black labor. By treating blacks as property, it was easier to hyperexploit black labor. "Race and property were thus conflated by establishing a form of property contingent on race—only Blacks were subjugated as slaves and treated as property. Similarly, the conquest, removal, and extermination of [First Nations'] lives and culture were ratified by confirming and acknowledging the property rights of whites in [First Nations'] land."[67] These distinctive and separate forms of exploitation of blacks and First Nations would define and explain what Harris called "the construction of whiteness as property."[68] Whiteness as property culturally defined and distinguished even implicitly the dichotomization between whites and nonwhites.

This racist formulation embedded the painstaking fact of white privilege into the very definition of property, marking another stage in the evolution of the complicated notion of property interest in whiteness. "Possession—the act necessary to lay the basis for rights in property—was defined to include only the cultural practices of whites. This definition laid the foundation for the idea that whiteness—that which whites alone possess—is valuable and is privileged."[69] Law professor Tracy Higgins would later refer to this principle as "a property right in 'whiteness.'"[70] Whiteness was everything. It was the foundation of literal as well as symbolic power. Poor whites managed to reap aesthetic and psychological rewards as a result of possessing the "property right in whiteness," on which they greatly relied. Whiteness became the "invisible knapsack" loaded with unearned assets that was given to white people. The "invisible knapsack" was loaded to the brim with white entitlements. Whiteness reinforced, perpetuated, and maintained the despotic position of whites in America and defined an American cultural identity as white.

An American Cultural Identity in Retrospect

The values, institutions, and culture of the early settlers, who mostly came from the British Isles, shaped the foundations for the development of an American cultural identity. There was an emphasis on America as a homogeneous society despite the presence of culturally and physically diverse groups of people. Horace M. Kallen, in his two-part essay, "Democracy versus the Melting Pot: A Study of American Nationality," explains this homogeneity. He notes, "The mass of white men in the colonies were actually, with respect to one another, rather free and equal."[71] Equally alarming is when Kallen takes on the meaningful task of explaining what he means by equal. "I refer not so much to the absence of great differences in wealth, as to the fact that the whites were like-minded" he explains. "They were possessed of ethnic and cultural unity; they were homogeneous with respect to ancestry and ideals."[72] First Nations, blacks, and later on Chinese and Mexicans, were peculiar and somatically different. Unlike whites in appearance, they presented a clear threat to America's cultural homogeneity. It made sense, then, that the entrance of Chinese women and families, for example, into the United States would be prohibited in 1875 with the passing of the Page Law, partly to maintain America's racial homogeneity. The Page Law debarred not only Chinese prostitutes from entering the United States but Chinese wives as well.

The Declaration of Independence and the Revolution engineered a distinctive America that presented to the colonists a decisive break with British rule. For John Jay, an architect of the *Federalist Papers*, the conception of America as "one united people, a people descended from the same ancestors, speaking the same language, professing the same religion, attached to the same principles of government, very similar in their manners and customs,"[73] clearly ignored America's diverse population. Ideals such as equality, democracy, individualism, "life, liberty, and pursuit of property," as is spelled out in Thomas Jefferson's *The Declaration of Independence* and the Constitution, characterized the "American creed," a creed that declared all American citizens as equal, yet is marred by racial and gender prejudice that would limit its universality.[74] "This ever raging conflict," as Gunnar Myrdal puts it, in *An American Dilemma*,[75] between the American creed and the "pre-rational racial dogma embraced by most white Americans" would eventually be put to the test.[76] In 1964, in his *Crisis in Black and White*, Charles Silberman refuted Myrdal's notion of "An American Dilemma" by pointing out that there is not really a dilemma because white Americans are comfortable being racists. During a roundtable discussion titled "Liberalism and the Negroes" held in New York the same year, James Baldwin restated the claim. Also, in 1967, Stokely Carmichael and Charles Hamilton, in *Black Power: The Politics of Liberation in America*, also rejected Myrdal's claim, and pointed to the fact that since all whites benefit from racism, it is in their best interests to work in maintaining such a system.[77] The "American creed" developed a cultural identity that was unique to America, and stemmed from a modified English culture rather than a fused European culture. In the words of Tocqueville, it was "a new race of people."[78] First Nations and blacks could not quite measure up, to cite Kallen, to "the measure and the standard of Americanism,"[79] which was based on whiteness. "Whiteness," as the eminent historian Eric Arnesen reminds us, "is, among other things, 'being white.'"[80]

Benjamin Franklin, one of America's founding fathers, had revealed his very desire for the homogeneity of America, and, to borrow the words of the critical race theorist David Theo Goldberg, "keeping America white."[81] Most telling was Benjamin Franklin's essay, titled "Observations Concerning the Increase of Mankind and the Peopling of Countries," in which he provided, without any reservation, his desire for more whites in America: "All Africa is black or tawny; Asia chiefly tawny; America (exclusive of the newcomers) wholly so. And in Europe, the Spaniards, Italians, French, Russians, and Swedes are generally of what we call a swarthy complexion; as are the Germans also, the Saxons only excepted, who, with the English, make the principal body of white people on the face of the earth. I could wish their numbers were increased."[82]

In this respect, Franklin bemoans the limited number of what he calls "purely white people" in America, and his desire for more white people in America led him to significantly ask, "why should [America] in the Sight of Superior Beings, darken its People? Why increase the sons of Africa by planting them in America where we have so fair an opportunity by excluding of Blacks and Tawneys and increasing the lovely whites."[83] It was a matter of excluding blacks and other racialized groups, since they were already in America. Certainly, Franklin and his contemporaries were acutely aware of race and the proper logics of racial hierarchy as an attempt to keep whites on top of the racial ladder.[84]

Thomas Jefferson had a solution for Franklin's desire for increasing the "lovely whites." Blacks had to be expatriated and shipped to another country. Perhaps blacks should be shipped to the independent black nation of Santo Domingo. This country was, for Jefferson, "inhabited already by a people of their own race and color; climates congenial with their natural constitution; insulated from other descriptions of men; nature seems to have formed these islands to become the receptacle of the blacks transplanted in this hemisphere."[85] Rather than convince blacks to form their own communities in America, it was fixed in Jefferson's mind that blacks and whites could never coexist in the United States of

America because of the acrimonious differences between the two races. For Jefferson, then, "blacks whether originally a distinct race, or made distinct by time and circumstances, are inferior to whites in the endowments both of body and mind."[86] Jefferson's outlandish speculation and ontological claim helped him to establish that whites were superior to blacks. Even though he distinctly knew that both "race(s)" belong to the same human class, for him, whites possessed "superior qualifications."[87] To borrow the words of Tocqueville, this racial "distinction . . . prevailed even in the equality of death. Blacks' inferiority was so pronounced that when the Negro died, [their] bones were cast aside."[88] The treatment of blacks' dead bodies was consistent with the social death that Patterson describes in *Slavery and Social Death*.

The symbiotic relationship of First Nations and whites, in the antagonistic view of Jefferson, then governor of Virginia, was that First Nations were to be civilized. "The idea that it was the white man's burden to make sure that [First Nations] became 'civilized' was born from the white imaginary."[89] If this were impossible, the only recourse was extermination. Even though First Nations, for the most part, were not anxious or thrilled to be a part of the dominant culture, according to Jefferson, they had to assimilate, or become "acculturated, that is, not only to confirm externally but to become habituated to the way of life, the practices, and customs of the [dominant] culture."[90] First Nations, in the words of Takaki, "had to adopt the culture of the white man."[91]

Even though assimilation was to bear on the ill treatment of First Nations, its presumption was to offer them a kind of exorbitant normality that blacks, for example, were unable to attain. However, for many First Nations, assimilation, which meant Americanization, was unreachable. The persistent effort to normalize First Nations cumulated into an 1830 law that amounted to their removal from their homes.[92] Assimilation became the basis for much of the government's policy toward First Nations from the 1880s to the 1930s. The passage by Congress of the General Allotment Act (The Dawes Severalty Act) of 1887 is illustrative. An extract from the act marked the unconcealed faith of First Nations: "Every Indian born within the territorial limits of the United States to whom allotments shall have been made under the provisions of this act, or under any law or treaty, and every Indian born within the territorial limits of the United States who has voluntarily taken up, within said limits, his residence separate and apart from any tribe of Indians therein, and has adopted the habits of civilized life, is hereby declared to be a citizen of the United States, and is entitled to all the rights, privileges and immunities of such citizens."

Thomas J. Morgan, the Commissioner of Indian Affairs, wrote in 1890 that assimilation became "the settled policy of the government to break up reservations, destroy tribal relations, settle [First Nations] upon their own homesteads, incorporate them into the national life, and deal with them not as nations or tribes or bands, but as individual citizens." In addition, it weakened First Nations' women's position in agricultural work by making First Nations' men head of the family unit as well as owners of the land. The Dawes Act would be the most important method of deterring First Nations from acquiring American citizenship. It was not until the Indian Citizenship Act of 1924 was implemented that First Nations were able to acquire American citizenship.

The republican ideals of equality and natural rights for all were put to the test on several fronts. It forced those in power to make an effort in bringing together the policy and practice of "Life, Liberty and Pursuit of Happiness," which was sacred to the American creed. Equality did not emerge in a vacuum. It was forever associated, to use the words of Morrison, "with another seductive concept: the hierarchy of race."[93] It is important to recognize that race in America took on a deeper and more disturbing meaning with the enslavement of blacks. In fact, slavery was dreadful for men but, not surprisingly, its ferociousness harbored itself in the body, mind, and soul of the slave woman.[94] The master, thinking of the slave woman as his property, might do to her whatever pleased him. He could have her murdered, mutilate her body, refuse to feed her, separate her from her children, or severely whip and rape her. Within the paradigm of heteronormativity, or what Adrienne Rich has termed "compulsory heterosexuality," black women experienced an enormous amount of sexual terror. To complete the picture, the rape of a slave woman was not considered a crime. Angela Y. Davis as well as Katie Geneva Cannon grippingly speak to this established and visible, imperative tradition of "stock breeding" with white men raping female slaves.[95] Davis explains that "rape, in fact, was an uncamouflaged expression of the slaveholder's economic mastery and the overseer's control over black women as workers."[96] Hence, the significance of this form of degradation of female slaves should not be considered through male dominance alone. It signified the reduction of human beings to animals.

Orlando Patterson, in *Slavery and Social Death: A Comparative Study*, has demonstrated that racial thinking was "the assumption of innate differences based on real or imagined physical or other differences."[97] These differences were in turn transformed into mere deficiencies. Racial identity, above all other identities, became a rationale for treating blacks as less than humans, and for white America to continue its vulgar practice of black enslavement. Later on, as I have already stated, Thomas Jefferson would try to resolve the inconsistency between enslavement and the necessary right to freedom by interpreting slavery as a fact of blacks' inferiority.[98]

Not surprisingly, for the power elites and the framers of the Constitution, the position on equality meant sameness in phenotype, language, and cultural representation that is derivative of whiteness. This led Jurgen Heideking, in "The Image of the English Enemy during the American Revolution," to declare that ideology, not ethnicity, was the touchstone of America's national identity.[99] Tamar Jacoby extends his argumentation and concludes that with America's identity "the emphasis was on ideas rather than ethnicity."[100] For sure, it was not until 1949, in his book *Social Class in America*, that W. Lloyd Warner introduced the word *ethnicity*, along with *class*, to operationally describe a group of people who were self-consciously fused around particular cultural traditions.[101] Yet the ethnic element in American nationality cannot be relegated to an epiphenomenal role. In Hector St. John de Crèvecoeur's *Letters from an American Framer*, Crèvecoeur wrote, in 1782, a much-quoted passage:

> What then is the American, this new man? He is either a European or the descendent of a European, hence that strange mixture of blood, which you will find in no other country. I could point out to you a family whose grandfather was an Englishman, whose wife was Dutch, whose son married a French woman, and whose present four sons have four wives of different nations. He is an American, who, leaving behind him all his ancient prejudice and manners, receives new ones from the new mode of life he has embraced, the new government he obeys, and the new rank he holds. He becomes an American by being received into the broad lap of our great Alma mater. Here individuals are melted into a new race of men, whose labours and posterity will one day cause great changes in the world.[102]

The "new man" whom Crèvecoeur wrote about was neither the First Nations nor the Negroes.[103] Years later, in 1924, Horace Kallen, in *Culture and Democracy in America*, would reinforce Crèvecoeur's notion of an American as white: "I do not discuss the influence of the Negro upon the esthetic material and cultural character of the South and the rest of the United States," he wrote.[104]

The concept of ethnicity, to borrow the historian Philip Gleason's words, "was quite recessive in the first years of the republic."[105] Nonetheless, ethnic diversity was not of much importance to those in power. In fact, as long as a person was white, a person did not have to be of "any particular national, linguistic, religious, or ethnic background" in order to become an American.[106] Eventually, the question whether all inhabitants on American soil should be looked on as Americans arose. Whether "Americans" thought of themselves as English or as the products of European amalgamation, they all had something in common which was their white skin.

What Professor George Lipsitz referred to as "the possessive investment in whiteness" started way before World War II.[107] "We hold these truths to be self evident that all men are created equally" Thomas Jefferson, in 1776, wrote in the Declaration of Independence. Ever since, "all men are created equally" has become part of America's public discourse. The British historian Eric J. Hobsbawn, on one occasion, argued that "words are witnesses, which speak louder than documents." It is partly for this reason that Samuel Huntington asks the provocative question, "Who hold these truths to be self-evident? Americans hold these truths. Who are Americans? People who adhere to these truths."[108] First Nations, blacks, Chinese, Mexicans, and other racialized groups could have never adhered to these "truths." How these groups perceived these "truths" is an important question, which remains underexplored.

The idea that "all men are equal" vexed some of the most prominent figures. In fact, for James Hamond, the former governor of South Carolina in the 1840s, it was "ridiculously absurd." A decade later, "a self-evident lie" was the phrase used by Senator John Pettit to denounce Jefferson's notion of equality.[109] As late as the 1980s, Pastor Richard G. Butler of the Aryan Nations noted, "When the Declaration of Independence talks about 'one people,' it's not talking about a nation made for Asia, Africa, [or] India."[110] Judging the rights of citizens based on the color of their skin has certainly been an American pastime.

Nonetheless, America, now this new nation comprising thirteen colonies, free from the tyranny of Britain, derived "its language, its laws, its institutions, its political ideas, its customs, its precepts, and its prayers from Britain."[111] Britain was the dominant influence on American culture. According to Arthur M. Schlesinger, the British tradition provided the standard for confirmation and assimilation into American culture.[112] Assimilation had a Eurocentric flavor and meant adopting the Anglo-Saxon way of life. Years later, among the many remarkable ideas to be found in Israel Zangwill's play *The Melting Pot*, was the adoption of the notion of assimilation. In the play, David Quixano, one of the characters, explains the melting pot. He tells us frankly that the melting pot "is God's crucible . . . where all the races of Europe—Germans and Frenchmen, Irishmen and Englishmen, Jews and Russians—are melting and reforming." First Nations, blacks, and the other racialized groups could thus not be a part of the melting pot; they were "the unmeltable ethnics." They failed to fit the mold of Americanness/whiteness. Given its Eurocentric bias, it is clear that the melting pot was only describing white ethnicities.

The "unmeltable ethnics," the racially inferior, no doubt functioned as a rationale for whites to sharply distinguish themselves from these groups.[113] Whites viewed nonwhites as savages, and their vision was the direct vehicle for the white colonists to appropriate First Nations' lands, and use blacks and Chinese labors. Blacks were slaves. Chinese first came to America to seek out the "gold mountain."[114] What was to be done with blacks and First Nations already in America became a pressing concern. The American Revolution against the British rule made the question of race relations an important one. It was the Naturalization Act of 1790 that would settle this once and for all. It determined who would be citizens of the United States of America, which in its effort to bestow citizenship only on white men, no doubt mocked the Aristotelian designation of a citizen as "one who rules and is ruled in turn."[115] Blacks and First Nations were, especially, vulnerable to the tyranny of being ruled. In the following section I will look specifically at the Naturalization Act of 1790 to show America's commitment to whiteness; how whiteness as a guarantor of American citizenship had serious consequences for nonwhites; how the law has constructed the relationship between citizens and how racial categorization would impact the very fabric of America's race relations, which served to define and protect an American cultural identity as white. This has inevitably shaped America's future on race relations and the symptomatic racial attitudes that exist in this society even today.

The Naturalization Act of 1790 and Citizenship in America

The Naturalization Act of March 26, 1790, claimed that "all free white persons who, have, or, shall migrate into the United States, and shall give satisfactory proof, before a magistrate, by oath, that they intend to reside therein, and shall take an oath of allegiance, and shall have resided in the United States for one whole year, shall be entitled to the rights of citizenship."[116] The lawmakers saw the 1790 Naturalization Act as very inclusive rather than exclusive and it never occurred to them that legal citizenship was limited to only white people.[117] This act served two main purposes. One, it was to suppress slave insurrections from occurring, and two, it was a way to discourage the resistance effort of First Nations against whites' infringement on their land.[118] For those entering the United States during and after 1802, a modification to the 1790 act set a five-year residence requirement for new immigrants. However, like the act of 1790, that of 1802 restricted naturalization to an "alien, being free and white."[119]

The act would eventually affect Chinese immigrants arriving in America in 1852, especially the Chinese who worked in the mines in California. The California legislature passed a tax law requiring all foreign miners who were not citizens to pay $3 a month. The law lasted until 1870 when it was reversed.[120] In the end, the Naturalization Act of 1790 normalized the racist practices of America, which connected whiteness with citizenship.[121] Cheryl I. Harris, in her article titled "Whiteness as Property," has expanded her thoroughgoing analysis to the changing definitions of citizenship as introduced in the act where "the franchise, for example, was broadened to extend voting rights to unpropertied white men at the same time that black voters were specifically disenfranchised, arguably shifting the property required for voting from land to whiteness."[122] Certainly, the expansion of the eligibility of nonwhites into the incorporation of American citizenship has been sluggish. For example, it was not until the implementation of the McCarran-Walter Act of 1952 that Japanese could become naturalized U.S. citizens. By racializing the qualification of newcomers into the United States, this act regulated free blacks[123] and First Nations and set limits on future access to citizenship for all racialized groups in America.[124] As shown in *Dred Scott v. Sandford*, in 1857, the Supreme Court held that blacks could not be citizens.[125] According to Justice Roger Taney, blacks had no rights that "the white man was bound to respect." This was highly problematic. The concerns were to be placed to rest when Dr. Van Evrie announced, "for those perverse creatures among us who clamor so loudly for Negro equality, or that the Negro shall be treated as if he were a white man, only desire to force their hideous theories on others, and would rather have theirs."[126] The fact of the matter is that "the Caucasian is white, the Negro is black; the first is the most superior, the latter the most inferior" he claimed with authority.[127] He would then produce a coupling of scientific and religious proof to support whites' supremacy.[128]

Blacks' inferiority penetrated into every aspect of America's daily life, from political debates to literature.[129] Mark Twain's novel, *The Adventures of Huckleberry Finn*, shows the dehumanizing process at work in society at the time. In the novel, there is a steamboat accident. Huck Finn's Aunt Sally asks, "Anybody hurt?" Huck Finn replies, "No'm. Killed a nigger." "Well, it's lucky," she retorts, "because sometimes people do get hurt."[130] This episode epitomizes the white conception of black human lives in those days. Ernest Hemingway, in his 1935 novel *Green Hills of Africa*, remarks in this regard that "all modern American literature comes from one book by Mark Twain called *The Adventures of Huckleberry Finn*. . . . There was nothing before. There has been nothing so good since."[131] Given its depiction of blacks, as Ralph Ellison acknowledges, *The Adventures of Huckleberry Finn* is an important document of America's culture,[132] viewing blacks and other nonwhites as unequal to whites. While all blacks and other nonwhites were looked on as inferior, nonwhite women's positionality was shaped and maintained by the intersectionality of race, gender, class, and ideology, which became embedded in America's cognitive and intellectual traditions and shaped the American cultural psyche. In this context, the issue of who is a "woman" becomes paramount. I return to the point later in my discussion.

The inferiority of all racialized groups was articulated by the lawmakers even before the Dred Scott case, when the Act Concerning Civil Cases was implemented in 1850. It states, "No Black, or Mulatto person, or Indian, shall be allowed to give evidence in favor of, or against a white man." In *People v. Hall*, in 1854, Hall, a white man charged with the murder of Ling Sing, a Chinese man, was convicted thanks to the testimony of three Chinese witnesses. But the California Supreme Court reversed the decision because, according to the Act Concerning Civil Cases, Chinese were also included in the law. The judge affirmed that the Chinese were "a race of people whom nature has marked as inferior, and who are incapable of progress or intellectual development beyond a certain point." Article XIX, Section I–IV of the California Constitution, adopted in 1876, was very specific on how Chinese were to be treated in California.[133] A succession of acts cumulated into the Chinese Exclusion Act of 1882.[134] This act suspended all Chinese immigration for at least the next ten years,[135] and denied citizenship to Chinese who were already in America. In addition to these legal clauses, lynchings, boycotts, and mass expulsions added to the anti-Chinese sentiments.[136] During the debate of the 1882 Exclusion Act, a senator wanted to know why, if First Nations could be located on reservations, the Chinese could not.[137]

In 1889, the Supreme Court supported this act as constitutional because, according to Justice Stephen J. Field, Chinese are of a different race. It was then impracticable to Americanize Chinese. The justice proceeded to claim that if the Chinese were not restricted, this "Oriental invasion [would be] a menace to [America's] civilization." The Chinese Exclusion Act was part of a tyrannical policy that was modified and extended in various ways to Japanese, Filipino, Korean, and Asian-Indian persons in the United States. Renewed in 1892, the Chinese Exclusion Act was extended indefinitely in 1902. It was not revoked until 1943 when Congress repealed the Chinese exclusion laws and allowed quotas for Chinese immigration. The implementation of the Immigration and Nationality Act Amendments of 1965 ended the quota system that was in place. The supposed racial inferiority of Chinese, as I have already pointed out, was on a par with the supposed racial inferiority of blacks and First Nations. Various measures had to be generated to reinforce racial inferiority. The racial binarism based on the "black" vs. "white" model led to consideration of all nonwhites as blacks. It was the foundation for America's political, economic, and social life, the very sovereignty of America's cultural tradition fixed in a hefty dosage of whiteness, which in the end would determine who is an American.

Whiteness would become the active and interactive process of determining who is an American. It is against this backdrop that the history of whiteness would reinforce, perpetuate, and maintain its institutionalization. What were the consequences for nonwhiteness? This might seem like a commonsensical question to ask, but I ask it in order to make us intensely reflect on the dialogic relationship between whiteness and nonwhiteness, and how nonwhiteness was measured and compared against whiteness, and was reduced to "otherness." "Otherness" humiliates and degrades the "other." David R. Roediger explains this well. He tells us that whiteness was not limited to the ways in which the racial "others" were treated; it impacted "the ways that whites [thought] of themselves, of power, of pleasure, of gender."[138]

The inferior status of nonwhite women has been depicted in the great American novels. The prototypical novel to which Morrison perceptibly draws our attention is Ernest Hemingway's 1937 novel *To Have and Have Not*. In the novel, Morrison tells us, "during a passionate scene of lovemaking, Marie asks her husband,"

> "Listen, did you ever do it with a nigger wench?"
> "Sure."
> "What's it like?"
> "Like nurse shark."[139]

While white masculinity is sustained and pumped up and the femininity that is put into play is white, in Morrison's view, black woman is "the further thing from being human. . . . [and] evocative of anything resembling" a white woman.[140] In the slightest overexaggeration, the quandary is laid out in Morrison's writing about the benefits that the cult of femininity bestows on white women. On the other hand, the assaulting cult of femininity and the metaphoric construction of woman, in many ways, quietly subjugated white women. However, it was an ethical impossibility for black women and other women of color to be seen as human beings much less as women. Nonwhite women were unable to escape their race. The female slave Sojourner Truth, "Ain't I a Woman?" draws our attention to the homogenizing and essentializing of the category "woman." Later on, "Ain't I a Woman?" would become the idiomatic manifestation of black feminists' contending the women's movement and second-wave feminism. In the autumn of 1984 the *Feminist Review* dedicated an issue, "Many Voices: One Chant: Black Feminist Perspective," to the question, in the hope of stimulating further discussions and debates of black women's experiences through the intersectionality of race, gender, class, and sexuality inequalities.

Engaged as Tocqueville was with "the prejudice of race," he sensed that the usage of the term *races* was something dishonorable. He recognized that racial prejudice was stronger in those states that had abolished slavery, and even more so "where servitude has never been known." Yet he marveled at American democracy, and the incorporation of white men into the body politic of America, exercising their political rights and civic responsibilities bestowed on them by the Bill of Rights and the Constitution. In the meantime, First Nations, blacks, other racialized groups, and women were excluded from democratic citizenship. What really stunned Tocqueville was that blacks and First Nations "ha[d] nothing in common; neither birth, nor features, nor language, nor habits. Both of them occupy an inferior rank in the country they inhabit; both suffer from tyranny."[141] There is nothing surprising about the treatment of blacks and First Nations. It was exactly how whiteness works.[142] Racial classification, an obvious but complex occurrence, began its opprobrious enterprise, the construction of an American cultural identity as white. Winthrop D. Jordan, in *White Over Black: American Attitudes Toward the Negro, 1550–1812*, claims that the mulatto classification was "to attract men who might be counted as white and who would thereby strengthen the colony's defenses against her foreign and domestic enemies."[143] Nonetheless, for Theodore W. Allen's *The Invention of the White Race*, "the 'mulattoes' distinction was a functional one. Being necessary and above all concerned with maintaining their ascendancy, members of the plantation bourgeoisie sometimes made accommodations in their thinking in the interest of having a 'mulatto' buffer between themselves and the plantation bond labor."[144] Eventually, the "mulattoes policy" underwent some changes. Many scholars have examined the changing in racial classifications and noted the details in the classification of mulattoes. Mulattoes' classification started officially in 1850, when the federal enumerator on the census schedule marked a person "B" (black) or "M" (mulatto).[145] According to G. Reginald Daniel, in *More Than Black? Multiracial Identity and the New Racial Order*, "the legal status of free mulattoes was ambiguous at best up to the time of the American Revolution, although European Americans had begun to chip away at their rights as early as the 1660s."[146] The rationale of the one-drop rule was to draw restrictions between blacks and whites, but more so, it was to assert the preeminence of whiteness. The absurdities of the racial classification system based on the one-drop rule are taken up by Adrian Piper's 1990 essay, "Passing for White: Passing for Black," where she draws on the complexities of being biracial.[147]

Between 1789 and 1791, the Bill of Rights, the first ten amendments to the American Constitution, was enacted to protect and secure the liberties and rights of white people. First Nations, blacks, and other racialized groups remained unprotected by these rights. First Nations were not citizens in the legalistic sense, and many blacks at that time were slaves. Acts, including the Fugitive Slave Acts of 1793, were implemented so as to strengthen and uphold the established idea that slaves were not persons, but properties. These acts were to stabilize the rights of liberty and property. For instance, a state's recognition of liberty cannot flout another state's classification of the property rights in slaves. "Any state law or state regulation, which interrupts, limits, delays or postpones the rights of the owner to the immediate possession of the slave, and the immediate command of his service and labor, operates, *pro tanto*, a discharge of the slaves there from."[148] To that end, the laws also denied lawful rights to free slaves.

Eventually, the pressing concerns for the men in power were to establish the determinate and constitutive conditions for the slaves to be liberated. Thomas Jefferson, the third president of the United States, and the author of the Declaration of Independence, had an optimistic and clear answer, which was American colonization. The fundamental underpinning for colonization was, in part, Jefferson's untamed desire to transform America into the homogeneous society that Benjamin Franklin longed for, where "men" would be free to pursue their own self-interest and exercise their "inalienable rights" and liberties. Eventually, it became obvious that slavery contradicted the self-evident truths that all people "are created equal." In the minds of the framers, only white men were created equal. Even after the Thirteenth Amendment of the Constitution outlawed slavery and the Fourteenth Amendment bestowed on blacks, at least in theory, the rights of citizenship, there remained a desperate effort to maintain white supremacy.

The Desperate Effort to Maintain White Supremacy

Slavery ended with the Thirteenth Amendment to the Constitution. An effective strategy to keep blacks subservient was to recruit them into "debt servitude" as sharecroppers. In addition, several Black Codes that supplemented an intrinsic and definitive white authority were implemented in the former Confederate States to define blacks' new rights and responsibilities.[149] For example, the Codes required that "ex-slaves employed by a white person" could not change jobs without permission from their employers.[150] Toward the end of 1865, Mississippi and South Carolina enacted the first and most ruthless Black Codes, and the other Confederate States quickly followed suit.[151] The Black Codes, in their desperate attempt to reinvigorate the slave system of uncontestable white supremacy, constrained the life chances of African Americans by maintaining them in structural subordination and dependency. In fact, as political scientist Rogers M. Smith insightfully points out, the Freedmen's Bureau, which derived from the American Freedmen's

Inquiry Commission, was a reaction to the Black Codes, and it was beginning "to transform the subjugating racial stratification in the nation's economic and cultural arrangements"[152] by endorsing civil and political rights to black men through suffrage. Having a black men electorate would have uplifted all blacks. Nonetheless, those writers influenced by William Dunning's and John W. Burgess's school of thought on Reconstruction were convinced of "Negro incapacity" and their lack of impulse to assert their political rights of citizenship and to exercise their suffrage.[153]

Thomas Andrew Bailey, a professor of history at Stanford University, and self-appointed defender of the Black Codes, zealously put forward the argument that the Black Codes were to guard the Negro from his own capriciousness.[154] While Bailey's justifiable formulation that average ex-slaves were virtually helpless and not prepared to live as free people has a ring of truth, he forgot to mention that it was largely because blacks, under the slave regime, were reduced to chattel, property, and eventually to three-fifths of a person for determining a state's share of the national taxes and its number of seats in the House of Representatives "according to the sacred script of the Constitution."[155] But Bailey's casting ex-slaves as socially, politically, and emotionally immature,[156] I think, is troubling and can be seen as an implacable dogmatism on Bailey's part. It is too bad that Bailey failed to recognize the capabilities of blacks and slaves.[157]

In many ways, "the enforcement of these Black Codes had encouraged free slaves to move to the North, bringing them into direct competition for jobs with the Irish immigrants."[158] Meanwhile, the Irish were facing tremendous discrimination because they were viewed as nonwhites. Roediger traces the process by which Irish workers defined themselves as white in order to obtain the privileges enjoyed by white people, which they could not obtain as Irish. In attacking blacks and Chinese, who had no political representation, the Irish workers secured their position by identifying with the dominant white culture. The descendants of the first generation of Irish immigrants were better educated and enjoyed better occupational mobility than their parents. President Abbot Lawrence of Harvard University draws our attention to the fact that the Irish, on the basis of their whiteness, have rapidly assimilated into America's dominant culture. "Universal political equality," Lawrence said, "should not be applied to 'tribal Indians,' 'Chinese,' or 'Negroes,' but only to whites who can assimilate rapidly."[159] First Nations, blacks, Chinese, and other racialized groups were inherently incapable of being assimilated. They were bestowed with "inborn differences," and hence inferior.

In terms of racial hierarchy, the North was no different from the South. While blacks in the South were reduced to slaves, in the North they were pariahs.[160] Loïc Wacquant reminds us that whites wittingly "strove to maintain an unbridgeable social and symbolic gulf with their compatriots of African descent."[161] Sociologists Douglas S. Massey and Nancy A. Denton note that "blacks were increasingly divided from whites by a hardening color line in employment, education, especially housing,"[162] and public transportation. For example, in New York City, there were separate buses for whites and blacks; in Philadelphia, blacks were allowed to ride only on the front platforms of streetcars.[163] As Takaki simply remarked, "the North for blacks was not the promised land."[164]

A few years later the Fourteenth Amendment claimed that it was unconstitutional for any of the states to deprive anyone of the rights of citizenship. The Fifteenth Amendment gave black men the right to vote on the premise that they could not be denied that right based on their race or former condition of servitude. Yet, in 1883, Justice Joseph Bradley struck down Congress's 1875 ban on racial discrimination in all places of public accommodations. For example, the Louisiana legislature, in 1890, passed a law that provided that "all railway companies carrying passengers . . . in this State shall provide separate but equal accommodations for white and colored races." One of the greatest victories that pertained to the institutionalization of white privilege was the abhorrently disingenuous decision to separate the so-called superior race from the inferior race in the 1896 landmark case *Plessy v. Ferguson*.[165] Blacks had to ride in separate carriages on the train.[166] In fact, the defense of *Plessy* and the review of the Louisiana statute were in the hands of four influential white men, Albion W. Tourgée, M. J. Cunningham, attorney general of Louisiana, and two other lawyers who assisted Cunningham in defending the statute. Justice Henry B. Brown delivered the majority opinion of the court. Understandably, Justice John Marshall Harlan, relatively isolated in his position, sensed that "the majority decisions violated rather than affirmed the Constitution."[167] Harlan's opinion of the court case is important, and it must be quoted at length:

> There is a race so different from our own that we do not permit those belonging to it to become citizens of the United States. Persons belonging to it are, with few exceptions, absolutely excluded from our country. I allude to the Chinese race. But, by the statute in question, a Chinaman can ride in the same passenger coach with white citizens of the United States, while citizens of the black race in Louisiana, many of whom, perhaps, risked their lives for the preservation of the Union, who are entitled, by law, to participate in the political control of the state and nation, who are not excluded, by law or by reason of their race, from public stations of any kind, and who have all the legal rights that belong to white citizens, are yet declared to be criminals, liable to imprisonment, if they ride in a public coach occupied by citizens of the white race.[168]

Engaged, as Harlan was, with the plight of blacks, did it mean that the black–white model in America included only the plight of blacks, excluding all other racialized groups—in this case—Chinese? It is clear from Harlan's speech, that the Chinese "are . . . absolutely excluded" from citizenship, that the black–white model was brought to the forefront. With minor exceptions, the model extended itself to include all nonwhites. For example, when the Naturalization Act of 1790 was challenged by Chan Yong, a Chinese man residing in San Francisco, because it denied him American citizenship, the court conferred in its ruling that the 1790 act limited citizenship to whites. Years later, in *State v. Wong Kim Ark*, the Chinese were considered to be part of the "colored race." Nonetheless, we cannot say for sure how the Chinese would have been treated on the segregated train because, to my knowledge, there is not much evidence to that effect.[169] What we do know for sure, and W. E. B. Du Bois summed it up exceedingly well, is that in the "Jim Crow Car . . . the races were mixed together." The "white coach was all white."[170] He goes on to explain, "The color line—the relation of the darker to the lighter races of men in Asia and Africa, in America and the sea" is the separation of colored people from the whites.[171] Will Kymlicka suggests as much when he acknowledges that "whenever African or Asian delegates to the United Nations in New York drove down to Washington to talk to American government officials, they passed into the land of Jim Crow, and were forced to use racially segregated restaurants and washrooms."[172] The color line was so rigidly drawn that all nonwhites had to accept the status of the blacks unless, they could pass for white as some blacks did. Taking my cue from Du Bois, "How does it feel to be the problem?" was not a question asked only of African Americans, but of all nonwhite people. The overall answer to this question would be clearly revealed in *People v. Hall*, in 1854, when the California Supreme Court determined that a California statute preventing Indians and Negroes from testifying in court cases concerning whites also applied to Chinese Americans. The black–white racial model was unmistakably applied to all racialized groups. It was quite telling, as Frank H. Wu, a law professor, reported. Wu stated that during World War II, on the night of the Harlem riot, a Chinese laundryman "hurriedly posted a sign on his store window which read: 'Me Colored Too.'"[173] When various nonwhites, Chinese, blacks, First Nations, and Mexicans, called themselves and each other colored, they invoked a shared political identity. In other words, the accepted undertones of the term *colored* was deformulated out of the dominant codes of racial discourse, and reformulated as signs of grouping and unity among isolated groups of people sharing common experiences that are historically framed by the psychic representation and the social, economical, and political reality of America's racism.[174]

The reinforcement of discrimination with the "separate but equal" Jim Crow laws, which started in the 1890s, continued until the court's decision in *Brown v. Topeka Board of Education* ended segregation in 1954. Under the Jim Crow laws, everything was separate, but nothing was equal. The de jure segregation in the South was matched by a de facto segregation in the North. In the North the "official" rules of segregation were pronounced in housing, schooling, entertainment, and employment.

The subordinate position of blacks was the "natural" outcome of white supremacy as a structure that was solidly in place. In fact, blacks and other racialized ethnic groups were not on the opposite side of the racial binary. All that mattered was white skin. Even the lowest of the lowest whites had something that a nonwhite person could never possess, which was white skin privilege. This was how whiteness worked. The Cherokee leader John Ridge (son of Major Ridge), for one, deeply wished that whiteness was less imposing. In fact, he was convinced of whiteness's presumptive hegemony. As such, his unrestrained contempt for whiteness is verbalized and documented by Theodore W. Allen: "An Indian . . . is frowned upon by the meanest peasant, and the scum of the earth are considered sacred in comparison to the son of nature. If an Indian is educated in the sciences, had a good knowledge of the classics, astronomy, mathematics, moral and natural philosophy, and his conduct equally modest and polite, yet he is an Indian, and the most stupid and illiterate white man will disdain and triumph over this worthy individual. It is disgusting to enter the house of a white man and be stared at full face in inquisitive ignorance."[175]

America's unabashed public attitudes and political response to racialized ethnic groups had been prominent and continued to shape the nefarious social and cultural practices of white America. Whiteness as the definitive concept of an American identity was not to remain isolated from present-day America. The exclusion of nonwhites from such an American cultural identity persists even to this day. In the next chapter I focus on the specter of whiteness and how it continues to deny nonwhites their American identity.

3

The Specter of Whiteness

Racialized ethnic groups including blacks, First Nations, and Chinese who were already in America were not expected to embrace the so-called cultural oneness and become a part of what the early twentieth-century Jewish poet and novelist Israel Zangwill called *The Melting Pot*, or what Will Kymlicka, the Canadian political theorist, has identified as the "Anglo-conformity model," where the existence of a unitary majority culture was evident. I have argued in the preceding chapter that racialized ethnic groups in America were not looked on as Americans and most of all were considered as inferior, which has important consequences in determining their places in American society as a whole. Certainly, while the history and classification of nonwhiteness is at the center of discussions and scrutiny, whiteness, as I have shown, is the taken-for-granted category, the norm, and hence it is invisible. Its invisibility, for AnaLouise Keating, "is [its] most common mentioned attribute."[1]

Taking my cue from Jean Genet's probing in his 1958 play, *Les Nègres*, where, at the beginning of the play, Genet asks the provocative question, what is a black?[2] the same question, I think, should be asked of whites and whiteness—"questions that are difficult to address" as Christopher Lane points out.[3] Because of whiteness normality, it is hard for whites, as Richard Dyer puts it, "to 'see' whiteness"[4] much less to examine, talk, and ask about it.[5] On the other hand, As Ruth Frankenberg cautions, "why talk about whiteness, given the risk that by undertaking intellectual work on whiteness one might contribute to the processes of recentering rather than decentering it, as well as reifying the term, and its 'inhabitants.'"[6] However, for the most part, whiteness remains invisible but only to white people. In her influential essay, "Declaration of Whiteness: The Non-performativity of Antiracism," Sara Ahmed draws our attention to the fact that "whiteness is only invisible for those who inhabit it. For those who don't, it is hard not to see whiteness. It is everywhere. Seeing whiteness is about living its effects . . . making whiteness visible only makes sense from the point of view of those for whom it is invisible."[7]

Furthermore, in terms of its performativity as "a stylized repetition of act,"[8] actions, and activities, there is nothing invisible about whiteness. In fact, there was nothing invisible about slavery, the Jim Crow South, or the Japanese internment camps. And today, there is nothing invisible about racial profiling, black ghettoes and superghettoes, and prisons. In her rich, complex, and influential book *Black Looks: Race and Representation*, bell hooks makes it clear that blacks and other people of color not only do see whiteness but also experience whiteness in their daily lives in such a dreadful way that it becomes terrorizing as well as brutalizing and encompassing.[9] Hooks, for good reasons, cannot give in to the traditional analysis of whiteness as wholesome and good. Instead, she breaks away from the "mythical norms" of whiteness—or, to borrow the words of the literary critic Roland Barthes, "the falsely obvious"[10]—by demystifying, debunking, and bringing to the forefront a broader opposition to whiteness. In the end, she offers a view of whiteness that mostly makes sense to blacks and other nonwhites.[11]

People of color, for a long time, knew, to use Langston Hughes's now classic phrase, "the ways of white folk." Racialized groups know what it means to suffer tremendously under whiteness as an everyday cultural practice. Blacks' fate was first slavery, then the Jim Crow South; now it is the prisons, ghettoes, and superghettoes,[12] bringing about, what Anders Stephanson, citing Cornel West in an interview, calls a "walking nihilism of pervasive drug addiction, pervasive alcoholism, pervasive homicide, and an exceptional rise in suicide."[13] Responding to blacks' predicament, West points to "anger, rage, and pessimism that remained relatively muted because of a well-justified fear of brutal white retaliation" that have inflamed blacks' wounds[14] and the wounds of all racialized groups in America.

First Nations experienced genocide, expropriation of their lands, and forced assimilation; the Chinese Exclusion Act, excluding Chinese from entering the United States, was adapted and extended in a variety of ways to Japanese, Filipino, Korean, and Asian-Indian persons in the United States; Japanese were placed in internment camps during World War II; Mexican Americans can trace their legacy to the Mexican people who have an inheritance in this country; more recently all Muslim Americans have been perceived as terrorists. It is for these reasons that Frankenberg's conclusion, according to which those who insist on not seeing whiteness suffer from a willful spiritual and social blindness, is fundamental.[15] Whiteness is widely perceived as racial dominance, "the natural, inevitable, ordinary way of being human."[16] I want to expand Frankenberg's argument and suggest that historically, whiteness has defined an American identity as white, and it continues to determine who is an American and what it means to be an American. Denying racialized ethnic groups an American identity gives us a good understanding of the distribution and propagation of racial otherness.[17]

Nonwhiteness—First Nationness, blackness, Chineseness, and Mexicanness—is associated with race, and whiteness, for the most part, remains an unmentioned racial identity. As David R. Roediger explains, when Americans talk about race, they often talk about racialized groups. "If whites come into the discussion, it is only because they have 'attitudes' towards nonwhites."[18] For whites, race tends to be positioned in such a way that it exists outside the political, economical, and social forces that have and continue to define whites as unmarked. Certainly, as Thierry Devos and Mahzarin R. Banaji acknowledge, even though white racial identity is socially constructed, it "is treated as cultural expectation,"[19] and most whites identify thoroughly with such a position. Yet the social construction of whiteness cannot be absolute unless we recognize the social and political consequences of race thinking in America. Race continues to shape and reshape the shifting and unstable identities that are tied to the racialized body.

Discussions of race have been traditionally applied only to demonstrate the perceived superiority of the "white race" over those who are looked on as nonwhite. Whites are individuals and Americans, glued together by the "bond of common paternity," as Arthur Mann once described it.[20] This bond is denied to First Nations, blacks, and other racialized groups who are marked as somehow different from Americans.[21] For instance, Arthur M. Schlesinger, in *The Age of Jackson*, willfully leaves out blacks and First Nations from America's history.[22] Also, in his work *The Uprooted: The Epic Story of the Great Migrations That Made the American People*, Oscar Handlin consciously excludes the uprooted from Africa, Asia, and Latin America who were decisive in the making of Americans.[23] Who, then, is an American? is not a question that has been asked directly. One of the main reasons this question needs to be at the forefront in the engagement with whiteness is because it calls attention to the pressing concern that First Nations, blacks, Chinese, Mexicans, and other racialized groups are denied their American identity because, to put it simply, they are not white.

It is not a secret from anyone that whites, benefiting from power and higher status endemic to their white privilege, are viewed as "owning" America.[24] This claim of ownership demands an articulation of racial and cultural differences that explains the discursive practices of racial and cultural hierarchization. First Nations, African Americans, Chinese Americans, and Mexican Americans are located on the fringes of American society. They are not sufficiently Americans. They are the hyphenated Americans, "two souls" in one body, as W. E. B. Du Bois describes nonwhite people in *The Souls of Black Folk*, and, as we will see later, they are unable to free themselves from the hyphenation, which is so cherished by cultural pluralism. The hyphenates, the liminal, the "anonymous Americans," to borrow Michael Walzer's term, are portrayed in terms of duality, an American as well as belonging to a racialized ethnic group. Belonging is configured and determined through daily regimes of social knowledge production or social intelligibility that is practiced daily. In the end, racialization becomes the signifier for determining who is an American.

Fueled, in part, by the concerns of who is an American and what constitutes an American's cultural identity, President Theodore Roosevelt, on October 12, 1915, stated in a speech to the Knights of Columbus at Carnegie Hall in New York City, "There is no room in this country for hyphenated Americanism."[25] Citing Theodore Roosevelt as authority, Schlesinger observes that "either a [person] is an American and nothing else, or he/she is not an American at all."[26] President Woodrow Wilson was also specific and up front in his observation that "any man who carries a hyphen about with him carries a dagger that he is ready to plunge into the vitals of this republic."[27] Racialized groups are not just Americans; they are, in fact, the hyphenated Americans. As part of the legacy of whiteness as associated with Americanness, many people have come to accept the notion that an American is white. Sadly so, whiteness appears inflexible. It permits a version of an American identity that is closely tied to the body, how one looks, rather than to one's loyalty and commitment to America. In fact, many studies have shown that nonwhites do not differ from whites "on a measure of implicit national identity, namely how much they associated American symbols with the 'us.'"[28] Yet the racialized bodies are not looked on as Americans. Nonwhite persons, in many instances, cannot live their own relationship to their body apart from the mediation of an interpretive schema that is not of their choosing.[29]

To concretely provide and epitomize the clear interlink between whiteness and Americanness, and how it continues to discursively exclude nonwhites from an American identity as vital, in this chapter, I examine how whiteness prolongs the idea that an "American = White." Questions about nonwhites and whites, inclusion and exclusion, normal and abnormal, inferior and superior, and ultimately the most basic question of who is an American are important. Since "American = white," nonwhites are always viewed as different, as aliens and therefore not Americans, and this fact is consequential in determining nonwhites' unequal position in America. In this sense, the call for "one America" by Presidents Clinton and Obama needs some reflection. What exactly is "one America"? This question is fundamental given that whiteness determines who is an American and America's cultural identity. The following section examines who is looked on as Americans. However, before I demonstrate how whiteness continues to determine who is an American, I want to look at specific elements of whiteness, which I call whiteness unbounded and unmarked.

Whiteness Unbounded and Unmarked

In fact, I have already shown that the definitive concept of an American cultural identity was based on whiteness. Whiteness is the cornerstone of America's cultural norms. In this sense, whiteness is more than a structural position benefiting white people, it is ideological as well. These cultural norms purposely and, in some cases, unconsciously reproduce whiteness and whites as different. This difference often conveys superiority. Certainly, one of the most straightforward explanations and definitions of white supremacy is formulated by Cheryl I. Harris. In her summation of white supremacy, she does not allude only "to the self-conscious racism of white supremacist hate groups." She refers "to a political, economic, and cultural system in which whites overwhelmingly control power and material resources, conscious and unconscious ideas of white superiority and entitlement are widespread, and the relations of white dominance and non-white subordination are daily reenacted across a broad array of institutions and social settings."[30] For this exact reason, nonwhites become the targets of an unconstrained and unisolated racism as a hegemonic force in America. Barbara J. Fields insightfully draws our focus on how racism functions. Nonwhites, she points out, "did not 'make' racism, nor were they free to 'negotiate' it, though they may challenge it or its perpetrators, and tried to navigate the obstacles it placed in their way."[31] Nonwhites are, in the words of Derrick A. Bell, "marked with the caste of color in a society still determinedly white"[32] not only in terms of structure and character but also, more importantly, in terms of what defines an American cultural identity.[33] Since American cultural identity is viewed as white, should we then talk about a "white culture"? Scholars, including David R. Roediger and Noel Ignatiev and John Garvey, have debated over the existence of a "white culture." Roediger insists on the nonexistence of a "white culture." It is, he writes, "an identity based on what one isn't and on whom one can hold back."[34] In other words, white culture is not merely missing; it is, in some respect, anticulture—striving on overpowering racialized groups who have "cultures." Even though Roediger offers a critical attention to "white culture," he does not recognize that "white culture" is alive and well, and quite often, it terrorizes nonwhites by imposing de facto the meaning of what is the norm in terms of racial, gender, class, sexual, and ethnic identities. This is, in fact, the power of whiteness; it appears invisible to those who inhabit it. It is "everything and nothing," to employ the words of film scholar and theorist Richard Dyer, and "the source of its representational power."[35] As I have shown in Chapter 2, historically in America, whites had to define themselves as "cultured" to set themselves apart and superior to First Nations, blacks, Chinese, and other racialized groups, who in their view were "uncultured." Whites see themselves as race neutral or color blind, the norm, and have a sense of themselves as entitled to judge the "other" against their own standards. For example, if blacks feel offended by whites displaying the Confederate flag on their cars or their lawns, many whites consider that blacks are being too sensitive. In their minds, in spite of its long-standing depiction of violence and terror against blacks, the flag represents whites' heritage and pride. In order to gain insight and to come to terms with the anguish of the "other," it would require a critical examination of the "self." For whites, the well-established and grounded notion of entitlement, which speaks to whites' attachment, to employ the title of a panel at the American Sociological Association on August 14, 2000, to "racial privilege: the view from above," is central. In fact, a good example of whites' entitlement is the frequent articulation by white men especially that "I" did not get the job because "I am a white male"; this is the active process of rehegemonizing whiteness and its performativeness of white male entitlement. Maleness and whiteness are bounded by an acknowledgment of their privilege and power as they manifest themselves.

While Rebecca Aanerud draws our attention to how white children are culturally whitened,[36] according to Seshadri-Crooks, some of the questions asked by the white children show that "white children do not come to 'accept' their whiteness, but consider themselves always already white."[37] For instance, "Why is she that color? Is she sunburned? Can she change?" Whites, without difficulty, can arrive at adulthood without thinking much as belonging to a racial group because they are part of the norm. In this sense, it is not about how white people experience their whiteness or the representations of whiteness in American society, as is the focus of some whiteness scholars including Karen Brodkin (1999), Richard Dyer (1997), Noel Ignatiev and John Garvey (1996), Noel Ignatiev (1995), Ruth Frankenberg (1993), and David R. Roediger (1991); it is about the normalization of whiteness, which "alerts us to deep relation between whiteness and the unconscious and thus of the specificity of dominant subject formation. In Lacanian terms, the discourse of whiteness can be said to function as condition of dominant subjectivity: It inserts the subject into the symbolic order."[38] At an early age, white children are trained to conduct themselves according to the norms of whiteness. Whiteness owes its hegemonic status not to its natural status but to the fact that, in the United States, it has been sanctioned and resanctioned repeatedly. And even though whiteness is constantly confronted and resisted, how whiteness works as a form of racial privilege, as well as the effects of that privilege on those who are recognized as white, must be given some serious analysis.

Whites in America, according to Penelope Ingram, "always experience the power that comes with their whiteness."[39] "Criticize Mexico—criticize your own country," a student asks of Professor Benjamin Alire Sáenz, a Mexican American who teaches a class on "Chicano Literature, Culture and Identity" at the University of Texas, El Paso.[40] Silently, the unarticulated plea is, "why don't you go back to your own country," which is a remark all nonwhites in America can hear. It is terribly confusing to nonwhite children, especially those who were born in America and are told to go back to where they came from, countries, places they know not of, only from what they have seen on television or read about in books, if they are old enough for such discernment. In the following section, I want to look specifically at the question, who is an American?

Who Is an American?

In 1782, Jean de Crèvecoeur, in his *Letters from an American Farmer*, claimed that America's culture had arisen from the melting of the "English, Scotch, Irish, Dutch, Germans, and Swedes" into this "new man," the American.[41] Philip Gleason points to the fact that for Crèvecoeur, an American is a multigenerational mixture of a variety of European nationalities,[42] excluding First Nations, blacks, Chinese, and other racialized ethnic groups, "the very element of America that has given it some of its more distinctive characteristics."[43]

Today, even though whites often think of themselves in terms of their ethnicity—Italianness, Greekness, or Jewishness, and so on—before they think of their whiteness as the privileged signifier,[44] Devos and Banaji acknowledge that "white racial identity . . . is treated as cultural expectation[45] . . . as a monolith, in the singular, as an 'essential something'"[46] and it is never in flux. However, whites as a race is never talked about because whites are the norm and discussions of race are traditionally applied only to demonstrate the perceived superiority of the "white race" over those who are looked on as nonwhite. Indeed, when the question is asked, who is an American? many researchers often find that whites view themselves as Americans and nonwhites are viewed as hyphenated Americans—Native Americans, African Americans, Chinese Americans, Mexican Americans, and so on.[47] A recent study was done by Devos and Banaji, in 2005, with African Americans, Asian Americans, and whites; what they found was that there is a propensity to view whites as Americans.[48] What this shows is "to be American is to be white."[49] In this respect, it has become apparent that

American and white are mutually constitutive in their attempts to confirm that whites are the only group that is seen as Americans.[50]

Ronald Takaki, in *A Different Mirror: A History of Multicultural America*, points to his experience of a taxi driver assuming that he was not American because he was not white.[51] The communal sense of America's past, a history that views an American as white, continues its menacing hold on all Americans. What is even more distressing is that Takaki's fellow academics, the learned and influential, the supposed enlightened, intellectually sophisticated, and intelligently reflective, sometimes marvel at Takaki's accent and will outwardly ask him how long he has been in America.[52] Even though there is no contradistinction between white and American, whiteness and Americanness, for the most part, function "interchangeably, though not always through the production of the same others."[53] In Takaki's case, his race, ethnicity, gender, and social class, in different ways, signaled his exclusion from an American identity, which is premised on whiteness. To be American is not to be First Nations, black, Chinese, Mexican, or a person belonging to a racialized ethnic group. To be an American is to be white. First Nations, blacks, Chinese, Mexicans, and other racialized groups are different and incompatible with what it means to be an American. Their cultural values are viewed as colliding with what white American cultural norms and values are. In the end, "keeping America White [is] as much an educational mandate of American culture."[54]

Since an American cultural identity, to use the words of Samuel P. Huntington, "is based on the seventeenth- and eighteenth-century settlers who founded American society,"[55] and, according to Benjamin Schwarz, their "customs and social relations, [their] standards of taste and morality were for 300 years America's, and in many basic ways they still are,"[56] then the twofold question is, Who is an American? And what defines an American and Americanness, two modes of subjectivity and identification? Are racialized groups including blacks, First Nations, Chinese, and Mexicans viewed as Americans? A well-known story about the Mexican War is illustrative. "When Americans marched into the Mexican city of Saltillo in 1847, they were greeted by a woman from New Jersey, who worked in a Mexican textile mill. 'Americans I am glad to see you,' she exclaimed. 'I have seen but one white man in eight months, a Negro from New Orleans.'"[57] "People speak of 'American' as if it means white," Frank H. Wu reminds us.[58] It was exactly the case when President George H. W. Bush reassured Soviet leader Gorbachev on National Public Radio that "we" Americans are Europeans.[59] Who are the "we" chosen by President Bush as Europeans? President Bush's language aims to unify all whites even those beyond its borders. Furthermore, there is a problem with this plural form "we," which helps to reproduce whiteness as Europeanness. A further examining of the word "we"

shows clearly how some groups are excluded from the privileged representation of America's cultural heritage, which is based on Europeanness or
whiteness. In other word, the multiethnic and multiracial America claims a
white European identity by marginalizing its non-European heritages.[60]

Nonwhite groups are, for the most part, viewed as "outsiders" from foreign places. "Do you speak English?" is always a question asked of nonwhites.
And those who do speak English, in many cases, are asked to speak slower
because their accents make their English difficult to understand. Asking
these kinds of questions clearly serves as a palpable reminder that nonwhites
are denied an American identity because they do "not fit the picture that is
America."[61] They are the "outsiders," people of a different cultural and racial
background, the racialized ethnics of America, within rather than outside an
antagonistic relation of self and "other," "us" and "them," the natural and the
unnatural, the pure and the impure. In the end, the insinuation is that only
white Americans can define and shape what it means to be American, the
hyphenated Americans—blacks, First Nations, Chinese, Mexicans, and other
racialized ethnic groups must basically "fit in."[62]

"Outsiders" are incompatible with "insiders," and there is sometimes an
aggression perpetrated by the "insiders" toward the "outsiders." Until now,
most whites especially, are not able to purge themselves from the gamut of
misconceptions they have about a nonwhite person, as Wu describes it, "a
visitor at best, an intruder at worst,"[63] irreconcilable foreigners, treacher-
ous, hostile, and strangers from a different shore, and "forever foreign," an
unnamable identity, designated merely as "foreigners." In fact, a foreigner
carries with him or her the foreignness of a foreigner, which is marked by
an illiberal culture. He or she is insufficiently American, possessing, as he
or she does, the dreadful markers of unassimilated alterity, such as a nonwhite skin color. Differentiation in skin colors has been and is connoted as
an indicator, pointing to the existence of different racial categories marked
by distinctiveness in which social meanings are ascribed within the concept
of racialization. Indeed, these meanings are "not fixed, but are rather multi-
accentual and polyvocal."[64] Nonetheless, according to Professor of Psychology and Women's Studies Kay Deaux, a study conducted by José Itzigsohn
shows that immigrants from the Dominican Republic, for example, are
positioned outside of Americanness. They feel that most Americans see
them first as black, and for this precise reason, they are reluctant to claim
"Americanness because they are not white."[65] In the end, nonwhites are, for
the most part, not accepted in white America. As they compete for jobs,
housing, education, and other resources, they experience various forms
of discriminatory practices. These discriminatory practices are associated
with differences of gender, class, and sexuality and do so in a structured
manner that goes beyond questions of racial identity.

Wu captures the predicament nonwhites face daily because they are systematically looked on as foreigners.[66] Whiteness = Americanness has posed a perpetual problem for nonwhites. Wu draws on the experience of "Asian" Americans and tells us, "'Where are you from?' is a question I like answering. 'Where are you *really* from?' is a question I *really* hate answering. . . . For Asian Americans, the questions frequently come paired like that. Among ourselves, we can even joke nervously about how they just about define the Asian American experience. More than anything else that unites us, everyone with an Asian face who lives in America is afflicted by the perpetual foreigner syndrome. We are figuratively and even literally returned to Asia and ejected from America."[67] Wu speaks to this denial of Asian Americans from an American national identity in no uncertain terms. As he points out, the question "where are you *really* from?" in many fundamental ways defines Asian Americans' experience as unified and connected by common racial interests.[68]

Most nonwhites in America can testify to the preceding line of interrogation—"Where are you from?"—and have become oversensitive to such a line of questioning because they understand it as a form of de-Americanization, a denaturalization of their American status. On the other hand, most whites would deny that this simple question—"Where are you from?"—has nothing to do with de-Americanization. For them, this question stems from curiosity, a genuine interest in the person. Nonetheless, what triggers such an interest? What are the motivations for asking such a question? In an effort to adequately provide answers to these questions, we must take into account an analysis that brings to the forefront the manner in which nonwhites are positioned in America as the "other" and how the dualistic conceptualization of self and "other" plays itself out. For nonwhites, the answer to the question "Where are you from?" is an irritating one because they consider that they are from a city or town in America. Yet if the answer is, for example, from Phoenix or Arizona, the follow-up question is, "No. Where are you really from originally?" These kinds of questions reflect the difficulty that arises from the limitation of the assimilation model, which suggests that racialized ethnic groups cannot be included in American cultural identity in the same way that whites are. Besides, this form of questioning is inscribed within paranoia circulating between and beyond the cultural and social norms of whiteness. Nonwhites must be constantly surveilled and interrogated. The surveillance sometimes takes the form of a white person greeting a nonwhite person in a different language, perhaps Japanese, Hindi, or Cantonese, because racial positioning assumes that the person does not speak English. The hyphenated Americans are boxed in because they are othered (and othering takes on various forms). The greeting of a nonwhite American by an unfamiliar white person in a language other than English—because it is assumed that English is not his or her native language—marks the conceitedness of whiteness.

Another form that this interrogation takes is the assumption that blacks, Chinese, Japanese, or Mexicans tend to identify with the country from which they are assumed to be. A form of self-ethnicitization is imposed on them, which in itself is a clear sign of not belonging, not "feeling" American.[69] Frantz Fanon has defined identification itself as a pathological condition since one experiences one's "being through others."[70] On the other hand, misidentification plays a foundation role in the dialectic of self and "other" and conceals the essentially "ambivalent structure of all identification."[71] Shefali Mileczarek-Desai, an Indian American, reveals that she always feels uneasy whenever someone asks her where she is from because she knows that she is supposed to name some "far-off place." India is seen as her country, even if only imaginarily, because she appears to be Indian. The truth is, she is from Phoenix, Arizona,[72] an Indian by descent, yet unable to transcend her Indianness as a signifier, the cultural specificity that works to exclude her from her Americanness and ties her to her Indianness. Her American identity has been dislocated, buried deep within her Indianness. She is seen through what Fanon names the "corporeal malediction" of her inescapable nonwhiteness.[73] In this sense, her inescapable Indianness is marked by a discernible divergence from whiteness. Whiteness is hopelessly enmeshed within the underlining logic of Americannness.

It is especially unsettling that people who are categorized as belonging (and belonging is reliant on the processes of exclusion) to a racialized group that had been in America long before America had declared its independence from British rule and sought to become a republic are bombarded with the needless question, how long have you been in America? This inopportune question clearly tells us that an American is viewed in term of whiteness. Striving to be both black, Chinese, or First Nations and American requires, what W. E. B. Du Bois refers to as "double consciousness,"[74] or what Frantz Fanon reveals as the doubling of identity, functioning as a narcissistic manifestation of the self in the "other,"[75] this "twoness" as Du Bois calls it.[76] It is partly for this reason that Afrocentrists particularly have suggested to African Americans that they must turn their attention to Africa for their cultural values because, as nonwhites, they are denied de facto an American identity and hence, cannot identify with American culture in a significant way.

The 1994 General Social Surveys (GSS) and the 1994 and 1995 Los Angeles surveys asked respondents the following question: "When you think of social and political issues, do you see yourself mainly as a member of a particular ethnic, racial, or nationality group, or do you think of yourself mainly as an American?" It was revealed that mostly whites saw themselves as Americans.[77] The respondents belonging to a racialized ethnic group also thought of themselves as Americans. Yet recent studies have also shown that racialized groups are always viewed as foreigners and are denied a full American identity.[78] In this sense, whiteness has a particularly harmful effect because it rejects its racial roots while disallowing racialized groups their American identities.[79] What is more fundamental, however, is that whiteness as well as racist predispositions are both a historically all-encompassing, particularistic, normative presence within the political, social, and cultural fabric of America's institutions, and the standard against which all nonwhite people are judged, measured, compared, and reduced to otherness. Otherness becomes the foundation for legitimizing exclusion, subordination, and exploitation of the members of the collectivity labeled as the "other."[80]

The desire "of" and not "for" the "other" becomes rather fundamental. The question, then, is what is the "self" for the "other"? Stuart Hall reminds us that "only when there is the 'other' can we know who we are." No identity occurs without the "dialogic relationship to the 'other.'"[81] It is clear, then, that if there is an absence of the "other," this absence creates an identity crisis, an echoing conflict for the "self." The unified "self" "refutes humanism's myth of the unified self,"[82] and hence puts it in trouble. Neither "self" nor "other" can be impounded since both are marked. They transmit and inhabit each other. In the end, there is no escaping from, what Roland Barthes calls "the binary prison" of the narcissistic "self" and "other."

Interestingly, Arthur Schlesinger Jr. recognizes America as "a racist nation"[83] that has and continues to disingenuously characterize itself as "a white possession."[84] Yet he is wary of the fact that "a cult of ethnicity has arisen both among non-Anglo whites and among non-white minorities to denounce the idea of a melting pot, to challenge the concept of 'one people,' and to protect, promote, and perpetuate separate ethnic and racial communities."[85] In the same spirit, in his 1987 book, titled *Cultural Literacy: What Every American Needs to Know*, Eric D. Hirsch Jr. longs for a more homogeneous America. And since he willingly erases the history of racialized groups in his long list of terms, one can then presuppose that homogeneous is a euphemism for a white presence and dictates who is an American, and who has the "right" to an American identity. Take the case of a telephone interview conducted in 1998 by a *New York Times* reporter with Ward Connerly, who was then the leading proponent of an initiative measure in California prohibiting affirmative action by the state government.[86] In the interview, one of the reporters asked, "Mr. Connerly, 'what are you?'" He replied, "I am an American."[87] According to Connerly, "the reporter didn't care for [his] answer." This is how the rest of the conversation went:

Reporter: "No, no, no! What are you?"
Connerly: "Yes, yes, yes! I am an American."
Reporter: "That is not what I mean. I was told that you are African American.
Are you ashamed to be African American?"
Connerly: "No, I am just proud to be an American."

Connerly admitted that "when he shared the story of his ancestry (Irish, North American Indian, French, and African), the reporter asked, 'Well, what does that make you?' And he replied, 'That makes me all-American!'"[88] Cheryl I. Harris's notion of "whiteness as property" is once again significant here, in the sense that if the "other" does not possess any of the characteristics of whiteness, it is definite grounds for the repudiation of an American identity and, at the same time, the demonization of a nonwhite identity with all of its complexities.[89] The expansion of the white self through "whiteness as property" starts and ends with the ownership of a white body, and it serves to protect the white self from any ontological interruption. So essential is the white self, that even in a discussion of otherness, it is voiced and rendered extremely discernible because the otherness of the self is celebrated in the perverse augmentation of white identity.

The hyphenated Americanness also came up when a question was asked by the 1995 Los Angeles respondents, referring to themselves as "just an American." The question asked whether or not "it was truer to say you are both an American and a member of a particular ethnic group." According to Jack Citrin, "only 17 percent of whites, compared to 54 percent of blacks, 59 percent of Hispanics,[90] and 59 percent of Asians opted for a dual identity rather than an exclusively American self-definition."[91] On November 25, 1998, David Broder of the *Washington Post* reported the findings of a 1998 survey conducted by *Public Agenda*. He noted that 80 percent of Americans in all racial groups said it is the schools' responsibility to teach students that "whatever their ethnic or racial background, they are all part of one nation."[92] Yet in *Two Nations: Black and White, Separate, Hostile, Unequal*, Andrew Hacker finds two nations in America, one nonwhite and one white, and decidedly unequal. More important, they are separated by two different cultures, a dominant culture and nondominant cultures, which remain intact. This separation presents a conflict over the realism of a presumed American identity as white.

Benjamin Alire Sáenz partly reconciles this quandary when he writes, "I am a Mexican American. American reemphasizes the place of my birth."[93] Like all hyphenated Americans, the problem is coming to terms with the existential dilemma of self-definition. In fact, Fanon warns us that one who is dominated and oppressed is forced to face the many challenges that present themselves to one's own self and identity. As a result, he or she asks this question constantly: "In reality, who am I?"[94] Am I an American? Or am I Mexican, black, First Nations, or Chinese? Can I be both black and American, or Chinese and American? Even though, within the prevailing racist structure, racial groups do work hard to shape their own identities, in the end, it is not how one defines herself or himself, but how society constructs and defines identity and the meanings surrounding this definition. In the end the ascriptive identity becomes real to the extent that it is lived as such. What comes to mind is how black identity, for example, was defined by the one-drop rule. Even blacks themselves had internalized the one-drop rule as the basis for determining their group membership. Yet what unites blacks with each other is not merely a set of common physical traits, the unmistakable "look." To a large extent, it is the common experience of being identified as black by a racist society and the castigatory and damaging effect of such racial identification, which creates the milieu for social exclusion to take place.

Racial identification is a process by which the knowledge of the racialized "other" is formed and produced in such a way that it appeals to racial common sense, as a technique of legitimate power. Yet moving beyond racial common sense, as an important effort to employ a more critical analysis of racial identification, seems to interfere with normative social working, teaching, or policing, for example. As such, multifaceted social experiences are extorted through, and become explained primarily in terms of, a racialized category of social insight that does not allow for the multiplicity and heterogeneity of exhaustive knowledge to be signified. "The Other," as Homi Bhabha explains, "must be seen as the necessary negation of a primordial identity—cultural or psychic—that introduces the system of differentiation which enables the 'cultural' to be signified as a linguistic, symbolic, historic reality."[95]

Blacks and other minority groups are collectively defined as members of a particular racialized group, "not as individuals or as generic Americans but as members of the liminal and fragmented real of the 'hyphenated American.'"[96] A nonwhite person feels this duality, what W. E. B. Du Bois calls this "twoness"—an American and a Negro, First Nations, Chinese, or Mexican—"two souls, two thoughts, two unreconciled strivings, two warring ideals in one dark body, whose dogged strength alone keeps it from being torn asunder,"[97] veiling their nonwhiteness under the facade of the constructed whiteness, and becoming an embodiment of this intense contradiction that reprehensibly engulfed them. Mitsuye Yamada, in her poem "Mirror Mirror," illustrates this "twoness" nicely when her son, Kai, complains that he is always asked where he came from. "The trouble is I'm an American on the inside and oriental on the outside," he explains.[98]

This racial liminality embedded inside and outside of the racialized body, not quite American nor quite Japanese, produces a boundary between the "American" self and the racial self, the borderlands of the body separating the nonwhite self from the "American" self, where there is no crossing over. In America, a nonwhite person is, to use Gloria Anzaldúa's words, "at home a stranger,"[99] pierced by a sensation of being mixed up, or not having a "true" identity.

Nonwhites are constantly marginalized through the hegemonic configurations of whiteness and its corollary blackness, Chineseness, Mexicanness, or First Nationness. For this reason, we have to consider seriously these very practices and signs of marginalization—racism, homophobia, misogyny, and class contempt, which are at the core of the dominant discourses. [100] Yet marginalization on both sides can provide an essential starting point for exploring the many ways that identity is inevitably interpolated through the relationality of whiteness and nonwhiteness. I think that what Homi Bhabha has labeled "cultural hybrids," where people have lived in more than one culture because of migration or exile,[101] needs to be invoked. In a sense, all hyphenated Americans are cultural hybrids, living in two different cultures, one American and white, and the other, a subculture and nonwhite, producing "a hybrid subject, almost the same but not quite, almost the same but not white,"[102] whose identities are shaped as "outsiders within." Identity formation, through hyphenization, signals a racialized position forged through the interstices of two separate cultural identities, alien to each other, but yet familiar as they forge a new and vibrant cultural hybridity. However, America's cultural homogeneity is antithetical to cultural hybridity. This fixity of identity and culture endorses a precarious brand of fundamentalism,[103] which, nonetheless, is unworthy of critical attention among the proponents of a homogeneous American cultural identity.

The twoness, which I have described above, is further explored in James Weldon Johnson's *The Autobiography of an Ex-Colored Man*. With equal insights, Johnson writes,

> Every colored [person] in the United States . . . is forced to take his[/her] outlook on all things, not from the viewpoint of a citizen, or a man, or even a human being, but from the viewpoint of a colored [person]. . . . And it is this, too, which . . . gives to every colored [person],in proportion to his[/her] intellectuality, a dual personality; there is only one phase of him[/her] which is disclosed only to the freemasonry of his[/her] own race. I have often watched with interest and often amazement even ignorant colored [persons] under cover of broad grins and minstrel antics maintaining this dualism in the presence of white[s].[104]

How many colored people in the United States of America have truly transcended this dualism? From the relentless borderland of otherness within Americanness comes the same metaphoric question that Fanon asks in his Introduction to *Black Skin, White Mask*: "What does the Black man want?"[105] In this sense, the same question can be asked of nonwhites: What does the person of color want? And even though the question may not be satisfactorily answered, it can, I think, promote some interesting concerns about an identity formation that assumes a prediscursive, objective truth, which for the most part is indoctrinated by the dominant ideological constructions of the subordinate groups.[106] In the end, I suppose that the nonwhite person unambiguously wants to be free from misrecognition.

A hyphenated American experiences a deep longing for what is at the moment impossible, that is, to be a bona fide American. A hyphenated American longs for a space where racial markers, as the distinctive characteristics in determining one's cultural identity, do not exist. For these Americans the liminality of Americanness is really worrisome. They want to "wear" their Americanness with respect, which, in this sense, would allow them to fully "feel" like Americans. Dr. Martin Luther King understood this very well when he wrote from his jail cell, "abused and scorned though [nonwhites] may be, [their] destiny is tied up with America's destiny."[107] Yet nonwhiteness and Americanness continue to be produced, reproduced, and perpetuated as mutually exclusive categories.

In the end, the hyphenated Americans are not connected but are separated from Americanness. It is a fact that nonwhites' loyalty to America is always treated with suspicion. During World War II, the identity of Japanese Americans was put into question; Mexican Americans are inevitably looked on as illegal immigrants; today, in post-9/11 America, American Muslims' identity is under attack. Racial profiling is endorsed by many Americans and is a predictable practice.[108] The identity of all nonwhite people as "true" Americans is questioned daily. This questioning "is tantamount to questioning their credibility as people."[109] On the other hand, a white person "is just white, just an American,"[110] even if he or she is Polish, German, English, French, Spanish, Italian, Greek, Irish, Scandinavian, Bohemian, or Jewish.[111] Whiteness is the glue that fastens all whites to the web of entitlement, the unspoken rules of white privilege, which is concealed by various unegalitarian ideologies operating in a subtle and yet all-encompassing manner. An American is just a state of being.

John McCain, a white man, and the presidential candidate in 2008, tells the American people to vote for him, a true American. Toni Morrison's question, "What parts of the invention and development of whiteness play in the construction of what is loosely described as 'America'?"[112] remains an important question that is not lost even amid our forgetfulness. It is well that the political scientist Andrew Hacker reminds us that "America is inherently a 'white' country: in character, in structure, in culture";[113] and Morrison's delineation also reveals that "deep within the word 'American' is its association with race . . . American means white."[114] Whiteness and Americanness, to use the terms of Ruth Frankenberg, are "conceptualized as bounded."[115] Whiteness is inextricably tied to power partly as an effect of a discursive "draining process," which is applied to both whiteness and Americanness.[116] In "Whiteness and Americanness: Examining Constructions of Race, Culture, and Nation in White Women's Life Narratives," Frankenberg interviews nine white women who are "sympathetic to, or involved in, antiracist or promulticultural activity" and view whiteness and Americanness as "'bad' because both were seen as definitively linked to domination."[117]

Whiteness continues to be a structural position maintaining white privilege. To understand fully whites' responses to whiteness, law professor Ian F. Haney-López, in his book *White by Law*, declares that whites are increasingly more mindful of their whiteness. "What finally is white[ness]?" he asks.[118] Drawing from Karyn D. McKinney's work, "'I feel "Whiteness" When I Hear People Blaming Whites': White as Cultural Victimization," white, in this sense, means "never having to say you're ethnic."[119] On January 27, 2003, an article written by Barbara Kantrowitz and Pat Wingert, "What's at Stake," claimed that 71 percent of Americans identified themselves as white,[120] because to be an American, in the words of Cynthia Hamilton, "one [has] to strive to be nonethnic."[121] Despite *Time* magazine's prediction that "the new face" of America is the bending of all the various ethnicities, "the new face" remains white.[122] Within this perspective, the conflation of ethnicity with race remains dangerous. Even though it is true that there are various white ethnicities, white ethnicities are often ignored. It is precisely for this reason that we cannot ignore white ethnicity. By ignoring white ethnicity, whiteness continues to be naturalized, and its hegemony redoubled. Without purposely addressing white ethnicity there can be no serious assessment of the construction of the "other" as nonwhite.[123]

Nonwhites are consistently denied an American identity. Larry F. Griffin and Katharine McFarland remind us that "in the event of a War, we"— meaning white Americans—"ask ourselves will 'they' align themselves with their ancestral homeland against America? Will their attempt to keep alive their culture and language fracture America? To whom and to what are they loyal—to their particularistic culture, whatever that may be, or the creedal political abstraction that is America?"[124] We do not have to look hard for the assumed answers to these questions. In America all nonwhites are looked on as suspect. During World War II, Japanese Americans were placed in internment camps. They were looked on as foreigners, citizen aliens, and denied an American identity. To use Giorgio Agamben's words, nonwhiteness is a form of "bare life"[125] in which all nonwhites are reduced to second-class citizens, and in some cases even classless citizens because they are locked into a remorseless caste system.

Most recently, in the wake of Hurricane Katrina, African Americans were denied an American identity and unremittingly redefined by American media as refugees. Given America's history, and judging from the full involvedness of the American media in reducing African Americans to refugees, this reduction nonetheless had no power to shock. While the media has reiterated a familiar racist American script, in the twenty-first century it has, even more so, left no doubt that race undeniably infuses the parameter of an American identity. Taking my cue from Morrison, in the problematic construction of Americanness, "race," as Morrison explains, "has always functioned as a metaphor, a necessary device for the construction, maintenance, and reinforcement of an American identity/culture as white."[126] It is clear, then, that in their pursuit of such an identity, racialized ethnic groups have been de-Americanized and excluded from the flawed norms of full democratic citizenship and the core presuppositions of the liberal lingo of equality and human community as is embedded within liberal political thinking. [127] The specter of whiteness, to employ the words of Karl Marx as cited by Eduardo Bonilla-Silva, "weighs like a nightmare on the brain of the living."[128]

The contemplation of a nonwhite haunting presence in America from the beginning of its formation is truly central in recognizing the growing complexity of America's cultural identity and "America's blindness to its own darker truths."[129] The Behind the Veil project at the Center for Documentary Studies at Duke University, as William H. Chafe and colleagues remind us, "speaks in myriad ways to the rich, complicated, heroic, and ultimately ambiguous texture of African American lives during the era of segregation,"[130] which like First Nations, other racialized groups, and whites alike contributed to the formation of an American cultural identity. Fishkin points to the many influences of African Americans, for example, on works such as *Huckleberry Finn*, *Moby-Dick*, and "Benito Cereno."[131] Taking into account the legacy of the merging of the many cultures in America is important in order to discard an American identity as white. But first whiteness would have to be denormalized. Denormalizing whiteness means understanding, engaging, and transforming, at all levels, the structures in place that normalize whiteness. For too long whiteness has been unmarked. Of course for blacks and other nonwhite groups whiteness has always been visible.[132] I will return to the denormalization of whiteness in Chapter 5.

As a matter of fact, in 1990, a cover story by *Time* magazine predicted that by 2056, most Americans will map out their ancestral affinity to the nonwhite continents, including Africa, Asia, and South America, but not to white Europe. "The New Face of America," according to *Time* magazine's 1993 special issue, is an amalgamated image of various racialized ethnic identities. This prediction has created some concerns for many white Americans because "the descendants of white Europeans are likely to slip into minority status."[133] For many, this new face of America can never be perceived as a good thing; it is like the "Rebirth of a Nation"; it is "breaking up" America's cultural homogeneity, to borrow from Lawrence Auster, and represents "the end of American civilization."[134] This can be a distressing experience for the dominant culture, putting it in a "kind of culture shock."[135]

"One America" and Whiteness

Is "one America" possible? Is "one America" another effort to deny racialized groups their American identity? Is "one America" the promotion of colorblindness? In *Putting People First: How We Can All Change America*, President William Jefferson Clinton remarks, "For too long we've been told about 'us' and 'them'. . . . But there can be no 'them' in America. There is only us." But President Clinton failed to come to terms with the fact that the "them" is inevitably positioned within the "us." Does the "us" mean only whites? "Can *we* become one America?" Clinton asked on June 14, 1997, in a commencement address to the graduating class of the University of California, San Diego. "Now is the time we should learn together, talk together and act together to build one America," he suggested.[136] In his "Remarks to the Democratic National Convention," Obama also claimed, "Now even as we speak, there are those who are preparing to divide us, the spin masters, the negative and peddlers who embrace the politics of anything goes. Well, I say to them tonight, there is not a liberal America and a conservative America—There is not a Black America and a White America and Latino and Asian America—there's the United States of America."[137] Obama, like Clinton, asks citizens to overcome their differences and become "one America."

What exactly does "one America" mean? Should Americans be so envisioned? Barack Obama ran a raceless campaign and made every effort to separate himself from "black radical leaders," or from any issues that might cause him to be perceived by white America as "too black." Does "one America" in this context mean gravitating toward colorblindness? And even if we understand "one America" to mean "one people, one nation, one destiny," the notion is dismissive of race, gender, class, sexuality, and other forms of inequalities that shape and determine one's position in American society.

This form of blindness always bears some remarkable insights. More fundamentally, "one America" does not take into account the problematics of whiteness as shaping and defining an American cultural identity as white. Could Americans share a common future in the absence of cultural heterogeneity? In fact, I think that it is more practical to frame public discourse around what the cultural critic Henry A. Giroux calls "a unity-in-difference position,"[138] in which a multiracial and multiethnic America would be the focus instead of "one America." If "one America" is metonymic for a culturally homogeneous America, in its larger context, "one America" in turn substitutes for an America that is based on whiteness.

More importantly, "one America" suffocates any meaningful dialogue about America's race problem. In 1997, Harvard University scholars Stephen and Abigail Thernstrom suggested that "the black condition, white attitude, and race relations have all improved dramatically";[139] and President Obama claimed that "a view that sees white racism as endemic . . . [expresses] a profoundly distorted view of this country."[140] The structural position of whiteness is at present consistently playing out.[141] Racism, even in twenty-first-century America, is even more prevalent and relentless. We cannot deny the persistence of racial discrimination, the hegemonic homogeneous majority, and the large unmeltable minorities with their own fundamentally different communities, such as the Chinatowns of America or the black ghettoes and superghettoes, which present important challenges for race relations in America For example, instead of interpreting Chinatowns and other Chinese communities such as Monterey Park in California as Chinese Americans' reluctance to become part of mainstream America, as Gwen Kinkead, in *Chinatown: A Portrait of a Closed Society*, suggests, one needs to reexamine America's history of racist exclusionary laws and harsh treatment that forced Chinese to form their own communities as a form of survival and resistance. In order to lay bare the manifestation of race relations in America, many scholars have characterized black ghettoes and other "ethnic enclaves" as America's internal colonies. Internal colonialism provides an effective entry point for analyzing racial oppression in the United States through the incantation of a colonial model.[142]

In opposition to colorblindness, the internal colonial perspective recognizes the saliency of race. It provides a fundamental challenge to not diminish the issue of race rooted in America's history based on oppression of racialized subjects. Racialized ethnic groups continue to undergo tremendous economic marginalization. Today, those nonwhites who are economically self-sufficient and popular are reclassified as honorary whites. "But what on earth is whiteness that one should so desire it?" W. E. B Du Bois once asked. Whiteness indicates the production and reproduction of white ascendancy, privilege, and domination. It is isolated and set apart from subordination, marginality, and disadvantage when juxtapositioned against nonwhiteness. Through an ambivalent and complex process of inclusion, honorary whites, by virtue of othering, are integrated into whiteness on a trial basis. I have already drawn our attention to the dilemma of O. J. Simpson in Chapter 1.

Honorary whiteness, that is, the entry of nonwhites into the so-called white club, is now quite common. Yet many nonwhites, rightfully so, take issue with this attraction to whiteness, and are quick, for good reasons, to point out how it afflicts people of color who confuse their real interest with the sense that identification with those in power is the key to recognition and approval. Identification itself is never a finished process; for the most part, it scripts the site of uncertainty. Given that the marginalized are unable to wholly escape their subordinate status, they subliminally accept the very standards of the dominant they think they are rejecting. Reading Fanon and Paulo Freire with and against each other on the topic of internalized oppression provides us with a shared premise on how it works. Drawing on the importance of the oppressed and oppressor model, Freire writes, "At a certain point in their existential experience the oppressed feel an irresistible attraction towards the oppressor and his way of life. Sharing this way of life becomes an overpowering aspiration. In their alienation, the oppressed want at any costs to resemble the oppressor, to imitate him, to follow him."[143] According to Fanon, "What is often called the black soul is a white man's artifact."[144] In the end, nonwhites are like, as Bill Clay rightfully characterizes, "dangling dolls on the strings of white puppeteers."[145] W. E. B. Du Bois has analyzed this problem in terms of the "double consciousness, . . . a peculiar sensation, . . . this sense of always looking at one's self through the eyes of others."[146]

Fanon warns us in his discussion of the "double consciousness" as a process that it is inevitable that the oppressed would internalize an identity that reflects the images put forth by the dominant groups.[147] In other words, how you identify yourself is to a large extent defined by how the dominant culture identifies you. To draw on a clear account of self-image formation, Fanon's much cited words, "in the white world the [person] of color encounters difficulties in the development of his[/her] bodily schema"[148] are accurate but worrisome. The dominant skillfully manages to conceal its hegemonic practices and gets nonwhites to believe in their "abnormality." The subordinates, in turn, adopt such "abnormality" as a part of their discordant psychic poise. A good example of how the dominant works is well accounted for in Michel Foucault's *The History of Sexuality*. In his work "A Foucauldian (Genealogical) Reading of Whiteness," African American philosopher George Yancy explores "how members of a society are trained to perceive themselves as having a certain sexual nature through the deployment of theories and practices that define that nature and so determine the realms of the normal and the abnormal."[149] Yet we must be wary of the deployment of truths about sexuality that regulate and stigmatize the racialized body.

Even though historical and cultural sociologist Orlando Patterson is hopeful that by the middle of the twenty-first century, America will have "no racial problem whatsoever," because "the racial divide" of material disparities between whites and nonwhites "that has plagued America since its founding . . . is fading fast,"[150] many blacks and other nonwhites continue to be marred by what he once described as the "social death" in his ingenuously radical work on slavery.[151] Today, "social death" has both a symbolic and a literal meaning. That the poor—and the poor in America are mostly blacks, Mexicans, and other racialized groups—are dying because they cannot afford proper health care is not without consequences. In fact, too many nonwhite people are located and continue to be allocated on the fringes of American society. According to neoclassical theory, championed by Milton Friedman and the Chicago school, the market itself, free of government intervention, was supposed to eliminate racial discrimination.[152] In fact, today, in the twenty-first century, racial discrimination is alive and flourishing.

The belief or hope that a nonracist society is here or close at hand is a dispossession of America's racist past, a failure to take into account First Nations' implicit extirpation, slavery, and other racially based exclusions and their enduring consequences in America's present racial problems. History cannot be forgotten; it is about remembering rather than forgetting. Remembering is a practice that permits severe breakthrough but also leads to confusion. It is not a quiet act of looking at past practices and events. America's shameful history compels a painful act of remembering that permits the mutilated past to make sense of the suffering of the present.[153] The absence of blacks, First Nations, Chinese, Mexicans, and other racialized groups in America's historiography creates an enduring pain that must be recognized. Such a history must be attended to because, as Maya Angelou, in her bountiful wisdom, tells us, "history, despite its wrenching pain cannot be unlived, but if faced with courage need not be lived again."[154] A concern with a history that hurts is not a backward orientation. To move on, we must recognize and come to terms with the "wrenching pain" of America's history. The "we" is all-encompassing, both historically specific and future oriented. It provides a location for the reevaluation of the collective subjectivity of protest and a way to understand its significance. In the end, the prevailing white power and privilege has to be given some serious consideration and incisive analysis. Struggles for racial justice and equality will continue to be at the forefront of America's race relations.

That many nonwhites continue to face several restrictive accesses to the "wages of whiteness," including high-paying jobs, decent housing, a good education, and a psychological sense of belonging to an America marred by the stain of a prodigious inequality, cannot be downplayed. Yet the focus on colorblindness, which amounts to a racial false consciousness, turns racial discrimination into a safeguard for whites' advantages and denies stratified racial differences. Can racial differences be overcome and celebrated in meaningful ways in America? The answer to this question can benefit from the acknowledgment that racial differences have shaped America's development, and continue to be a largely embedded American pastime. One of the most astute developments is Eduardo Bonilla-Silva's theory of "colorblind racism," which shows clearly that there are several ways in which whites talk about blacks without sounding racist. A good illustration, he notes, is given by "Karen, a student at MU, [who] agreed with the premise that blacks are poor because they lack the drive to succeed."[155] She is not alone. In the United States, the anchored notion of the fomenting "underclass" has remained entwined with race, and the mass media and public officials have perpetuated the correlation by finding ways to talk about the poor with an invidious racist subtext.[156] The manner in which the media knowingly talks about the "underclass" and the language it employs racializes. This is what J. L. Austin, in *How to Do Things with Words*, calls the performative quality of language, a perlocutionary act, which is what is brought about or accomplished by saying something.[157] Yet the media lacks a detailed language to verbalize about those who oppress—"how they feel about, think about, react to, make sense of, come to terms with, maintain privilege over, and ultimately renounce the power to oppress."[158] A postracial America can never be realized in the near future. Racialized ethnic groups continue to be policed.

The Policing of the "Them"

Nonwhites continue to be treated as the "them" and as second-class citizens. Along with the second-class status of nonwhites, the state continues to be the perpetrator of a racially unjust society. It was not so long ago that President Franklin D. Roosevelt enacted his blatantly racist Executive Order 9066 directed at the Japanese. More than 110,000 Japanese were incarcerated in internment camps during World War II, in barefaced refutation of their alleged rights as Americans. In spite of the harsh treatment of Japanese by the U.S. government, many Japanese Americans were fighting on the side of America, dying in the name of American democracy.

At present, The Patriot Act (the United and Strengthening America by Providing Appropriate Tools Required to Intercept and Obstruct Terrorists Act of 2001)[159] is illustrative of the state's roles in perpetuating and reinforcing its racist practices. In the wake of 9/11, all Muslim Americans are viewed as terrorists, and in order to legitimize its racism, the U.S. government must implement "homeland security," an implementation supposedly meant to "impede another 9/11" and "keep America safe from terrorist attacks." Even though racism has changed over time, taking on new forms and serving different purposes, racism "as inherently integrated within a racist system of colour privilege, and/or/thus [is] inevitably placed within an untenable position within research on 'racial' oppression for non-White people."[160] Michael Omi and Howard Winant explain that there is nothing intrinsically white about America's racism.[161] Yet whiteness allocates, Frankenberg explains, "everyone a place in the relations of racism." Going along with Frankenberg, I think that it is harder for a white person to say, "Whiteness has nothing to do with me—I'm not white" than to say "Racism has nothing to do with me—I'm not racist."[162] For sure, racial domination is not as straightforward as it used to be. It has become more sophisticated and manifests itself in institutionalized power and white privilege. Racism comes in a new form. "New" in this sense does no longer depend on the racial categorization that produced First Nations' extermination, slavery, Chinese exclusion, Jim Crow South, or, more recently, the ghettoes, super-ghettoes, and prisons.

In the following section I look at the new racism and how it is anchored in constructing and reinforcing difference. Difference, in this sense, is taken to mean cultural specificity, that is, what is different about the nondominant cultures, and the implications stemming from such difference.

The New Racism and Difference

The new racism is not just "subtle, institutionalized, and apparently nonracial practices that maintain white supremacy," as Bonilla-Silva and Ray describe it.[163] The central task of the theory of white superiority, as Oliver Cox explains, is not to serve as a diagnostic demonstration that "white is superior to all human beings but to insist that whites must be supreme."[164] This is the conceitedness of whiteness. It imprints on the white self a presumptuous view of itself. Through its self-congratulatory mode it overrates its own character, personal vanity, and pride, and consequently falls prey to its own conceitedness.[165] White supremacy is not about membership in extremist white supremacist groups such as the Ku Klux Klan (KKK), the White American Resistance (WAR), the Aryan Nations, the Silent

Brotherhood, the Church of the Creator, or the National Association for the Advancement of White People.

This new racism is made visible through discourses and practices that are racial and are couched in terms such as *diversity, multiculturalism*, and *culturalism*, as I demonstrate in Chapter 5. Racist ideology is now being expressed through seemingly nonracial discourse.[166] In spite of Paul Gilroy's assumption that "the era of the new racism is emphatically over,"[167] the new racism is replicating a variety of racialized logics that make a distinction in differences through racialized categories and promote the notion that groups are essentially differentiated.[168] It is definitely a defense of white privilege, or what Professor Charles W. Mills has defined as "the racial contract."[169] A report presented by the Lewis Mumford Center on April 3, 2001, reveals that blacks and whites continue to live in separate neighborhoods, and Asian and Hispanics are more isolated now from whites than they were in the 1990s.[170] Bob Jones University continues its banning of interracial dating.[171] Yet we are made to think that there is "a declining significance of race"[172] and that racism has ended.[173]

It is true that, through laws like the Voting Rights Act and the Civil Rights Act, racialized groups are granted the political status of citizen, but they are still denied full social membership into normative Americanness. In fact, as Bonilla-Silva and Ray note, "Racism has changed in form and not in substance."[174] Today, American citizens live in a new racialist climate, not one that talks openly about nonwhites' inferiority. Rather, culture is substituted for race, and rather than providing the basis for understanding how race functions in this society, cultural differences, as an ideological device for subordination and social control, promote and nourish racial thinking.[175] Moreover, cultural differences, and not intolerance, "structured inequality, and social injustice," become "the enemy of democracy." [176]

Cultural differences are encoded, made universal, and constrained within a distinct culturalism, which is not only unhelpful but actually disabling.[177] We can see this clearly after 9/11. The focus on culturalism sets the stage for the comparison and measurement of the dominant and civilized against the countercultures and uncivilized, which, for Huntington, is a clash of civilization between Islam and the West. In fact, the clash of civilization must be allowed to play itself out and thus it has been uncritically employed as an indomitable explanation for 9/11. Nevertheless, Professor Mahmood Mamdani suggests "a more historical and parochial reading of culture, one informed by the idea that the clash is more inside civilizations than between them."[178] In the same vein, Paul Gilroy concludes that "the fissures, folds, and leaks within civilizations deserve more attention than the much-vaunted clashes between them."[179] In fact, it is easier to resolve, at least on the surface, clashes within cultures by setting up cultural borderlands that separate the dominant from the subcultures. Clashes between cultures, nonetheless, bring into play binary oppositions such as civilized and uncivilized cultures, the West versus "the rest." It enables a discourse that promotes "the rest" as having an illiberal culture. In America, this form of knowledge dissemination is used to think about and define subcultures as separate from the dominant, which has proliferated into, for example, an irrational Islamophobia.

The detectable appearance of culturalism, in its many forms, has not declined in culturalism's meaning and interpretations. For the most part, it nurtures intolerance and bigotry toward groups that are perceived as racially and culturally different. In addition, it naturally creates "cultural hierarchy" based on the ideology of white superiority.[180] One of the precise invariant outcomes of white superiority is the essential and multifaceted oppression of nonwhites. At this juncture, "internal colonialism" explains the exploitation and discrimination of racialized groups in America. Internal colonialism is best defined as a structure of social relations based on an intricate and exhaustive control and mistreatment of racialized ethnic groups.[181] This definition harks back to colonialism, which had, for good reasons, preoccupied Fanon's thinking in his provoking book, *Toward the African Revolution: Political Essays*. Fanon saw colonialism as the direct result of dehumanization, a product of ethnocentrism and its exclusion of the "other."[182] In the United States, the exclusion of the racialized "other" from an American identity is deplorable.

In 1993, in the *New Yorker*, the American Indian College fund ran an advertisement in large, bold capital letters. The advertisement read, "SAVE A CULTURE THAT COULD SAVE OURS." What is meant by "ours"? Does this mean that First Nations' culture is no longer marginalized? It was not so long ago that First Nations culture was viewed as savage. I am apprehensive of the invocation of "ours" in these situations. "Ours" too often means the cultural norm that remains unmarked. How plural is "ours" in the construction of America's single culturality? The "ours" has colonized American cultural identity. First Nations, blacks, Chinese, Mexicans, and other marginalized cultures are situated in the shadow of whites' subjectivity. They are recognized not as "ours" but as "them."

The idea is to celebrate cultural differences and at the same time keep intact a unified dominant culture specifically adhering to the norms of whiteness. Or, put differently, "mention differences—and continue doing what you've always done,"[183] keeping whiteness intact. Yet the interpositions or dynamic between and among subcultures does not function according to a clear logic. There are always the "in-betweens," the "other" within the "them," the liminal "them," which are particularly challenging for identity categories because they rely on authenticity. Consequently, the othering of the "other" inevitably manifests itself and serves as a means for silencing and marginalizing those who do not fit into the normative cultural identity.

Saving First Nations' culture would be the only way to guarantee their alienation from the dominant culture and the sustenance of cultural borderlands. It would prevent First Nations from crossing over the cultural borders, separating whites from nonwhites. Even though borderlands are "sites of crossing, negotiation, translation, and dialogue,"[184] cultural border crossing is detrimental to the crossers. It puts subjectivities at risk of cultural fragmentation, in which new identities are formed. In this sense, cultural fragmentation counts for something. Even though the discourse of culture itself undercuts any effort at cultural self-constitution, a self-constituted identity can be brought into play in and through the very impossibility of achieving such an identity. Nonetheless, I want to expose and analyze the complexity of the hyperrealism of dominant versus subcultures, which embraces a dangerous oppositional binary and its certitude of representation in America. "Binary oppositions are a 'violent hierarchy,'"[185] which inevitably leads to domination and privilege on the one hand, and subordination, exclusion, and marginalization on the other hand. Yet the subordinate subject "can become an incalculable object, quite literally, difficult to place"[186] within these fixed cultural binaries.

In fact, the dialectic at play throughout the process of cultural representation and adjustment structures and maintains power and privilege in all spheres of America's institutional and social relations. On the one hand, this form of power can create a self-constituted identity. A good illustration of the formation of a self-constituted identity is depicted in Toni Morrison's *Beloved* "through the voices of African American slave women"[187] in an effort to invoke and scrutinize the "self."

> Beloved
> You are my sister
> You are my daughter
> You are my face; you are me
> I have found you again; you have come back to me
> You are my Beloved.
> You are mine
> You are mine
> You are mine.[188]

From the preceding analysis, this "self" is a "self" of its own construction; it is a site for creating a new subject position for black women. On the other hand, this form of power impoverishes the spirit and deteriorates the human condition, resulting in the social decay that informs the daily lives of nonwhites. When I employ Fanon's phrase "cultural hierarchy," this is partly what I have in mind.

In post-9/11 America, the need to reemploy cultural hierarchy is more urgent than ever. Clearly, cultural hierarchy is not critically addressed in the discourse of multiculturalism because one of multiculturalism's goals is to maintain and strengthen the very cultural hierarchy that it seems to reject. Even though multiculturalism's idea and practice allows for recognition of nonhegemonic cultural group identity, it continues to reinforce America's cultural hegemony as white. Yet for many conservative scholars, including Arthur M. Schlesinger, Dinesh D'Souza, Samuel Huntington, and Nathan Glazer, "multiculturalism has come to signify a disruptive, unsettling, and dangerous force in America,"[189] and it is reshaping the very fabric of America's cultural homogeneity. Schlesinger fearfully points to the "disuniting of America"[190] with the emphasis on multiculturalism. Huntington anxiously suggests that "America could lose its core culture, as President Clinton anticipated, and become multicultural."[191] In fact, the emphasis on multiculturalism as a celebration of cultural otherness, where otherness is viewed as un-Americanness, suffocates the dream of "one America." Cultural otherness, we will see later, operates as a metonymic form of the new racism clothed in its old ways.[192] The question, then, is whether the "other" can be turned into a "self"? And what are some of the implications for otherness within the self? How can American "live" its cultural heterogeneity? The quandary of multiculturalism will be the focus of the next chapter.

4

The Quandary of Multiculturalism in America

The diversification of American society is reflected and reinforced by the shift from assimilation (the melting pot) to multiculturalism (the mosaic). Against this background, multiculturalism, as a way of nurturing America's diversification by encouraging racialized ethnic groups to maintain their distinctive cultures, seems especially appealing. Lately, especially in Europe, there is a new emphasis on interculturality, fueled partly by the globalization process. It is expressively relevant that people from different cultures interact with each other so as to reexamine their own cultures and the cultures of other groups.[1] The idea of interculturality is expected to promote positive interaction among people from different cultures so they can learn from each other and gain a better intercultural knowledge. Culture, in this milieu, becomes an essential part of who we are as human beings because it shapes the way we give meaning to our world. More fundamental, culture, as Anne Phillips recognizes, is "one of the mechanisms through which social hierarchies are sustained."[2]

To speak of multiculturalism is to speak of a plurality of cultures that are unique and distinct from each other. According to Will Kymlicka, multiculturalism is, in relation to culture,[3] "a microcosm of the social,"[4] which, as the term suggests, should not restrict cultural homogeneity but promote cultural heterogeneity. If it is true that multiculturalism as an egalitarian principle is committed to the idea that all groups have a role to play in truly shaping a country's cultural identity,[5] in terms of an American cultural identity, where whiteness is treated as cultural expectation, the pressing task, then, is how would multiculturalism implement such an idea? In other words, how has multiculturalism dealt with the construction of America's cultural homogeneity? What is at risk in the very dialogue of multiculturalism seeking to recognize cultural otherness and hold on to the conventional thinking where cultural otherness is celebrated as un-Americanness?

How can multiculturalism free itself from the inescapable racialist ontology from which it has evolved and detach itself from its legacy of cultural hierarchization? Can it create new cultural spaces where respect for racial differences can flourish in spite of the othering and diasporic significations that had and continue to plague racialized groups in America? One significant result of othering, as Jean Baker Miller suggests, is that white Americans "are denied an essential part of life—the opportunity to acquire self-understanding through knowing their impact on others."[6] How can racialized groups be included into America's cultural identity if one of multiculturalism's main goals is to exclude and set apart the dominant culture (official) from the nondominant culture (unofficial)?

Multiculturalism has shaped academic thinking about cultures, has guided public policy issues on racial dynamics in the United States, and has influenced the general public's understanding of race relations in America. If we take seriously the Canadian philosopher Charles Taylor's description and explanation of multiculturalism as an appearance of a "politics of recognition"[7] and what feminist and political theorist Nancy Fraser describes as the "identity model,"[8] recognition means the recognition of the multiplicities of intact cultures, deriving from racialized ethnic differences that are different and oppositional from the dominant culture. Yet recognition signals distribution as well, since cultures that are considered illiberal are nonnegotiable and unacceptable. This particular strategy to recognize cultural differences, as Eduardo Bonilla-Silva positions it, as "differentialist racism" within particularly racially defined groups, is an acute form of racial essentialism, which is largely true of multiculturalism. In other word, multiculturalism is not resistant to de facto essentialist construction of cultures. For example, what constitutes gender inequalities within the parameters of "culture" needs continuous requestioning and, I suppose, requires an overhaul of the ways nondominant cultures are understood by the dominant culture, as well as a shift from the "I" (here the "I" denotes the dominant viewpoint) that denotes accuracy and facts.

Even if the interests of racialized groups are apparent in specific ways in their attempt to reclaim their so-called blackness, First Nationness, or Chineseness within these given cultural groups, there are internal differences stemming not only from gender differential but from sexuality as well. Gender functions as an act of cultural inscription and is inevitably positioned within a designated cultural group. Given patriarchy's horrible predispositions, women's positions in these groups are often established as subsidiary. It is the otherness of the "other" that cannot be accounted for by multiculturalism in its quest for cultural recognition and celebration.[9] The point is that we can see the limitations of multiculturalism in terms of its treatment of cultural identity as fixed.

Taylor argues that through a dialogical process, our identities and concepts of ourselves as free and equal agents are formed by certain cultural scripts that are at our disposal.[10] However, Taylor forgets to mention that these cultural scripts are predefined by our social conditions. Since racialized groups' cultural identities comprise, for the most part, norms of identification and treatments associated with otherness, the clear line between recognition and cultural marginalization is deplorable. My purpose in this chapter is to focus on multiculturalism and its emphasis on the celebration of cultural otherness as a way of projecting and marking otherness as un-Americanness. The projection of the specificity of cultural otherness, in this sense, is appropriated and reappropriated, and continues to be alienated from cultural oneness or Americanness. Accordingly, cultural otherness provides the yardstick for exclusion of racialized ethnic groups from an American identity. The anxiety of prominent scholars who consider multiculturalism as a threat to America's cultural homogeneity, another form of de-Americanization of racialized groups, is deeply misguided. Nonetheless, these concerns are not without warnings. It is another attempt on the part of the antimulticulturalists to reinforce the notion of an American cultural identity as white. Racialized groups continue to be the unmeltables. The brilliance of multiculturalism is to keep these groups unmeltable, setting them apart from America's meltables so America's cultural homogeneity remains intact. To maintain homogeneity it is necessary to repress cultural heterogeneity by excluding and silencing differences. The very desire to exclude racialized ethnic groups from America's cultural oneness and to celebrate and recognize America's cultural manyness as cultural otherness where otherness is correlated with un-Americanness is precisely the quandary of multiculturalism.

In the following section, I would like to examine specific characteristics of multiculturalism, in order to demonstrate that recognizing and celebrating nondominant cultures does not solve the problems of cultural marginality, which continues to preserve the familiar cultural fabric of America's society as white. More so, cultural recognition does not signal economic redistribution, which is an issue I address later in this chapter.

Defining Multiculturalism

Notwithstanding the foregoing concerns, multiculturalism is frequently presented in many discussions as a totemic issue pertaining to the diversifying of the workplace, schools, and higher institutions of learning.[11] In this sense, it can be seen as a logical response to promote diversity, a radical break with a previously American past of assimilation. If promoting diversity in the public sphere is one of the functions of multiculturalism, well, then, fastening the core supposition of affirmative action to multiculturalism is not so recondite. Yet for Nathan Glazer, in *We Are All Multiculturalists Now*, "affirmative action has nothing to do with the recognition of cultures. . . . It is about jobs and admission."[12] The real question is whether affirmative action fails to deal with the cultural. Can it be separated from multiculturalism? My concern here is not to debate the pros and cons of affirmative action, however.[13] By asking these questions, we can see clearly that the meaning of multiculturalism has become increasingly unclear, and for this reason many authors are deterred from using the term.[14] Susan Moller Okin, a feminist political philosopher, captures, at best, the difficulty of defining multiculturalism when she admits that she finds it hard "to pin down."[15] Also, Paul Gilroy acknowledges that "there is no consensus on how the term 'multiculturalism' should be defined or employed."[16]

The most common definition of multiculturalism is one extracted from the *HarperCollins Dictionary of Sociology* by the French sociologist Michel Wieviorka. Wieviorka states that multiculturalism is "the acknowledgement and promotion of cultural pluralism. . . . [It] celebrates and seeks to protect cultural variety, for example, minority languages. At the same time it focuses on the unequal relationship of minority cultures to mainstream cultures."[17] While this definition is particularistic, I use it in order to show that one of the real purposes of multiculturalism is the maintenance of what Frantz Fanon terms *cultural hierarchy*.[18] Joanne Harumi Sechi, a Japanese American author, confesses, "I was made to feel that cultural pride would justify and make good my difference in skin color while it was a constant reminder that I was different."[19] Race is fundamental and is the ultimate indicator of one's cultural identity; it is one of the primary organizers of America's social relations. It is the racialization process that keeps culture intact. It is precisely for this reason that the literary theorist Walter Benn Michaels's conclusion that cultural recognition "is not a critique of racism but is a form of racism"[20]—which, for Fanon, "vitiates American culture"[21]—is welcome here. In fact, it is the appeal to race that makes culture an object of concern, giving meaning to ideas like America is losing its homogeneous cultural identity and, therefore, needs to preserve its cultural identity.[22] And while multiculturalism's focus on culture takes attention away from the real issues of racism in the United States, we need to be alerted to the actuality that "culture" has become a metonym for "race."

In "Multiculturalism's Unfinished Business," one of the most far-reaching and systematic attempts to review multiculturalism, Professors Christopher Newfield and Avery F. Gordon point to the changes in meanings and the various methods of multiculturalism since the 1970s in the United States.[23] To locate multiculturalism is, at best, to place it into two opposing camps.

On the one hand, one of the functions of multiculturalism is to deal with the problematic race relations in the United States. In the 1980s, for example, it was the locus for race relations and it supported renewed disapproval of racial inequality and white supremacy. On the other hand, the overextension of cultural diversity, although inevitable, has forced the opponents of multiculturalism to perceive it as "disuniting," or "fraying" an American identity and its presumed homogeneity that the founders worked so hard to promote and preserve.[24] At this juncture, I would argue, this seeming threat to America's national identity is just another attempt to reclaim an American identity as white. In the discourse of multiculturalism, nonwhites, the unmeltables, are the metaphoric subjects who are seen as not Americans and as "raced ethnic," aliens to America's cultural oneness.[25]

Specific Characteristics of Multiculturalism

In some self-proclaimed, multicultural countries like Canada[26] and Australia,[27] the emphasis of multiculturalism on rethinking the initial epistemology of the liberal rights claims, but not the practice of liberal rights, is in place as a policy to protect minority cultures. Without a doubt, the liberal state will primarily recognize and concern itself only with those cultural groups that will adhere to and benefit from the existing rules of "the political and cultural games."[28] Multiculturalism starts from the premise that society comprises different cultures, one dominant and the others nondominant. It is through these cultural dichotomies—dominant and nondominant—that multiculturalism in America gains its support. While credence is given to the cultural traditions of the hegemonic white majority, the need for cultural recognition of racialized ethnic groups becomes a "right" instead of a necessity.[29] For instance, some well-intended liberals draw on the need to correlate the rights of racialized groups with that of human rights as a form of promoting "liberty, democracy, and social justice,"[30] which, in turn, defines an abstract form of universalism that is at the core of the liberal state.

The role of the liberal state is to make sure that the norms and values deriving from the dominant culture are always in place, but at the same time concessions must be given to racialized ethnic and other marginalized groups. The role of multiculturalism is to promote cultural identities, deriving from distinctive group identities, and to intractably fasten itself to inassimilable differences as a way of destabilizing "the liberal belief in a universal subjectivity (we are all just people)."[31] These cultural identities are looked on as authentic and deriving from values and group norms as a manifestation of power. The idea is that cultural identities are "natural" parts of our social lives as human beings. Hence, identities become essentialized instead of being seen as social constructions. And this authentic essence, as an ever-present and completely dispersed modality of social relations, limits our capability to develop new knowledge and forms of resistance. Rightly, the filmmaker, writer, and composer Trinh T. Minh-ha views the harm of authenticity as problematic.[32] She reminds us that authenticity "is rife; as a product of hegemony and a remarkable counterpart of universal standardization, it constitutes an efficacious means of silencing the cry of racial oppression."[33] In the end, what motivates multiculturalism is not a genuine concern for cultural diversity, but the maintenance of the Fanonian notion of cultural hierarchy. The marginal position of nondominant cultures as the natural order of things is assumed within the framework of multiculturalism.

In the United States, multiculturalism is a fact of life.[34] It is a recent and significant reflection of America's racial and ethnic heterogeneity that has come to define America from the start. Multiculturalism has gained a tremendous amount of ground among academics, politicians, commentators, and laypeople. One function of multiculturalism, as a given strategy to deal with the problematic race relations in America, is to organize and attempt to recognize the United States as a multiracial and multiethnic society. If one willingly ignores the various strata of its conceptual complexities, surely multiculturalism is one of the most significant political achievements in America in recent years. Multiculturalism is a political alibi for tolerance, or as Peter McLaren puts it, a "key signifier of 'tolerance,'"[35] which has to envision resistance in order to contain itself and properly demonstrate its progressive relativism. Its emphasis on the tolerance of racial and ethnic differences, masquerading as an antiracist project, is at the forefront of America's race and ethnic relations.

That white Americans are now interpellated as being tolerant of nonwhites certainly marks a turning point in America. Even if one does not put up with the tension that arises from a culturally diverse society like America, any expression of intolerance is not particularly attractive. To be intolerant is to be "politically incorrect," to violate the spirit of multiculturalism and cultural diversity, and, in the end, to be labeled as uncivilized, barbaric, and irrational. Therefore, tolerance as a core value has been encouraged and expected. The German political theorist and sociologist Herbert Marcuse refers to this social attitude as "repressive tolerance."[36] In other words, cultural differences, beliefs, values, habits, and observances are tolerated as long as they do not interfere with or disrupt the dominant culture.

Tolerance is an important conception, especially given its enduring presence within the liberal ethos of multiculturalism as a politics of cultural recognition. Yet tolerance, as a concept, harbors a deep intolerance. One who is tolerant is equally intolerant.[37] In an interview that Jacques Derrida conducted after 9/11, the French philosopher warned that tolerance "is most often used on the side of those with power as a sign of condescending concession power."[38] In this sense, tolerance must be located in the existing social relations of power that symbolize and presume the very discourse of tolerance itself. In the end, tolerance is not about eradicating the power of the powerful or, in other words, making the powerful powerless; it is about negotiating with them in such a way that they may not exercise their power. For those who have been intolerant, the task at hand is now to be tolerant. Yet it does not destroy the desire to be intolerant, nor does it annihilate the inordinate power structure of which white Americans are invested as defining agents of an American culture.[39]

In the post-9/11 era, to be openly intolerant of Muslims is a widely endorsed and tenable position because tolerance in this case is perceived as providing a breeding ground for Islamist militants. The Nation of Islam, even before 9/11, was placed on the government's list as a dangerous organization.[40] More recently, with the 9/11 attacks, black American Muslims and Muslim Americans in general are viewed as terrorists. This view of Muslim is widespread and has become a normative feature of post-9/11 America. Even the Bush administration has been determined to invade and bring about a regime change in Iraq intended to liberate Muslims from the yore of Islam.[41] Nathan Glazer points to the "sharp discord between some key Muslim values and American cultures."[42] For this reason, the restless resurgence of an American cultural identity in discourse as well as in practice, opposing Muslims, has become visible. And since blacks have been de-Americanized, this anti-Muslim sentiment permeating in America has been worrisome for most non-Muslim blacks. It is not surprising that mainstream opposition to Islam is not endorsed by most blacks in America, because blacks have no real stake in America and experience ill treatment as a marginalized group.[43] Nonetheless, Islam has fueled the idea that Christianity in America is fundamentally undermined; its hegemonic position is somewhat challenged by Muslims. Accordingly, like black and Mexican communities where social control is evident, policing the Muslim communities has now become quite marked.

Tolerance is imbedded in the discourse of normativity, and for this reason inequality is masked within this discourse. Inequality has to be accepted because the basis of a democratic nation is premised on the conception of an unequal society that can only be rectified through the promotion of tolerance. Hence, neighbors appear to be tolerant, schools teach tolerance, the state advocates tolerance, and religious and secular civic associations propagate tolerance.[44] Tolerance is that which organizes and imposes what Mahmood Mamdani calls a "rational self-restraint" from expressing our feeling of insurmountable intolerance for the constructed social "others."[45] Its inconsequentiality as a moral or ethical principle reveals itself. Not to mention that, as a political principle, tolerance is entrenched with antidemocratic elements dividing society into groups that are entitled to claim respect as a right and groups that are required to petition tolerance as a favor. The craze for schooling everyone to be tolerant brings about the antidemocratic connotations of tolerance.[46]

In the end, tolerance cannot exist without intolerance. It is forever dependent on intolerance. As Slavoj Žižek acknowledges, "the traditional liberal opposition between 'open' plural society and 'closed' nationalist-corporatist societies founded on the exclusion of the other has thus to be brought to its point of self-reliance: the liberal gaze itself functions according to the same logics, in so far as it is founded upon the exclusion of the other to whom one attributes the fundamentalist nationalism, etc."[47] Given that in the United States there is the presence of a hierarchy in which the dominant (tolerator) is placed in a position of power over the nondominant (tolerated), the discourse on tolerance becomes paramount. Yet this dialectic does not simply capture the unequal status of the two groups; rather, it draws our attention fully to the primeval structure of toleration as a form of social relations.

The power asymmetry based on the dualistic concept of the tolerator (white self) and the tolerated (nonwhite other) is at the heart of multiculturalism in America, which is rarely recognized and acknowledged. For sure, this oppositional model cannot fully explain the intricacies of actually living in a multicultural society that is shaped by whiteness, and the different ways in which subjects are situated based on such categories as gender, race, ethnicity, sexuality, class, religion, age, mental and physical abilities, and geography. Iris Marion Young, in *Justice and the Politics of Difference*, points to ways in which these identities are embedded in social relations and are "tightly defined by domination and subordination."[48] Is it possible, then, for us to move beyond these fixed identities? For those groups on the margins of the symbolic order, is Homi Bhabha's notion of the "third space,"[49] the liminal space of ambivalence where the racialized agent is discursively confined, enough? Can the very status of the "other" be reinscribed in a different way? Is cultural hybridity the answer? Being nonwhite in America is to be positioned on the margin of society; to be a member of a nondominant culture. Through the discourse and practice of multiculturalism, the cultural advantages of whiteness are perpetuated and maintained. Can the complex divide between the white self and the nonwhite "other" be overridden? The burden of this restricted binary serves the primary purpose of keeping in place the phallocentric logic of the ideology of white supremacy,[50] which is concealed behind concerns that multiculturalism is putting an end to America's cultural homogeneity.

On April 9, 1990, *Time* magazine published a cover story, titled "Beyond the Melting Pot," that asserted that because the United States has a larger black, Hispanic, and Asian population, America is no longer a melting pot. In fact, it is more of a "mosaic or even a lumpy stew."[51] It has "jumped out of the 'melting pot' and into the 'salad bowl'"[52] because the melting pot cannot melt the unmeltables.[53] This is not to say, as the economic journalist of *Business Week* Michael J. Mandel has suggested, that "the melting pot is not still melting."[54] Whites, as the dominant ethnicity, even if they have just arrived in the United States, continue to be melted into America's cultural oneness. In other words, the idealized image of an American cultural identity continues to be associated with whiteness.

Who consumes multiculturalism is a question that needs to be asked. Events such as the Labor Day parade in New York City, Puerto Rican Independence celebrations, Black History Month, and Mexican Day celebrations are spaces and times where objectified otherness is produced and the essential "other" given a visible aura. To use Canadian folk singer Faith Nolan's words, "for the Wasps to gaze upon, for the vultures to devour,"[55] these kinds of social events offer "objectified spectacles," different modes of existence, which can be compared and measured against the white American culture. The fascination with what bell hooks discerns as the "commodification of Otherness"[56] appears as an acceptance celebration of diverse culture, and signals the idea of cultural enrichment as an "epistemological object,"[57] only to give rise to cultural exchanges that are, most of the time, based on immeasurable judgments about otherness and that, in the end, assist in nourishing cultural stereotypes. Cultural stereotypes provide the backdrop for the creation of hollow, cultural boundaries between the dominant (white) culture and the nondominant (nonwhite) cultures, the "us" and "them" scenarios, combining and fusing the "them" into a seamless whole.

Nonetheless, there is no breaking away from otherness. More fundamental, otherness, in many cases, bars and disallows members of racialized groups from developing a vigorous cultural identity of their own. The reinscribing of otherness on the racialized ethnic communities keeps intact the system of cultural hierarchy, where nonwhites' cultures are located at the very bottom and are viewed as inferior, deviant, and unusual. It is precisely these cultural differences that matter in the enhancement of multiculturalism's goal to maintain otherness.

Cultural differences, for the most part, are disruptive of the status quo and create anxiety for the status quo seekers. As such, these differences can never occupy a privileged status. Trinh T. Minh-ha reminds us that there are two kinds of social and cultural differences; those that threaten and those that do not. The acceptable differences induce, to borrow her words, "an attitude of temporary tolerance."[58] Multiculturalism, then, is expected to promote and perpetuate the kinds of differences that do not threaten. These nonthreatening differences are important in promoting the good life that has become important to liberal thinkers such as Will Kymlicka (1995), Charles Taylor (1994), and Iris Marion Young (1990). At the same time, however, these thinkers are preoccupied with universal traits, which are supposed to be shared by all members belonging to a specific cultural group.

Even though each subculture is recognized as distinct, what is played out is an emphasis on a duality of cultures, the dominant (white) and the non-dominant (nonwhite), the "us" and "them," instead of a plurality of cultures as well as a plurality within cultures. Furthermore, cultures themselves are multicultural in their genesis and foundation, the "us" and "them" is embedded within the notion of the necessary dichotomization of cultures, the dominant and the nondominant, where the dominant culture, for the most part, remains invisible, unmarked, and closed. Since the dominant culture defines its identity in terms of its intractable difference from the nondominant and conscientiously guards itself against their pressures for incorporation, the dominant culture is always threatened by the nondominant culture and avoids genuine links with the nondominant cultures.

"SAVE A CULTURE THAT COULD SAVE OURS," reads the advertisement in the New Yorker for the American Indian College fund, and points to the importance of individuals being bona fide members of a given cultural group.[59] Being a member of a cultural group provides a normalizing place for nondominant cultures, but at the same time restricts access to the dominant culture. In instances where the survival of a culture is threatened, it is fundamental for that culture to be preserved and protected.[60] Protecting or saving First Nations' culture, for example, and their traditional way of life, is the easiest way to organize and maintain cultural borders. Given that First Nations' culture is separate from American culture, this advertisement highlights the real dangers of cultural border crossing.[61] Cultural borders like the color line, because of the wrenching fear of the "other," the fear of the very idea of a multiethnic and multicultural America, serve as a form of protection and stabilization. It is fundamental to grasp how fear harbors itself in the beings of many whites, lending credence to the very question that Lucius T. Outlaw Jr., professor of philosophy and Africana and Diaspora Studies, asks, "And what is [truly] feared? Contamination, genealogically and culturally, by those more or less radically different, presumed inferior non-European Others,"[62] exotic, untamed, deviant, and unrestrained. Samuel P. Huntington's book, Who Are We? The Challenges to America's National Identity, has made some helpful observations in highlighting this fear, the threat of Mexicans (since all Mexicans are viewed as immigrants), for example, to America's cultural identity.

Along the continuum of cultural and racial categorization that has been an inherent part of America's racial history, whiteness, then, has to be compared with nonwhiteness, where nonwhiteness must be reduced to otherness. While otherness presents a challenge to one's own self-identity, othering, in itself, is another way of ensuring whites' superiority. And in order to adhere to such forms of superiority, cultural borders have to be set up and positioned in such a way as to demarcate the core and peripheral cultural spaces that are secured and unsecured, to make a distinction between "us" and "them," the civilized from the primitive, the included from the excluded, the "we," the same, the familiar, from the "they," the unfamiliar and unknown, occupying the other side of the border, the constrained cultural space of the "other." The other, in its strangeness, in its foreignness, mirrors and represents what is no stranger to the self, but yet it is projected outside of the self. [63]

The cultural borders of "us" and "them," rigidly in place, perform the policing function of maintaining such a demarcation. The borders are culturally imposed and ideologically reproduced by a whole system of cultural as well as racial symbols, which determine the members and nonmembers. This is exactly what I would call cultural apartheid—that is, an unavoidable solidification of cultural borders maintaining not only difference from but also inequality with the dominant culture. First Nations, blacks, Chinese, Mexicans, and other racialized groups cannot cross the cultural border and escape the visible social meanings that are discursively inscribed on the racialized bodies and further construed through gender and class configurations. Entrance on the other side is prohibited for "them." In fact, cultural borders are indeed scalable. However, its scalars are socially and psychologically scared. Yet it is important to recognize the extent to which marginalized groups have succeeding in naturalizing, in the most diverse forms and to their own advantages, their cultural practices, which are deeply rooted in their histories as marginalized groups.

While replacing the melting pot metaphor with the salad metaphor, it is hard not to miss the unavoidable difficulty of power among the "ingredients" that remains intact. At best, the melting pot "still contains plenty of unmelted pieces,"[64] placing multiculturalism as the normative responsive to keep cultural borders intact. In fact, even white immigrants, or what Horace M. Kallen calls "the Atlantic migration," the newcomers to America, melt quite easily and, in most cases, by "the measure and the standard of Americanism" that the newcomers accomplish,[65] they are able to easily cross over to the white side of the cultural border. There is no crossing over for First Nations, blacks, and other racialized groups who have been in America from the beginning of its formation. They continue to be treated as foreigners, aliens to America's cultural oneness. For precisely this reason, they have been forced to develop and establish their own "societal cultures," which provide, according to Kymlicka, one of the most forceful voices on group rights to its members with consequential ways of life across a full range of human activities, including "social, educational, religious, recreational and economic life, encompassing both private and public sphere."[66] Is secure access to "societal cultures" for racialized ethnic groups, to a large extent, undermined by basic concerns of opportunities and income?

In fact cultures are far from being fixed, essentialist categories; they are always in a state of flux and are opened to negotiation and renegotiation.[67] In other words, cultures are totally imbricated with rights and materiality. Their implicit meanings are constantly changing and continue to be contested and hybrid because there is a constant struggle to re-create themselves outside of the norms of the mainstream culture. Furthermore, in terms of gender configuration, because the cultural practices devalue the status of women in society as a whole, what we have within the rubrics of multiculturalism is the promotion and preservation of the otherness of the "other" or "minorities within minorities."[68] For women, this is a "double bind," which for many multiculturalists is largely ignored. It is one of the dangers of "culturalism within multiculturalism."[69] In this sense, to borrow Okin's words, "multiculturalism [is] bad for women."[70] Sandra Harding, the philosopher of feminist and postcolonial theory, says it best when she observes that "there are no gender relations per se, but only gender relations as constructed by and [within] . . . cultures."[71] While there is no "clash of cultures"[72] between the dominant culture and the nondominant cultures, there is more a "clash of cultures" within and between these nondominant cultures because they all must compete for recognition or acceptance by the dominant culture. Also, to be a member of a particular cultural group, one must adhere to its requirements. Because multiculturalism emphasizes the authentication of culture and the suffocation of individuality, we can clearly see the skepticism and problems that multiculturalism poses.

In "Race into Culture: A Critical Genealogy of Cultural Identity," Walter Benn Michaels draws our attention to the racism that is embedded in multiculturalism. Even though the racial extent of culture has propagated, because the focus went from race to culture, the task of multiculturalism is to "rescue . . . racism from racists."[73] Now whites can talk about poor black people, for example, with an invidious racist subtext without appearing to be racist. The disturbing tendency to blame the victims for their poverty, for example, is one aspect of the new form of racism, a "racism without racists," to borrow from Eduardo Bonilla-Silva's 2006 book title.[74] In fact, neoconservatives believe that we are now living in a postracist era, which applauds "the end of racism"[75] and "the declining significance of race."[76] Yet today the best jobs, schools, and neighborhoods remain reserved for whites. Particularly insightful in this regard is psychology professor Aída Hurtado's argument according to which "racism is a burden that is not completely understood by those who do not share the stigma. Ignoring race, however, does not erase it as a variable in social interactions."[77]

In an attempt to advance the notion of America as a white nation, American intellectuals have been driven to reflect on or deflect a multiculturalism that goes up against the notion of assimilation.[78] For many, assimilation has outgrown its purpose, which was to integrate the "not-so-white" whites—Irish, Jews, Italians, and Greeks—into America, into "becoming Americans." "Becoming white," which is a privileged status, is synchronistic of "becoming Americans."[79] First Nations, blacks, and other nonwhites can never be white. In fact, Gunnar Myrdal, in *An American Dilemma*, suggests that African Americans, for example, are "exaggerated Americans," in the sense that they are even more incorporated into American culture than some whites.[80] The African American Professor of Economics, Thomas Sowell, points to the fact that "little or no African culture survives among American Negroes."[81] Yet assimilation has not worked for African Americans and other nonwhites—even though some nonwhites may experience some aspect of whiteness by becoming honorary whites. The urban sociologist Robert E. Park explains why assimilation has not worked for nonwhites who have been in America for over three hundred years. It is not because blacks and other nonwhites' cultures appear to be foreign and alien to America's cultural tradition. In fact, nonwhites, especially African Americans and First Nations, are "entirely native to the soil," as Park puts it. The distinction, which sets nonwhites apart from whites, is primarily based on phenotype and racial characteristics, which are correlated with cultural traits.[82] It determines membership into normative Americanness. The key to assimilation, then, is white skin.

Is multiculturalism a distraction from the power differential between whites and nonwhites? Does it promote the notion that the nondominant cultures are homogeneous? Can it provide space for conflicts within the groups stemming from differentiated interests? Are these groups united by the same struggle for racial equality, for example? Are the differences that exist within these groups important? Is multiculturalism an antiracist project? These are not easy questions to answer, given the many understandings and misunderstandings of multiculturalism's goals. The Left, for one, has been critical of multiculturalism's failure to address power relations since racialized ethnic groups are situated differently from whites. Multiculturalism is also flogged by the Left for promoting the notion of group authenticity or shared oppression and for its failure to examine gender, class, age, religious, and sexual differences located within the groups themselves. These differences are important because they help to shape one's situatedness within a group and the larger society as a whole, and how one experiences the various forms of discriminatory practices and unequal treatment.[83] A nondominant culture cannot be at ease with its difference from the dominant culture "unless it is also at ease with its own internal differences."[84]

Multiculturalism and Cultural Diversity

The focus of multiculturalism is to enhance cultural diversity and encourage public protest against racial and cultural differences. A large number of universities are emphasizing cultural diversity on campus. Diversity in itself is a troublesome and difficult concept. For example, is a white working-class student from the Bronx in New York City who attends an Ivy League university such as Yale University contributing to the diversity of the campus? Or does diversity mean racial, cultural, and perhaps sexual diversity? We may have strong views on these questions because "while we are not all the same or fungible," we are diverse internally and externally. Our differences are "relational, shifting, unstable, and constitutive."[85] Yet diversity seems to be the motto for the enrichment of students' college experience. It is important because the university is, as Professor Henry Louis Gates concludes, "an institution of legitimation—establishing what counts as knowledge, what counts as cultures."[86]

In higher education, syllabi, curricula, and scholarships mark a shift from the focus on the works of dead, white, European men, to now include a more diverse array of authors and texts. Even the student bodies have become more diverse in terms of racial and cultural difference and socioeconomic classes. Today, what is being taught, by whom, and for whom, for the most part, is quite different than it was in the 1960s. Nonetheless, many of the nontraditional programs and departments, such as Black Studies, Women's Studies, and Asian Studies, continue to exist under substantial tensions and present many challenges. Multiculturalism has become a matter of much heated controversy, and it is allegedly blamed for the emphasis on diversity that is placed within the educational system through the curricula and the courses that are offered in colleges and universities.

In many of the colleges and universities there is an "ethnic" course requirement for students to complete in order to graduate. The rationale for these courses is to provoke students' intellectual interests in different subcultures and to sensitize them to cultural differences as intrinsic to a "good" education. The fundamental question, nonetheless, is whether this approach to education replaces or displaces cultural hierarchy. For sure, the university, as a structured space with its own laws of functioning, has extended its hiring practices to include highly qualified racial minorities and white women.

However, is the university relatively autonomous or structurally homologous with the dominant structures in place? Is the university a necessary and integral agent of cultural production and hegemonic power? Does it, or can it, exist independently of a multifaceted institutional framework that sanctions, facilitates, empowers, and legitimizes white supremacy? Today, white supremacy is portrayed in a more legitimate and intellectualized light, distanced from the imagery of ignorance and violence associated with white supremacist groups like the Ku Klux Klan, the National Association for the Advancement of White People, or the Aryan Nations.

The institution of higher education is now the focus of much critical work purporting to report on, and effect real changes in, the lives of nondominant groups. However, the university has not dismantled its prominent and long-standing cultural norms of white male elitism. The structural power inside the university obscures the potentiality for general critique, let alone any dismantling of the power structure that is in place. It is important to look at the ways in which it silences the marginalized within its walls.[87] Nonwhites, attending predominantly white institutions, experience this quiet, but discursive silence, as Professor Roger Wilkins explains. It is basically about the many ways in which whites encroach on and upset nonwhites' "psychic space," with indifference, an automatic manner of classifying, primitivizing, and dehumanizing them without any awareness. And, even though racial positioning manifests itself in many different ways, what is more complicated is when whites begrudgingly give nonwhites stares that without a doubt say, "What are you doing here."[88]

Can we conclude from the preceding analysis that the educational system promotes a genuine critique of the dominant culture that is in place? Providing students with "ethnic" classes is one thing, but offering class materials that challenge the status quo, and aid students to move away from normative answers to normative questions and develop independent judgment, is quite another thing. In fact, I think a class on "Western History" can be just as "productive" as a class on "Race and Ethnicity" if in the former, Western civilization is situated within the broader contours of nonwestern histories, and students are able "to 'unlearn' what they've been taught."[89] In the end, though, it would be a mistake not to recognize that the educational system is still rooted in the prerogative of whiteness, and white students, especially, have to become translators of "cultural text" in order to benefit from such specific and important knowledge. "My beliefs," as one student declares, "do not always show the values that this course is intended to instill in our beliefs."[90] It is exactly for this reason that we have to pay closer attention to the importance of such knowledge. The dissemination of such knowledge will help students to clearly and creatively think, read, and write. Further, it will provide a framework to critique and expose artificial usage of language, falsified allegations, mixed-up representation, false arguments, and misinformation about a culture in which they are invested.[91]

Allan Bloom, in *The Closing of the American Mind*, has surfaced as a leader of an intellectual reaction against cultural diversity. A report titled "Defending Civilization: How Our Universities Are Failing America and What Can Be Done About It" shamelessly "calls upon all colleges and universities to adopt strong core curricula that include rigorous, broad-based courses on the great works of Western civilization as well as courses on American history, America's Founding documents, and America's continuing struggles to extend and defend the principles on which it was founded."[92] The valorization of America's cultural identity as shaped by a European heritage has, not surprisingly, pushed Arthur M. Schlesinger to ask with headiness, "Would anyone seriously argue that teachers should conceal the European origins of American civilization?"[93] For Samuel P. Huntington, the rejection of Western civilization is the rejection of America's identity.[94] In "In the Borderlands of Chicano Identity, There Are Only Fragments," Benjamin Alire Sáenz argues that America's identity is forever associated with Western civilization.[95] For this precise reason, there has been what the political and social scientist Christian Joppke calls a "seismic shift" from the idiom of multiculturalism to one of civic integration[96] because multiculturalism is a threat to America's cultural homogeneity.

The argument that multiculturalism is a threat to America's cultural identity is not without significance. A clear reason for this unnecessary concern is that cultural pluralism signifies cultural "multiplicity in a unity," in the phrase of the official source, Horace M. Kallen, writing in the *Nation* in 1915. In his article Kallen puts cultural pluralism in opposition to the notion of a homogeneous culture that delineates America's national cultural identity. Newfield and Gordon suggest that cultural pluralism "redivides the public along familiar lines. Some stress multiplicity and some stress unity. The former are wary that pluralist unity is a nice word for assimilation of [racialized ethnic] groups to Euro-American or even Anglo-Saxon norms. . . . The former group worries about cultural autonomy; the latter is preoccupied with cultural commonality. The former denounces the cultural dominance of the majority, while the latter rejects the cultural separatism of the minority."[97]

Should cultural pluralism be reduced to a bare noncritical multiculturalism even in its most radical expression? There is no doubt in my mind that multiculturalism has captivated an important facet of America's society, but as I have already argued, multiculturalism's emphasis on recognizing and celebrating cultural differences keeps the dominant culture intact and bars the nondominant from inclusion into the dominant culture.

However, we will see in Chapter 5 that inclusion into America's cultural oneness is not the answer for eliminating cultural hierarchy. It is the recognition of America's cultural manyness that can truly promote America as a multiracial and multicultural society.

Multiculturalism as a Threat to America's Cultural Homogeneity

Recent studies have examined what Rogers M. Smith has termed "the multiple tradition" of an American cultural identity.[98] In fact, many studies have focused on three elements of an American identity: liberalism, republicanism, and ethnocultural Americanism.[99] Smith suggests that various combinations of liberal republicanism dominated America's laws in determining who were to be American citizens.[100] In short, liberalism restricted rights only to white men, and the courts justified these restrictive measures by means of appealing to principles drawn from republican and ethnocultural characterizations of American citizenship.[101] As I have shown, liberal republicanism was constitutive in framing and promoting America as a homogeneous nation based on an Anglo Saxon heritage. Therefore, First Nations, blacks, Chinese, and other racialized groups were excluded from an American identity because they were looked on as racially and culturally inferior.[102] Biological and scientific explanations were employed to support and substantiate nonwhites' inferiority.[103] Eventually, there was a shift from biological to cultural explanations for blacks and other nonwhites' inferiority.[104]

Samuel Huntington, in *The Clash of Civilization and the Remaking of World Order*, explains America's cultural identity. He claims that from the very beginning of America's founding its cultural identity was a derivative of Western civilization and heritage, which shaped the American creed of "liberty, democracy, individualism, equality before the law, constitutionalism, and private property" as its core values.[105] Arthur M. Schlesinger concurs and adds that Europe, not Africa, nor Asia, nor the Middle East, should be complemented for those "liberating ideas of individual liberty, political democracy, the rule of law, and cultural freedom"[106] that have shaped America's cultural identity.[107] In fact, for Schlesinger, European (white) culture is the pinnacle of civilization, unlike Africa, Asia, and the Middle East (nonwhite), whose cultures are "based on despotism, superstition, tribalism, and fanaticism."[108] Groups in America, embodying such traits as Schlesinger describes, violate the very criteria for an authentic American cultural identity. They are excluded from Americanness, and placed on the borderland of an American cultural identity. Americanness, as we know, has systematically acknowledged racial implications. Cultural identity is linked to racial identity as the major principle by which social relations in America are organized.

Multiculturalism, for the assimilationists, has altered the symbolic ordering of American cultural identity. For Nathan Glazer, this "is the price America is paying for its inability or unwillingness to incorporate [nonwhites] in the same way and to the same degree it has incorporated so many [European whites]."[109] In the same spirit, Huntington is concerned that "a multicultural America will, in time, become multicreedal, with groups from different cultures espousing the different political values that are rooted in their own culture."[110] This, he concludes, represents a threat to America's cultural identity.[111] This seeming threat to America's cultural identity is not without significance. It is another attempt to reclaim an American cultural identity as white.

Huntington's concern is inane because it is easy and simple to "live with differences," which is inherent within the multicultural ideals. In fact, multicultural ideals grow out of the very idea of "living with differences." Differences are important but cannot be employed as a way to determine and maintain equalities at all cultural and socioeconomic levels. Encouraging differences is one thing but using them as a tool for employing discriminatory practices is quite another. I think that accommodating the idea of "different but equal cultures" would be a starting point for truly embracing difference. However, can multiculturalism promote the idea of "different but equal cultures"?

The goal of multiculturalism is to make sure that these cultures remain, for the most part, unassimilated, and situated in opposition to the dominant American culture. Multiculturalism, in this sense, is caught in the process of informing instead of transforming racial and cultural differences and the prevailing power relations that attend to these differences.[112] Racialization continues to link nonwhites to a racialized cultural identity, which continues to preserve cultural differences as alien to America's cultural oneness. American identity continues to be based on an Anglo-Saxon, Protestant foundation in its celebrations, language, and main traditions. And because what defines an American identity is premised on the notion of the Anglo Protestant culture, which emphasizes Protestantism and English as its main forms of linguistic expression, some scholars such as Huntington consider that, for example, Mexican Americans are eroding the dominance of English language as a marker of an American identity by their insistence on treating English as a second language, notwithstanding the fact that three hundred years of history has chosen English as the primary language of America.[113] More so, what Jack Citrin and his colleagues make clear in "Testing Huntington: Is Hispanic Immigration a Threat to American Identity?" is that "Huntington's somber case scenario for the future envisions a split America: two de facto nations, an English-speaking 'Anglo-America' and a Spanish-speaking 'Mexamerica' that, like

Quebec in Canada, regards itself as a distinct society."[114] America will then become a "bilingual, bicultural society like Canada."[115] For Huntington, the threat looms large because Spanish is now becoming an "official" language in the United States.[116] "Evidence suggests," Huntington notes, "a weak identification with America on the part of Mexicans."[117] In the same vein, Republican senator Lamar Alexander from Tennessee, in a 2006 debate on immigration where there was a vote of 63–34 in the U.S. Senate, pleaded to make English the official language. Alexander stated, "English is part of our national identity. It's part of our spirit. It's part of who we are." While white racial nationalism remains smugly intact, Mexicans and other racialized groups who resist and challenge America's identity are interpreted as "viciously nationalistic."[118] The core culture that delineates an American national identity is what Kallen unabashedly refers to as "cultural racism." For Kallen, cultural racism "is not a racism of color as in imperial Britain and America's Southern states. It is a racism of culture. It claims that the American idea and the American way are hereditary to the Anglo-Saxon stock and to that stock only; that other stocks are incapable of producing them, learning them and living them. If, then, America is to survive as a culture of creed and code, it can do so only so long as the chosen Anglo-Saxon race retains its integrity of flesh and spirit and freely sustains and defends their American expression against alien contamination."[119] Kallen's emphasis is not on biology but on culture. Kallen's cultural racism shows its connections with racist thinking that deem racialized ethnic groups as inferior to whites.[120] Accordingly, nonwhites should be excluded from America's cultural identity. Today, racist discourses and practices no longer rely on the claim that nonwhites are biologically inferior to whites. What is far more dangerous, I think, is the biologization of the complex cultural practices of nonwhites, which are presented as predetermined. It apocryphally accounts for the racial inferiority of countercultures. These cultural messages and institutional practices are a conscious necessity for constructing and establishing difference, excluding and setting apart the dominant (official) from the nondominant (unofficial); they serve as the yardstick for exclusiveness or inclusiveness into America's cultural identity.

Among the most vocal protesters against multiculturalists is Huntington. America, he claims, "is not a national community of individuals sharing a common culture, history, and creed but a conglomerate of differences, races, ethnicities, and subnational cultures,"[121] which are supposed to be incorporated into American social and political landscapes. Lawrence Auster, in "The U.S. Must Restrict Immigration to Prevent Cultural Disintegration," joins Huntington's bandwagon by pointing his finger at the influx of immigrants—and here *immigrants* has a specific connotation that is attached to nonwhites—as adding to the challenge of the "end of American civilization."[122]

When members of the dominant culture feel "invaded" by the members of the nondominant cultures, they are angry. One of the white students that Karyn D. McKinney interviewed in her study was at an amusement park with her parents. She claimed, "No one spoke English. I have never been so annoyed. . . . I am definitely very ethnocentric in that I think that my culture and my ways are the best."[123] Lately, "nationalists" has been a metonym for "racists." "We" like Mexican Americans, but "We" think they should all go back to Mexico. "We" are not racists. "We" are just nationalists.

Even though most Americans would argue that cultural diversity is important, it is quite another thing, to use the words of Kymlicka, "to be swamped by it."[124] It was the British prime minister, Margaret Thatcher, who once remarked that "once a minority in a neighborhood gets large, people do feel swamped. They feel their whole way of life has changed,"[125] not for the better, but for the worse. Comments such as "it is not our country anymore"; and "why don't these people speak English?" are frequently heard. Speaking another language besides English contradicts what the dominant consider their cultural identity and history.[126] The question that the dominant culture asks itself is not so much the kind of society that "we" desire to live in, but who is American? Under the veneer of American nationalism, Mexican Americans and other racialized groups presenting a threat to America's cultural homogeneity is at the forefront of public discourse.[127]

Margaret Thatcher once marveled at America's cultural homogeneity by remarking that America was the only nation that has "so successfully combined people of different races and nations within a single culture."[128] Monoculturalism, and not multiculturalism, was what Thatcher had in mind. According to Schlesinger, the "monoculturalists are hyperpatriots, fundamentalists, evangelicals, laissez-faire doctrinaires, homophobes, anti-abortionists, pro-assault-gun people, and other zealots. They inveigh against ideas and books they deem blasphemous, atheistic, socialistic, secular humanistic, pornographic, and/or un-American and seek to impose on the hapless young their own pinched, angry monistic concept of America."[129] In other words, monoculturalism not only universalizes the suppositions and conditions of a distinct American culture,[130] it also refers to an "ethnoracial Eurovision"[131] positioned as the unconcealed ideological premise for America to derive its cultural identity. Today, given the growing concern of recognizing different cultures, multiculturalism signals a shift from monoculturalism's "univocity and singularity" to multiculturalism's "antihegemonic thrusts."[132] Monoculturalism remains marked and invisible. Unlike whiteness and nonwhiteness, where the connection is dialogical at best, the symbiotic relationship between monoculturalism and multiculturalism is nonexistent; there is an emphasis on either one or the other.

From the preceding analysis, we have come to see multiculturalism as a threat to America's cultural homogeneity. The assimilationists are blind to racialized differences. Beginning in the 1970s, another motto for blindness to race has been impounded and popularized by the neoconservative argument that America was founded on colorblindness. One of the most sophisticated arguments they use is that the American Constitution was founded on colorblindness. Justice John Marshall's assertion, as is revealed in *Plessy v. Ferguson*,[133] is that the American Constitution is color blind. In my mind, this colorblindness, which amounts to being racially transparent, emphasizes the very reality of the construction of race that it purports to eliminate. The daunting fact is that America was never founded on a color-blind society. The words,[134] "We hold these truths to be self-evident that all men are created equal" and unalienable rights are bestowed to them, were never applied to nonwhites.[135] They were not applied to white women either. In fact, the founding fathers were preoccupied with promoting racial domination in terms of whites' supremacy and nonwhites' inferiority. Counting on the lack of analytical maturity among the masses, they made use of science, religion, mythology, and other sources of assumed knowledge to propagate and legitimize this racial binary. The inferiority of nonwhites appeared to be rational, acceptable reinforced, perpetuated, maintained, and disseminated through political as well as social means. The social milieu itself was the production of an undergirding whiteness where nonwhites had no place, except as de facto inferiors. The white child pointing at the black person cries out, "Look, a Negro . . . mama, see the Negro! I'm frightened."[136]

What Is at Stake?

Should American civilization illuminate aspects of the encounter of First Nations and blacks who were already in America from its very inception? The continuing emphasis on European culture as the pinnacle of American history and civilization serves the specific purpose of reinforcing and maintaining the interests of whiteness as a social privilege. The problem is that European culture is always taken for granted and unmarked; it is never problematized in the ways that other cultures are problematized. Africans, Asians, and Middle Easterners are still viewed and understood by many as savage and barbaric, far beyond the reach of civilized Western values and morality. Should First Nations, blacks, Chinese, Mexicans, and other racialized groups, then, be subject to this extolling of whiteness or Europeanness as cultural domination and the legacy of white supremacy?

The overextension of cultural diversity and the emphasis on multiculturalism, according to Schlesinger, is a platform for "reviving old prejudice"[137] and breaking the bonds of an American culture as white.[138] In other words, scholars such as Schlesinger assume that multiculturalism signals the impossibility of having a homogeneous America based on white American culture. Huntington, for one, is angered by this, and makes it clear that "American identity has come under concentrated and sustained onslaught. . . . In the name of multiculturalism they have attacked the identification of the United States with Western civilization, denied the existence of a common American culture and promoted racial, ethnic, and other subnational cultural identity."[139] In fact, it is the claim of America as a homogeneous nation that is prompting scholars to wittingly argue for a return to the homogeneous America that had unfolded at the beginning of America's history. Homogeneous America means this "new man" about whom Jean de Crèvecoeur wrote in his *Letters from an American Farmer*, in 1782, and excludes First Nations, blacks, Chinese, and other racialized ethnic groups who want to be fully fledged Americans. The "new man" was definitely not a "multicultural woman," a seminal being, pliant, irregular, unbounded, and evolutionary.

Without taking into consideration multiculturalism's core objective of de-Americanization, the reinforcement of the notion of nonwhites' cultural separatedness from the dominant culture is appropriate and necessary. Antiracists have rushed to defend multiculturalism because they too have projected a fear of the return to assimilation that continues to be advocated by conservatives, nationalists, some communitarians, and other groups on the far Right. Accordingly, this anxiety about multiculturalism on both sides, I will later show, is unwarranted because the cultural practice of whiteness, which is linked to an American identity, assumes normality and exclusivity. Assimilation into the American culture, for the most part, requires a white skin. Under the guise of multiculturalism, the cultures of racialized ethnic groups have been marginalized and alienated from the dominant culture.

How much of multiculturalism can the dominant culture tolerate without "losing" its whiteness? America has worked very hard to preserve its core culture and its claim to a white identity. Within the spectrum of antimulticulturalists' sentiments, writers, including Allan Bloom (1987), Arthur M. Schlesinger (1991), and Dinesh D'Souza (1991b), are quite hostile to the fact that everyone is now forced to deal with issues of cultural diversity. For them, cultural diversity should be nonthreatening, and kept at a distance. It should be met in Chinese, Japanese, and Ethiopian restaurants located in big cities. The emphasis on cultural diversity promoted by the multiculturalists has gone too far; it is too close for comfort, confirming antimulticulturalists' worst suspicion that America is heading toward the loss of its cultural homogeneity.

Cultural homogeneity eases the anxiety of having to confront cultural differences, even if in the form of the liberal notion of *recognition*. For Bloom and his colleagues, multiculturalism and diversity have taken permanent hold in American society. It has gone too far, causing many antimulticulturalists to be on the defensive. Huntington speaks to this: "The various forces challenging the core American culture and Creed could generate a move by native white Americans to revive the discarded and discredited racial and ethnic concepts of American identity and to create an America that would exclude, expel, or suppress people of other racial, ethnic, and cultural groups. . . . It could produce a racially intolerant country with high levels of intergroup conflict." [140]

For Huntington, multiculturalism creates a backlash and is responsible for the "making of serious white nativist movements."[141] What would keep all Americans united, in the form of cultural manyness instead of cultural oneness, is important. For sure it is not multiculturalism. I have already shown that multiculturalism promotes cultural otherness, which is looked on as un-Americanness. In fact, with multiculturalism's deployment, America's cultural homogeneity remains tightly smug. The problem for the antimulticulturalists of Huntington's sort, as Sara Ahmed explains, in "The Politics of Good Feelings," is that "when we are 'in' multiculturalism we are 'out' of our comfort zone."[142] It is partly for this reason that Glazer can announce with an edge of irony that "we are all multiculturalists now,"[143] which is unworthy of celebration, especially for those who do not embody cultural diversity. Against this backdrop, it is not surprising that a white student would unequivocally claim that "one thing that really upsets [her] is Black History Month."[144] How does multiculturalism deal with the racist sensibility that permeates American society?

Multiculturalism and Racism

The emphasis on race and racism, to a large extent, is avoided by the multiculturalist discourse in the first place, and is replaced with an emphasis on cultural diversity as a way of expressing "cultural particularities and pride."[145] In the context in which multiculturalism is currently being configured, cultural diversity, even though it seems desirable for any society, frequently considers culture, to use Chandra Talpade Mohanty's phrase, "as noncontradictory, as isolated from questions of history,"[146] constituting and reconstituting the relative position of those in power, which diversity cannot alter. It is difficult for those in power to detach themselves from certain social practices. Multiculturalism, as we will later see, is not the answer to incorporating racialized groups as fully fledged Americans into the dominant culture. In the end, what multiculturalism does is reproduce whiteness and maintain its dominance. Strategies, such as multiculturalism as a way to make nondominant cultures visible, tend to replicate and reinforce the ideology of racism, sexism, homophobia, and white privilege.[147]

Racism, a virulent structural as well as ideological stance that explains and justifies the differential treatment of the socially constructed "others" based on their alleged racial inferiority, remains situated and encoded within the imperializing discourse and practice of multiculturalism. Even so, for Taylor, "the demands of multiculturalism [have been built] on the already established principles of the politics of equal respect"[148] and therefore multiculturalism recognizes the cultural identity of racialized ethnic groups. Notwithstanding the claim of multiculturalism to recognize cultural differences, it is the racialized ethnic communities, with the help of the state, that are burdened to retain and cultivate their different cultures through cultural events such as festivals of music, costumes, foods, and dance.

The integration of racialized groups into America's political life has taken place without confronting the basic structures of marginalization and domination. The general tone of this critique is well captured by Newfield and Gordon who speak to this in explicit terms. They contend, "This makes racism [for example], more difficult to acknowledge and control: phenomena that might be at least partially attributed to racism, such as crime in racially segregated, low-income neighborhoods. . . . It downplays white supremacy as a system of privilege, favoritism, discrimination, and exclusion."[149]

Robert Blauner extends Newfield and Gordon's analysis to show that "racism and racial oppression are not independent dynamic forces but are ultimately reducible to other casual determinants, usually economic."[150] And even though marginalized groups struggle for inclusion and recognition by reclaiming their "blackness," "Asianness," and "First Nationness," it is necessary to conclude that multiculturalism, while assuring the loyalty of nonwhites, masks accountability for the problematic of racism and other forms of unequal practices that are solidly in place. If, in the first place, as the liberal ethos promises, equality is for all, then feminists, for example, would not have pressed for "differential rights"[151] for women. In the end, feminists' pressing for "rights" that differ from men's does not solve the fact of women's unequal position in society. In fact, as I have already pointed out, the term *woman*, in itself, is highly contested. As such, the key for promoting cultural pluralism in America is to recognize the many different cultures within the larger American culture, not to incorporate them into the dominant culture. The cultural othering of multiculturalism is one of its main objectives.

Multiculturalism and Cultural Othering

Every discourse in multiculturalism is ingrained in its history and grounded in human practice. The ideals associated with multiculturalism, rather than being neutral, are in no way autonomous and exceptional. Multiculturalism has been prearranged to confront the challenge that minority cultures present to the dominant culture in terms of incorporation and inclusion into the dominant, and the embedment of that challenge in muliticulturalism's practice of "othering" is not without significance. Othering positioned itself between two unequal cultural spheres, the dominant (white) and the subcultures (nonwhite), and there are numerous factors, including race, class, ethnicity, and sexuality, that shape and determine a woman's situatedness. In other words, as Kathleen M. Brown, in *Good Wives, Nasty Wenches, and Anxious Patriarchs: Gender, Race and Power in Colonial Virginia*, reminds us, white women are embodied in the privileges and virtues of true womanhood.[152] White, exceedingly white—submissive, vulnerable, innocent, pure, pious, nurturing—is what women are; nonwhite women— exotic, promiscuous, and impure—are not included in the term *woman*.[153] As James Weldon Johnson, the author of *The Autobiography of an Ex-Colored Man*, wrote in his book *Along This Way*, "In the core of the heart of the race problem the sex factor is rooted."[154]

Multiculturalism legitimizes the most discriminatory actions and reactions of those in power. Judith Butler cautions us that "there is no opposition to power, which is not itself a part of the very workings of power."[155] The question that America faces and must confront as a pluralist society is how to vindicate its cherished traditions of cultural exclusiveness without breaking the bonds of its so-called cultural homogeneity. This exclusion is inevitable because the dominant culture, far from being advanced and secure, demonstrates a continuously reformulated fright over the constructed meaning of "ours" and "them," and the suspected defining presence of the "them" within the "ours."

As a way of actually abjuring the new racism or cultural racism, culture is replaced with race and the qualities of social groups are predetermined, made normal, and restricted within a defined culturalism based on biological determinism. In other words, culture and race are perceived as having the same self-evident application, even though the emphasis on racial difference has been shaped by the notion of cultural differences in America. Cultural difference is the process through which the declaration of culture and the focus on culture differentiates, discriminates, and excludes racialized groups from an American cultural identity.

Cultural difference is the hallmark for multiculturalism's emphasis on recognition, which in the end does lead to misrecognition. As Nancy Fraser puts it, "To belong to a group that is devalued by the dominant culture is to be misrecognized, to suffer a distortion in one's relation to one's self"[156] and his or her group membership.[157] For Taylor, then, misrecognition "can be a form of oppression, imprisoning someone in a false, distorted, reduced mode of being."[158] Given that misrecognition has a cultural and a material foundation, the question is not so much how misrecognized groups, in the case of racialized ethnic groups, can secure recognition. Instead, it is how this recognition is administered since one has to be recognized by the group as a member of that group. In defining group membership, whether it is determined by communities—it is requisite that communities should be able to decide on their own membership[159]—or otherwise imposed, an enormous amount of problems surface because identities are multiple, heterogeneous, and unfixed. Recognizing First Nations, blacks, or Chinese as members of their assigned group gives that group as well as its members a particular essence; and it does not necessarily promote respect for the individual subjectivities beyond their groups as well as the groups themselves. Those who do not meet the decisive requirements for group membership have to suffer the consequences. In this sense, misrecognition might not be such a bad thing after all because it frees one from conforming to group norms. One should be able to decide for oneself, if one is equipped with such strength, what customs and traditions one wants to adopt or completely repel altogether, even at the cost of not being a "true" or "proper" member of the group.[160] Justice is not inevitable just because laws promoting justice exist. Liberal thinkers have argued that group membership is important for individuals to enjoy certain group rights, even though the rights of women have not been taken into consideration. Will Kymlicka points outs that "membership in a cultural community may be a relevant criterion of a liberal theory of justice."[161]

Should universal justice be promoted since it was implemented within the white, heterosexual male symbolic order? Without belaboring this point, nonwhites, women, homosexuals, the poor, and the disabled are still viewed by the dominant in stereotypical ways. And even though marginalized groups, in this case nonwhites, struggle for inclusion and recognition founded on reclaiming their nonwhiteness as is encouraged by multiculturalism, it is compelling to conclude that multiculturalism masks accountability for the problematic nexus of otherness as un-Americanness. The pressure to maintain one's culture, whether one wants to do so or not, is an abridgement restricting individual freedom to choose.[162]

Multiculturalism is not even, to borrow the words of Norma Alarcón, "a quick metaphoric fix signaling inclusion,"[163] it is all about exclusion from an American identity. Of course, it allows racialized groups to make their culture accessible by adhering to the liberal ethos of promoting cultural pluralism and culturalism. However, it allows for the segregationist impulse to separate cultures, dominant and nondominant, "high" and "low," and for culture borders to remain in place; it does not allow the nondominant cultures to withdraw from their constrained status as the "other." In this case, Everett V. Stonequest is mistaken when he asserts that racialized groups are always the ones that are expected to do the melting.[164] As I have already argued in Chapter 2, racialized ethnic groups are the unmeltable, and as such, they represent a threat to America's cultural homogeneity. However, he is correct when he acknowledges that the dominant group "does not expect to adjust itself to the others; it is the subordinate group, which is expected to do the adjusting, confirming, and assimilating" and to be self-critical.[165] Multiculturalism does not concern itself so much with assimilation—not that assimilation is a good thing[166]—its emphasis is on cultural otherness instead of cultural inclusiveness, which is fashioned and refashioned through its policy of cultural recognition. In the end, it reinforces power asymmetries. Fanon's theory of cultural hierarchy is once again brought to light. Its purpose is to rework America's past of exclusion of racialized groups from an American cultural identity and to construct a present where the exclusion become more pronounced in an effort to maintain whiteness as a cultural praxis.[167]

Historically and culturally America has always promoted its nation as white. Consequently, according to Schlesinger, 'to deny the essentially European origins of American culture is to falsify history."[168] Schlesinger asked if it would really do America and the world good for America to rid itself of its European tradition.[169] This question seemingly poses, in itself, a need to celebrate and applaud the cultural homogeneous United States of America. When European whites, including the Scots, Swiss, Irish, Germans, and Dutch enter the United States, they become the American that Crèvecoeur describes as "the new man," who is ready to assimilate into America's cultural oneness. For Schlesinger and his contemporaries, the emphasis on multiculturalism interrupts and fractures the immanence of America's cultural homogeneity. Once again, notwithstanding multiculturalists' anxiety, which remains fatuous for the many reasons I have already pointed out, multiculturalism keeps America's cultural homogeneity intact. Instead of embracing the recognition and celebration of cultural otherness as the discursive condition for exchange and acknowledgment of the politicized subject's position as "other," an important goal of truly recognizing and celebrating America's cultural manyness would be to envision an alternative to multiculturalism. The alternative that I am alluding to is postmulticulturalism.

Postmulticulturalism does not subscribe to the racial script of America, in which racialized groups, especially blacks, are the ones responsible for

America's race problems. In America, because race is correlated with non-whites, blacks especially have courageously and persistently fought many civil rights battles on behalf of "the race." For this reason, it is easy enough for the white proponents of colorblindness to erase "something they think they never had to begin with,"[170] and for nonwhites who are victims of "white-wishing" to promote colorblindness as a way of advancing the notion of "one America." In this regard, there is a need for a more elaborate discourse that productively speaks about the oppressor instead of the oppressed; that questions and challenges how those with the power "feel about, think about, react to, make sense of, come to terms with, maintain privilege over, and ultimately renounce the power to oppress."[171] If multiculturalism is to be a vehicle for addressing race relations in the United States, it must take into account strategies that incorporate those (usually whites) who are often both the ones with the power and the most misinformed about what it means to live in a multiracial and multicultural society.[172] However, the white self would have to be transformed into a postwhite self. Since multiculturalism cannot convert the white self into a postwhite self, and dissuades to aid this conversion, postmulticulturalism, then, would be the new possibility. But first, there has to be some transference of an American monocultural state into a multicultural state that would be consistent with the values of its multicultural and multiracial populace. The second step is the denormalization of whiteness. While these processes are not mutually exclusive, I think, for good reasons, that these undertakings would be inevitably complex. It is this complexity that I will present in Chapter 5.

5

Postmulticulturalism

We have seen the limits of multiculturalism in coming to terms with the incorporation of racialized groups into the dominant culture. One of the reasons for such a limitation is that multiculturalism is situated within a monocultural state. A monocultural state is antithetical to racial and cultural differences—even though race, for the most part, as I have already indicated, is a marker for determining cultural differences. In this respect, there is a need to move beyond multiculturalism as a function of normalizing cultural practice and to take on new cultural practices that would profoundly transform America's cultural homogeneity (cultural oneness) into cultural heterogeneity (cultural manyness). However, to move beyond multiculturalism toward postmulticulturalism, America needs to transform itself from a monocultural state into a multicultural state. Only a multicultural state can embrace the new cultural forms that are created. Postmulticularism would work against American cultural oneness and promote cultural manyness as Americanness.

The transformation from a monocultural state into a multicultural state is not enough. For postmulticulturalism to be effective, whiteness would have to be denormalized, "split open," "exploded," and "tortured"[1] so as to create a postwhite self. Yet we have to be careful that this postwhite self is not appropriated in such a way that whiteness becomes the refractory signifier of defeat and deficiency and the downfall of white supremacy.[2] Affirmative action and the quota system are viewed as repellents for white males' power position and as challenges to white supremacy. Consequently, these are singled out for aggressive attacks by many whites, especially white men. Note the tiresome comment, "I didn't get the job because I am a white male." Through this discourse, white males' sense of entitlement is at the forefront. And for them, this entitlement assumingly is slipping away from their overly tight grip.

If, as the preceding analysis shows, whiteness is in some sort of crisis because its implication is now unfixed and unclear, the denormalization of whiteness and white privilege would have to conceive of positive ways to be white. To request that whites renounce their whiteness or declare whiteness to be insignificant would be catastrophic. However, renouncing whiteness as a marker separate from race would be quite another thing. In fact, it would emphasize that being white is not being different from being black, First Nations, Chinese, or Mexican. I need to make it clear that the post-white self that I am alluding to is not on a par with the Supreme Court's decision to recast whites as a racial group competing on the same footing with nonwhite groups. The Supreme Court is interpreting race-based remedies to address America's history of racial discrimination of disadvantaged blacks and other nonwhite groups as reverse discrimination.[3] *Regents of the University of California v. Bakke* in 1978 and *City of Richmond v. J. A. Croson Company* in 1989 illustrate this phenomenon.[4] The postwhite self can only be envisioned when whiteness is denormalized and stripped of its presumptive hegemony.

Notwithstanding whiteness as being historically specific—initially the Irish, Germans, Italians, Greeks, and Jews were not considered white—whiteness, as a normalized, unmarked structural position, maintains privilege and power that never admit to its own existence. Ruth Frankenberg, rightfully so, is vexed by the unmarkedness of whiteness.[5] She made clear that "whiteness as an unmarked norm is revealed to be a mirage or indeed, to put it even more strongly, a white delusion."[6] Nonetheless, whiteness assumes a visibility that defines America's cultural identity as white and defies America's multicultural and multiracial society. A multicultural society is not the same as a monocultural state. Besides, any discussion of America's cultural oneness in the face of its cultural manyness would be incomplete without some understanding of how America's monocultural state helps in the development and maintenance of a homogeneous cultural identity. It is only then that we can truly make real the transformation of a monocultural state into a multicultural state. In the following section I examine first the specific elements of America's monocultural state.

The Monocultural State

From the beginning of America's development, the emphasis on promoting America as a homogeneous nation, with a Eurocentric focus, was recognized and endorsed in spite of the presence of a culturally and racially diverse group of people. Furthermore, the practice of contrasting the superiority of the dominant culture and the inferiority of the nondominant cultures provided the distinctive classificatory process for inclusion in and exclusion from an American cultural identity. Given that racialized groups were excluded from such an identity, the state had to learn to deal with any conflict arising from the multiracial and multicultural presence within the United States. As a way to harness the multicultural mix, it was important that the government naturalize America's cultural homogeneity. Although America's cultural homogeneity finds its way in the language and practices of white professionals, intellectuals, and ordinary white people, the American government took steps to develop legal frameworks that consolidated America's homogeneous cultural identity. American cultural homogeneity was established and maintained through the institution of slavery and the allocation of First Nations to Indian reservations.

As a way to address racial and cultural differences, the first Naturalization Act of 1790 recognized only white men as Americans. In addition, laws were implemented to prevent racialized groups from entering the United States and from being naturalized. What immediately comes to mind is the Chinese Exclusion Act of 1882. Men in power were aware of the different cultural practices of the Chinese, and in an effort to keep America pure from the "yellow peril," they ratified the Chinese Exclusion Act. It prevented Chinese, Japanese, Filipinos, Koreans, Asian Indians, and Southeast Asians from entering the United States during that period.

The United States, for a long time, promoted the notion of the melting pot and assimilation.[7] For First Nations, blacks, Chinese, and other racialized ethnic groups, assimilation into the dominant culture has been impossible. Blacks and other nonwhites remain culturally unassimilable. Eventually, through cultural pluralism and multiculturalism, cultural differences, which remain constructed and socially marked, came to be recognized and celebrated. To gain full membership in a specific cultural group, all individuals had to assimilate into the group culture. Through recognition and continuing interaction, common understanding across these differences was promoted.[8]

Unlike Canada and Australia where multiculturalism is an official policy, in the United States, multiculturalism remains an unofficial policy. Nonetheless, multiculturalism is a form of prescription controlling America's multiethnic and multiracial society where cultural hierarchy remains intact. Given the logic of cultural hierarchy, the dominant culture dictates the norms and values of society. Groups who are recognized as culturally different must still adhere to the norms and values of the dominant culture—the ways of the majority—which shape the public culture.

What is a public culture? A public culture is a body of values and practices that, for the most part, are not governed by legislative laws, even though the constitutional and legal values are largely embedded within the public culture, promoting the very bases for thinking about race, gender, sexuality, and religion. It functions as the prevailing ways according to which all people in the United States are expected to live their lives. These ways are based on America's liberal democratic principles. The public culture interacts with other norms and identities such as gender, heterosexuality, class, and nationality. Whiteness, as a way of thinking and acting, defines and shapes these social identity categories by constructing the "other" as demonic.

Racialized ethnic groups are expected to fully participate in the public culture and abide by its norms, values, and expectations. Yet the prevailing assumption is that nonwhites are invested with essential characteristics and blemishes that contaminate the public culture. Given that their position within the public culture is that of the "other," they are perceived as a threat to the public culture. Consequently, they have to deal with various destructive racial and cultural stereotypes and the harmful ways in which they are envisioned as objects, rather than as subjects able to create their own existence and shape their life choices. These stereotypes, for the most part, find their way into the public discourse. The media always find full-fledged faces of blacks and Mexicans to make the six o'clock news and the newspaper headlines on crimes. In this sense, the idea of pluralism, which stresses the rights of the individual to create his or her own place in America's society, is called into question.

These stereotypes are classificatory strategies for defining differences. They have serious racial implications and operate in such a way that they stigmatize an entire group of people. For instance, blacks and Mexicans are stigmatized as violent drug pushers and gangsters. They are systematically associated with criminal behavior. Muslims are regarded as terrorists, and Indians and Chinese are said to smell like garlic. These forms of stereotyping are passed off as natural and serve an essential purpose. They set up cultural borders, separating the insiders from the outsiders, the normal from the abnormal, the superior from the inferior, and the "us" from the "them." It is precisely for this reason that stereotyping the "other" remains unchallenged and becomes part of everyday culture. Hence, in the public cultural sphere, racialized ethnic groups are constantly policed and regulated.

The monocultural state allows for the recognition and celebration of cultural differences through various festivals. I call this practice the *performation* of culture; it actually performs the cultural expectations of blackness, First Nationness, Chineseness, or Mexicanness. In other words, it responds in practice to the stereotyped scenarios written by whites. However, these festivals, such as the Labor Day parade in New York City, Puerto Rican Independence celebrations, Black History Month, Hispanic Heritage Month, and Mexican Day are celebrated within restricted public spaces, in such a way that these regulated celebrations do not collide with the public culture. For a limited time and in a restricted space the private sphere of the "other" is allowed to become public. For the most part, these private cultural spaces are highly racialized. The state, by homogenizing and essentializing the cultures of the "other" through stereotypical expectations, decides when, where, and how to exhibit nondominant cultures in their so-called purest forms.

In fact, there are no pure ways of being culturally African American, First Nations American, Chinese American, or Mexican American, because of the following reasons: (1) each of these cultures is an artifact: it is the synchronization of two separate cultures, African and American cultures or Mexican and American cultures; (2) in many cases, more than one cultural tradition comes together within each culture, which is thus opened to different interpretations; and (3) by negotiating between the dominant and subordinate positions, a different form of cultural expression erupts. And, in many cases, this new form of cultural expression serves as resistance against the dominant culture.[9] Homogenizing and essentializing cultures serves the specific purpose of refurbishing racial thinking. And, in spite of Paul Gilroy's argument that racial thinking has disintegrated because "'race' has lost much of its common-sense credibility,"[10] culture, in this sense, reconstructs and reinscribes racial thinking.

Sadly so, race is not over as yet.[11] In fact, race has a substantive presence in shaping and defining culture.[12] I think this is what Richard Dyer is getting at when he states, "And since race in itself—in so far as it is anything in itself—refers to some intrinsically insignificant geographical/physical differences between people, it is the imagery of race that is played out."[13] Culture, clinging to race, is, in my mind, one of the most commanding offsets to racial thinking. There are several ways in which racist positioning is used to describe an entire group of people. It often operates furtively, and avoids direct actions that are directly associated with racial results—for instance, all Muslims being terrorists. Racially profiling Muslims at the airport in order to keep Americans safe from terrorists or to prevent another 9/11 is acceptable. This points to the many ways racism is brought into play without being understandable. In post-9/11 America, institutionalized racism, as "an underlying cultural logic; . . . a complex social force,"[14] is harder to pin down. "It is being reconfigured without 'race' as a classificatory device for demarcating difference."[15] Its focus is on culture.

Substituting culture for race cannot discard race as the signifier of cultural identity because race and culture remain conjoined in America's cognitive and legal tradition. In other words, it is the racialization of culture that enabled whites to separate themselves from blacks and other nonwhites. Black ghettoes and superghettoes and other racialized ethnic enclaves are consequential in highlighting how the cultural differential works on a daily basis. The appeal by some scholars[16] that "it is time to be done with race and all of its oppressive logics and implications,"[17] is to promote Paul

Gilroy's "raciology"[18] and to move in the direction of a postracial society. Any need to transcend race, after all, would have to foreclose on a critical analysis of historicizing America's racism as an ongoing ideology and structure in place, which continues to see blacks, First Nations, and other racialized groups as second-class citizens. This need would have to do away with examining the interconnectedness of race and culture. What is culture without race? I think is a question that remains at the heart of the discussion of America's monocultural state.

In the end, a postracial society only serves to reinforce and maintain whiteness as the cultural norm. In other words, in its very attempt to get rid of race, the concept of race is reaffirmed. I suppose, when we focus on culture, socioeconomic inequality and its multiple dimensions are buried underneath the discourse of culture. Blacks and other nonwhites' poverty level in America is then explained by a "culture of poverty" instead of by systemic racism.[19] The upshot is that everyday racism and its multiple layers experienced by racialized ethnic groups in America's cultural, socioeconomic, and political spheres is played down. This new form of commonsense racism is quite prevalent. In general, racism, nowadays, is talked about as a form of ignorance and a lack of exposure to nonwhite people. This is like concluding that wife beating is done by primitive and backward men.

To avoid confrontation, in some cases, members of racialized groups suppress cultural markers such as languages and clothing, and even go so far as to alter their appearance—by not looking too ethnic—in the hope of being accepted. They try to become the model minority always striving for the majority's acceptance and approval, to measure up to the lifestyle, values, behavior, expectations, and norms modeled from the mainstream culture. The perception of model minorities is, at its worst, revealed in what W. E. B. Du Bois refers to as the double consciousness, always looking at themselves "through the eyes of others, of measuring one's soul by the tape of a world that looks on in amused contempt and pity."[20] In the end, the model minorities experience what I would call "white-wishing," that is, a desire to be white, to acquire a physical look that they can never possess, and thus suffer from an anxiety partly of their own making. They are caught up in what Frantz Fanon calls the "bodily schema"[21] of their fragmented selves. I am black, First Nations, Mexican, Chinese, Japanese, or East Indian. I am not white but I want to be white.

Bearing witness to the fragmented self, a space in between the imagined self and the ascribed self, "black is beautiful" makes no sense within the context of white-wishing. Some of the white-wishers have gone so far as to alter their physical self—plastic surgery, hair straightening or dyeing, and skin bleaching—in order to achieve a "white look" that would allow them admittance into whiteness. And even though as a nonwhite person you may, as Fanon puts it, "make European culture [your] own,"[22] and gravitate toward whiteness, I think there is always a split between the performative act of whiteness and the embodied presence of nonwhiteness. Nonwhiteness, because it is visually imprinted on the body, makes crossing over the color border impossible. In this sense, colorblindness is in big trouble. Nonwhites, in spite of their subjective experiences and choice of identity, cannot escape from the social meanings that are inscribed on their racialized bodies.

White-wishing inscribes on the racialized body a deformed bodily schema that is weighed down by the injurious and self-defeating internalized whiteness. Internalized whiteness promotes the split between whiteness as a power position (structural) and nonwhites' daily experience of whiteness (personal). Nonwhites have internalized the mythical norms of whiteness—pure, wholesome, and good—that positioned nonwhites as oppositional to whites. In short, internalized whiteness creates a self-hatred, a certain amount of ambivalence about embracing one's blackness, First Nationness, Chineseness, or Mexicanness. Instead, one gyrates toward whiteness. In the end, individuals are alienated not only from members of their own group but also from the other racialized groups.

For members of racialized groups, being ascribed to a particular cultural group, for the most part, is inescapable, unless they can pass. A cultural group is in itself problematic, in that, in order to keep itself intact, it relies on the establishment of cultural sameness, which, as a form of identification, obscures racism, sexism, classism, homophobia, and the other facets of inequalities. Meanwhile, those who are looked on as belonging to a given cultural group must, at the same time, adhere to the public culture, which is embedded with signs of racial superiority and concealed authority. To give an example, it is a religious practice for Hindus to place the ashes of a person who is cremated into a flowing river. Hindus living in California would not place such ashes in the Sacramento River. In addition, chopsticks are a cultural symbol assigned to all Japanese Americans, but Japanese American students cannot expect cafeterias at the universities to have chop sticks. And orthodox Muslim American students would not insist that the school cafeterias serve curried chicken only if the chicken is slaughtered in accordance with Muslims' practice.

In places where cultural practices and values contrast with the norms and value system that governs society, the state implicitly or explicitly regulates these cultural practices. Members of a racialized cultural group have to become accustomed to the norms of society even if it means temporarily shredding their own cultural identities.[23] Even though some practices—for example, female circumcision or Chinese foot binding—are rather common in certain cultures, they are viewed by those outside those cultures as horrifying, and evoke their utter dismay. It is hard to imagine that female circumcision or Chinese foot binding, which denies women their auton-omy, according to the many arguments put forward by some feminists, would not be upheld by the patriarchal state. Nonetheless, it is central that racialized groups do not pose a problem for the dominant culture. Hence, pressures to conform to the norms and values of society are prevalent.[24] These pressures sometimes take on supplementary meanings and implica-tions of their own.

In the United States, Sikhs are not exempt from the motorcycle law that mandates wearing a helmet or from the official dress code of the police force. At the universities, for example, nonwhite students engage in what the Marxist philosopher Peter McLaren calls an "articulatory whiteness."[25] It would be strange if Mexican American students expected the professor to present his or her lectures in Spanish, or if black students chose Afri-can American Vernacular English, also referred to as Ebonics, as a form of communication within the normative codes of the university culture. Whiteness is not just mythical because it creates and fashions itself on the illusions formed around the ontological superiority of the white subject, it is also multistructural in that it unites whiteness across differences such as race, class, gender, sexuality, religion, and geography.[26]

Since 9/11, some Muslim Americans are pressured into hiding their Muslim identity because, as Will Kymlicka explains, "People who too vis-ibly or publicly identify themselves as Muslim today are suspected by some of being 'unAmerican.'"[27] Kymlicka's notion of polyethnic rights—the right to wear one's traditional attire in public—is being put to the test. It was recently debated whether or not Americans who are Sikhs should be forced to take off their turbans during security checks at the airport. These kinds of debates are intended to reinscribe racist positioning, which bears on the distinction between the self and "other." In addition, racist position-ing, for the most part, becomes a site for the denial of American identity. Also, it marks Americans' growing discomfort with noticeable differences, which conjure up images of un-Americanness. The "othering" of the "oth-ers," in most cases, manifests itself in an unpleasant manner.

Women, caught between the synchronizing of their racialized and gen-derized bodies, are made unfit as equal participants in the public culture and are thus denied access. The state plays a crucial role in determining which groups are allowed a degree of autonomy. I think the question still remains, who is allowed to speak on behalf of each group without being reproved while in the process of reproving others? In the end, multicul-turalism allows for certain group members to speak for or represent the group and prohibits other members from such an opportunity. Those who speak for the groups, or the token individuals, are the ones who are quickly elevated.

Should America promote a dominant culture in the presence of its multiethnic and multiracial mix? If there is to be a dominant culture, what should it entail? How would America be able to incorporate its diverse racial and cultural groups into a single American culture? In a globalized world where a person's alliance is not tied to one country, is talking about a single American cultural identity obsolete? In the face of transculturalism[28] where there is this push to create global communities or cities, which are urban and cosmopolitan and are constructed and shaped by Western modernity, is there now a global cultural identity? Should we be wary of a global culture as another form of cultural boundedness? Even though these are some concerns, for some scholars the need for a single American identity remains important.[29]

Once, Dr. Martin Luther King pondered the question, What would it take for America to achieve a genuinely inclusive society where all Americans are looked on and treated as Americans? For the nondominant cultures, cultural inclusiveness into America's homogeneous cultural identity can only be achieved in a multicultural state. A multicultural state would swap America's cultural homogeneity and replace it with cultural heterogeneity. The question, whether a multicultural state and the complex cultural relation it would embody could contribute to positive social changes that are supposed to alter America's homogeneous cultural practice, is germane. Since in a monocultural state a homogeneous cultural identity is not only inescapable but a legitimate goal of the state, because we cannot expect a monocultural state to work in the best interests of the nondominant group, America's transformation from a monocultural state to a multicultural state is necessary.

In the next section I examine what an American multicultural state would look like. The task at hand is to reconstruct strategies that would enhance the starting point for the remaking of an American cultural identity that would replace America's cultural oneness with America's cultural manyness.

The Multicultural State

Before examining what America's multicultural state would look like, it is important to ask whether in a multicultural state, racialized groups would exist as outsiders or aliens to America's cultural oneness. Would America's cultural oneness take precedence over America's cultural manyness? What would an American multicultural state look like? For sure it would not look like the United States in its present form where the dominant culture as white remains unmarked and dictates the norms and values of a society that benefits the white hegemonic group. A good starting point is that in a multicultural state, the social, political, and economic institutions would not identify with an American cultural tradition based on whiteness.

I will draw on Kymlicka's description of a multicultural state to put forward my own vision of a multicultural state. He writes,

> First, a multicultural state involves the repudiation of the older idea that the state is a possession of a single national group. Instead, the state must be seen as belonging equally to all citizens. Second, as a consequence, a multicultural state repudiates any nation-building policies that assimilate or exclude members of minority or non-dominant groups. Instead, it accepts that individuals should be able to access state institutions, and to act as full and equal citizens in political life, without having to hide or deny their ethnocultural identity. The state accepts an obligation to accord recognition and accommodation to the history, language, and culture of non-dominant groups, as it does for the dominant. Third, a multicultural state acknowledges the historic injustice that was done to minority/non-dominant groups by these policies of assimilation and exclusion, and manifests a willingness to offer some remedy or rectification for them.[30]

He goes on to say that "these three interconnected ideas"[31] are fundamental for a multicultural state. How are we to avoid the dominant culture imposing its norms on the nondominant groups? And what happens when nondominant groups are not acceptable because they present challenges to the majority culture?

The oppositional position of nondominant and dominant cultures not only establishes and reinforces the hegemony of the dominant culture but also relies on specific criteria to determine membership into these groups where cultural hierarchy remains in place. Instead of thinking in terms of dominant and nondominant as Kymlicka does, which is consequential for promoting and maintaining cultural hierarchy, America's multicultural state would move beyond the binaries of dominant and nondominant, central and peripheral cultures, superior and inferior cultures. Since the center remains culturally homogenous, for this reason, we would need a different vocabulary that dehegemonizes the discourse about identity, nation, and self; a discourse that would speak about culture in America by replacing the dialectic of dominant and nondominant cultures. Only then could America truly incorporate its multicultural and multiracial society into its cultural manyness. Members from different cultural groups would interact and complement each other, increase each other's awareness about cultural differences, and expose each other to new forms of cultural realization. I think that cultural diversity would truly be achieved if it remains open to the value of other cultures while shaping a heterogeneous American culture. The problem is not the nondominant groups' access into the dominant culture, but changing the representation of nondominant cultures as the "other" to where "otherness" is looked on as Americanness.

A multicultural state cannot establish one culture over the other. All cultures should be looked on as equally important, and as a part of shaping a heterogeneous American culture. With this in mind, "group-differentiated" rights, in terms of cultural recognition and celebration, would be obsolete. This is not a move toward culture blindness, but toward the integration of the value of the nondominant cultures into America's cultural manyness. The idea is that all groups have a role to play in influencing a country's cultural identity.[32] Each cultural group should contribute to America's cultural heterogeneity.

Membership into ascribed groups would be voluntary. In other words, you can choose to be a member of your ascribed group in the cultural mosaic or choose not to be a member of that group. Since a multicultural state consists of diverse communities, its members would have membership in these communities. However, membership would not be based on group authenticity since these groups are constantly changing. Of course, this challenges and upsets the communitarian spirit of authenticity and individual rights that forms the bases of much liberal thinking, even though authenticity is quite bothersome because of its exclusivity. One would think that liberalism's obsession with individualism would make liberals more attuned to individuals' differences within a group identity—not in terms of group recognition as is espoused by many liberal thinkers.[33] However, this is not the case.

Whites are individuals; nonwhites belong to a racialized ethnic group. Granting a cultural pedigree to marginalized groups—such as the rights of Sikhs to wear a turban, or the right to be tested for a driver's license in a language other than English—is another instance of cultural hierarchy. In a multicultural state the right to be different would not be granted but automatic. Other characteristics of a multicultural state would include the daily use of sign language for those who cannot hear and speak; or the right for groups such as orthodox Muslims who want to lead culturally enclosed lives to do so without being viewed as unpatriotic or un-American. Still, given the impact of globalization on culture, I think it would be difficult for groups to be isolated and self-contained.

The discourse about the need for cultural recognition and accommodation of racialized groups has to be replaced by a new discourse as well as new practices that truly promote America as a multicultural society. There would be no need for laws recognizing and protecting nondominant cultures since minority cultures would be incorporated into the majority culture. Instead of celebrating America's cultural oneness, the new emphasis would be on celebrating America's cultural manyness where whiteness as shaping the dominant culture would have begun to disintegrate. Organizations, political systems, and institutions would represent the multicultural aspect of the population by including racialized groups, women, and other marginalized groups as key players in decision making and daily social functions. These groups would not be granted these positions as a form of concession in a society in which the white power structure remains intact.

In a multicultural state these groups would no longer be ignored in political decision making because the solution for promoting America's cultural manyness lies, in part, in the visible representation of racial and ethnic groups. The integration of many dominant voices in discussion about America's multiracial and multicultural society has the potential of moving America in the right direction. It is only then that America will be able to nurture and disseminate multicultural norms and values and be reimagined as a truly multicultural society. Instead of viewing racialized groups as threats to America's cultural identity, or the influx of racialized immigrants to America as the "end of American civilization," as Lawrence Auster claims, a multicultural state would embrace differences as enriching America's cultural identity.

Because racialized groups are de-Americanized and are looked on as foreigners, it is a difficult task to ally "otherness" with Americanness. Not only would there have to be a shift in the cultural psyche, but America's social, political, and economic institutions promoting whiteness as Americanness would have to be reconfigured. The state and each group, through open dialogue, would have to divide authority over controversial matters and focus on shared values that are important to a multicultural society. Whiteness, instead of being unmarked and invisible, would have to be seen as just another feature of America's multicultural state. I am referring here to a postwhite subject who would provide the possibility for a different America, and, ultimately, a different answer to the question, who is an American?

Instead of concealing the model of power and subordination under the veil of a multiculturalism situated within a monocultural state, a truly multicultural state would recognize a plurality of cultures. The entrenchment of cultural pluralism properly becomes more complex within a multicultural state. The naturalization of the dominant culture and simultaneous recognition of the subcultures will disappear to create a new cultural heterogeneous space: American culture as multiethnic and multiracial. The focus of recognizing a multicultural America would not be a matter of rhetoric but should be an entrenched practice. With the discarding of America's cultural homogeneity as white, an American culture in its multiple dimensions would be inclusive of nonwhiteness.

In the United States, before the beginning of the twentieth century, the use of European languages—including German, Italian, and Swedish—in private as well as public arenas was prevalent. With World War I and the proliferation of anti-German sentiments during that period, the state insisted on the usage of English. Persons using any other language besides English were looked on as un-American. English language, as the public language, continues to be important for active participation in the public culture, and the state supports and endorses the systematic usage of English. There have been several debates in Congress as to whether English should be America's official language. In 1996, Congress passed the English Language Empowerment Act. With this act in place, many states have endorsed English as the official language. English language provides a fundamental aspect of America's cultural identity and it represents and promotes an American way of life. I am not requesting a return to these European languages. Since, in a multicultural state, pluralingualism is a cultural asset, other languages besides English would have to be made official and easily accessible by any person living in America. In other words, English should not be treated as the "first" language. California allowing its residents to take their driving test in another language besides English, or the inclusion of a provision in the Voting Rights Act that permits New York election authorities to provide election materials in Spanish to Puerto Rican voters, is a good starting point. If, as in Canada where bilingualism is an official policy, America would legally adopt some form of bilingualism where both English and Spanish are official, America's multicultural state would be moving in the right direction. However, we have to be wary that language legislation in America does not become restraining, as has Quebec's language laws.

Given the history of the United States where whiteness is unmarked, a multicultural state is not enough; we will also have to denormalize whiteness. It has to become an antiracist project aimed at "emptying the armory of binary logic" as Peter McLaren puts it,[34] and at the same time provide a space that can serve as a facilitator for whiteness to shed its presumptive hegemony. It is only then that social and cultural norms that maintain whiteness's despotic position can be challenged. In other words, whiteness "as the natural, ordinary, inevitable way of being human"[35] has to be discarded. A good strategy, which started with whiteness scholars, is the interrogation of whiteness as a way of thinking about the "self" and the "other."[36] However, we have to move beyond the interrogation of whiteness and imagine new and positive ways to present the postwhite subject, a subject that would render inane cultural hierarchy. In Chapter 4 I pointed to the dangers of cultural border crossing. In a multicultural society, border crossing would not be detrimental for the crossers because the borders would be diffused and indeterminate. It would also broaden the notion of interculturality where the focus is on cultural fixity rather than cultural fluidity. Cultural fluidity is important to construct the values of a multicultural society. It is only then that American society can move in the direction of genuine cultural celebration.

The efforts by whiteness scholars[37] in interrogating and making whiteness visible "to dislodge [whiteness] from the position of power"[38] is paramount. Naming whiteness is the beginning of interrogating its social norms and values. Yet "whiteness studies," in its thrust to generate spaces to address the position of whiteness, which I discussed at length in Chapter 3, may have recentered whiteness, to use Michele Fine and her colleagues' words, "as an essential something."[39] Rather than discussing how white people live their lives and the rules and norms that frame their existence, it is more fruitful to inaugurate new discussions about whiteness. Despite the important insights "whiteness studies" has allowed, to date, there has not been much attention paid to how whiteness infuses ways of thinking about America's cultural identity. In other words, these scholars have not looked at the ways whiteness determines who is American. Nor have they examined the institutionalized relation between being nonwhite and being a foreigner, an alien to American cultural oneness.

Do "whiteness studies" demonstrate a political commitment for developing a postwhite subject? Can the subaltern speak through "whiteness studies"? Can "whiteness studies" reconfigure whiteness as a tool for the promotion of antiracist, antisexist, and antihomophobic projects? Is "whiteness studies" the first sign of the denormalization of whiteness? Such questions provide the conceptual base for any discussion of whiteness and how it can be denormalized.

Whiteness Studies

In the 1990s, in the United States, the concept of whiteness emerged as a category of analysis in literary criticism and cultural studies.[40] Since then, in many other disciplines as diverse as history, gender studies, film studies, media studies, humor studies, linguistics, art history, rhetoric and communication, material culture, and dance,[41] there has been a growing body of influential, academic literature that focuses on whiteness.[42] The need to examine whiteness to promote critical analysis of racial formation and cultural practices in the United States[43] is seen as essential. David R. Roediger, whose work on whiteness is well known and important, explains that "whiteness studies" is not new and it is not "a white thing."[44] In an article published by the *Chronicle of Higher Education*, in 2006, and titled,

"Whiteness and Its Complication," Roediger suggests that "whiteness stud-ies" seem to decrease in popularity in academic institutions. He writes, "The field of whiteness studies in the United States has no journals, no professional association (which it does have in Australia), no book series, and no presence as an academic department anywhere. Yet, despite its modest proportions, it is at times castigated as if it sits atop the academic food chain, begging to be brought down to size."[45] Nonetheless, the field of "whiteness studies," in America, has come about because whiteness, being at the center of America's institutions and systems, must be interrogated in order to resolve the many issues to which it calls attention. In order to gain new perspectives, "whiteness studies" is positioned inside an indefensible location within research on white privilege that enables the racial subju-gation of nonwhites.[46] Yet most whites remain naively clueless as to how nonwhites experience the effects of whiteness in their daily lives.

The representation of whiteness in blacks' and other nonwhites' imag-ination as "the mysterious, the strange, and the terrible,"[47] is even more important, as bell hooks rightfully argues. James Baldwin, the celebrated African American novelist, explains this best when he draws our attention, as hook also notes, to his experience as the only black person in a white community in Switzerland. In his *Notes of a Native Son*, a collection of pathbreaking essays, Baldwin expresses the most distinguishing manifesta-tion of whiteness. What he expresses, which hooks draws on in making a similar case about whiteness, is instructive of how whiteness functions and hence is worth quoting at length to capture the substantive significance of his analysis. He writes,

> I thought of white men arriving for the first time in an African village, strang-ers there, as I am a stranger here, and tried to imagine the astounded popu-lace touching their hair and marveling at the color of their skin. But there is a great difference between being the first white man to be seen by Africans and being the first black man to be seen by whites. The white man takes the astonishment as tribute, for he arrives to conquer and to convert the natives, whose inferiority in relation to himself is not even to be questioned, whereas I, without a thought of conquest, find myself among a people whose culture controls me, has even in a sense created me, people who have cost me more in anguish and rage than they will ever know, who yet do not even know of my existence. The astonishment with which I might have greeted them, should they have stumbled into my African village a few hundred years ago, might have rejoined their hearts. But the astonishment with which they greet me today can only poison mine.[48]

Baldwin's monumental work points to the naturalization of whiteness. And, as hooks highlights, it shows the way in which whiteness exists without the knowledge of nonwhiteness, even as it collectively asserts control, which is important when analyzing whiteness.[49] It is precisely for this reason, as Toni Morrison explains, that there has to be a shift "from the racial object to the racial subject; from the described and imagined to the describers and imaginers; from the serving to the served."[50]

In "whiteness studies," whiteness and its primary trajectories can be traced either as a driving force within the history of class struggle[51] or as an individual and varied "lived experience."[52] Ruth Frankenberg's position in *White Women, Race matters: The Social Construction of Whiteness* is arguable because she contends that "naming whiteness and white people in this sense helps dislodge the claims of both to rightful dominance."[53] In fact, naming whiteness reminds us only too clearly that it is not exactly from the voices of the repressed and the oppressed. It is first of all for the "other," and outside the self; and it is from voices coming from the pinnacle of whiteness, the norm that always authorizes the powerful to speak for the powerless and silences the "others."[54] If, as Judith Butler explains, "citational practices" is a process that names and privileges,[55] does "whiteness studies" generate and privilege the effects of that naming? Would renaming whiteness work? It is Frankenberg's hope, nonetheless, that by investigating and naming whiteness, it will be possible to engender and work toward antiracist forms of whiteness, or at least toward antiracist strategies for an alternative form of whiteness.[56] David R. Roediger, *The Wages of Whiteness: Race and the Making of the American Working Class*, adheres to Frankenberg's hope by repositioning the class struggle as an antiracist project. His historical explanation of white racial formation describes, with allurement, the political perspective of "whiteness studies" by imagining for whites a political identity outside the equation of power and privilege with white skin.[57] Indeed, if naming whiteness remains separate from antiracist discourse and practice, it would probably produce studies that are removed from any thought of its political signification.[58] However, we have to be careful in interpreting antiracism as a site for struggles and its commitment to justice and equality as a nonappearance of racism. In examining Jane Lazarre's *Beyond the Whiteness of Whiteness: Memoir of a White Mother of Black Sons*, we can conclude that memoir and "whiteness studies" can amalgamate in ways that are definitely antiracist and responsive to how structures of race shape and inform our personal relations and daily experiences.[59]

In April 1997, "The Making and Unmaking of Whiteness" conference at the University of California, Berkeley, was another effort at "examining and naming the terrain of whiteness," which, in my mind, was long past due. In the same year, *The Minnesota Review* published a special issue on whiteness. From August 12 to 16, 2000, at the annual meeting of the American

Sociological Association, in Washington, DC, there was a section devoted to "the current status of whiteness." Many books and articles on "whiteness studies" have been published since then, including Matt Wray's *Not Quite White: White Trash and the Boundaries of Whiteness*, in 2006; John Tehranian's *Whitewashed: America's Invisible Middle Eastern Minority*, in 2008; and *The Making and Unmaking of Whiteness*, edited by Birgit Brander Rasmussen and colleagues in 2001.

Whiteness Studies: Some Concerns

There are many good reasons for critical engagement in the study of whiteness. And reorienting whiteness is a necessary requirement, if its purpose is to denormalize whiteness and develop antiracist forms of whiteness. Writing in the early 1990s, hooks already renounced "whiteness studies" on the grounds that these scholars "are able to enact it as a lived practice or not." She says, "Many white folks active in antiracist struggles today are able to acknowledge that all whites (as well as everyone else within white supremacist culture) have learned to overvalue 'whiteness' even as they simultaneously learn to devalue [nonwhiteness]. They understand the need, at least intellectually, to alter their thinking. Central to the process of unlearning white supremacist attitudes and values is the deconstruction of the category 'whiteness.'"[60] Hook's remark begs the question: Does the deconstruction of whiteness advance an essentialist approach to race? And if the answer is yes, as I suspect it is, then "whiteness studies," in of itself, relies on essentialist ideas about race.

"Whiteness studies" literature, with few exceptions,[61] has, in the words of Alastair Bonnett, professor of social geography, "tended to retain an uncritical, ahistorical, common-sense, perspective on the meaning of whiteness."[62] Whiteness, how whites live their lives and "think of themselves, of power, and of pleasures,"[63] as the historian Eric Arnesen puts it, "has become hip."[64] More recently, there is a reorienting of whiteness as an attempt to rethink whiteness as a bendable set of cultural and symbolic representations that provide meaning, significance, and power to the social category white. Hence, many whiteness scholars have placed a lot of emphasis on groups, including Irish, Jews, and immigrants, whose claims to whiteness were greatly contested.[65] Also, the incontestable presence of hybridity, an identity considered impure and inauthentic, has been interpreted by some scholars as potentially undermining whiteness.[66] What remains unexplored, however, is how whiteness defines who are Americans and their rite of passage into normative Americanness, which has important consequences for racialized groups in America. Chapter 2 of this book already points to this dilemma when it discusses whiteness as the decisive conception of an American identity.

By giving serious attention to issues of whiteness, "whiteness studies" make that which is invisible visible.[67] It shows how being white is a guarantor for impeccable privileges given to white people. In addition, it critically engages with whiteness and revolves toward a kind of "truth claim." This impulse toward an ardent "truth claim" where white privilege must be confessed and explained should be looked on with a great degree of caution. For me, there are many unresolved questions that are reasonable to ask. Who are the beneficiaries of a "self-reflective whiteness"? Is "self-reflective whiteness" another way of skillfully reenacting the white subject position because, for many whites, whiteness, it is assumed, is in some kind of "crisis"; as Charles Gallagher remarks, "a fundamental transformation" of whiteness is occurring.[68] Is there a crisis of whiteness, or an anxiety about whiteness promoting a "me-too-ism" of white victimhood?[69] Does the government's attempt to compensate for unequal treatment of nonwhites through preferential hiring and admission policies challenge whiteness? Charles Gallagher's work points alarmingly to the growing prevailing assumption that whiteness is in some kind of crisis.[70] What makes this a crisis in the first place is, of course, the impression that we are living in a period of interference and challenge to white supremacy, and it is no longer justifiable or even sustainable because of numerous attacks on white privilege by nonwhites.[71] And even though Gallagher points to the difficulty in illustrating that white privilege remains uncontested, for the most part, in social spaces, he draws on numerous examples to demonstrate the primacy of white privilege.[72]

Some whiteness scholars wish to triumph over white privilege by abolishing whiteness altogether,[73] which I think is desirable but at the same time impossible because without changing the very structure of power, it is impossible for whites to transcend their whiteness and automatically give up the privileges that come with whiteness. The deconstruction of whiteness is a good starting point in order to put forward a critique of whiteness. However, as we will see later, in order for us to reinscribe a postwhite self, one of the essentials would be to denormalize whiteness. I will return to the denormalization of whiteness later in the discussion.

How can whites confront race privilege and achieve the conditions of a nonracist space within a racist space? Does it create a space for overcoming whiteness notwithstanding its alleged nature of being, its metaphysical status? Has the Foucauldian notion of power and its deployment continued to function in "whiteness studies"? Is promoting "whiteness studies" another way of legitimizing whites' privilege as a safe space to theorize about whiteness? Is it about the removal of "unearned assets" given to whites? Is it about supplanting white supremacy? To what extent can "whiteness stud-ies" help us answer these questions, or are the issues of "whiteness studies" new ones altogether? Are "old" answers sufficient to address "new" ques-tions? Is whiteness transforming itself as some scholars have argued? [74] To be sure, these are not easy questions to be answered in a single text.

Some of the concerns that "whiteness studies" come up against are wor-thy of contemplation. In his Introduction to "*Out There: Marginalization and Contemporary Cultures*, Russell Ferguson suggests that whiteness is no longer the ubiquitous paradigm. It is positioned at the center as well as the periphery.[75] Thinking about whiteness as unmarked and decentered is itself impossible unless whiteness is no longer the norm. In some seminal writings by whiteness scholars, the truth claim encompasses a reference to what Robyn Westcott refers to as "the author's racial situatedness."[76] "Let me state," Richard Dyer begins, "that while writing here as a white person about whiteness, I do not mean either to display the expiation about my guilt of being white, nor to hint that it is also awful to be."[77] One of the implications is that "I" am white—"I" am not a raced being—"I" am a human being. "I learned absolutely no lore of my German ancestry."[78] Yet, at this juncture, "I" acts as a carrier of authority.

In addition, Frankenberg's acknowledgment that "white feminist women like [her]self could no longer fail to notice the critique of white feminist racism,"[79] is to acknowledge the naturalization and normalization of whiteness, which has been legally and constitutionally retained for cen-turies. The practice of speaking as a white person does not involve a separa-tion from one's self since one's subjectivity is fully steeped in the protocol of speaking from the position of one's situatedness. In other words, as a way of illuminating the position from which whites speak as whites, white-ness is made visible against the backdrop of an invisible nonwhiteness.[80] What we are witnessing here is what Butler calls "another self glorification where whiteness is equated with moral rectitude."[81] In fact, to engage in the sort of ardent self-positioning—"I am white"—requires, I think, some sort of self-reflection about one's situatedness, which shapes how one views the world. To sum it up, "the whiteness of whiteness studies" is dominated by white scholars who speak and write from a particularly privileged position. In fact, "whiteness studies" has fastened itself in the minds of many white scholars as a right to speak about and for the "other."[82]

Having taken into account Alastair Bonnett's description of "intro-spection practice" as an abstract and textual tool, where one is speaking as a white person, where one has the right to speak about, and conceivably even for, all white people, is important. It is, after all, puzzling that not much thought has been given in "whiteness studies" to the interconnect-edness between symbolic forms and preoccupied utterances as important dilemmas that haunt the study of whiteness, which rehegemonizes rather than dehegemonizes whiteness. [83] If the hope of "whiteness studies" is to decenter whiteness, whiteness will reemerge in a new and different form. Since whiteness naturalizes the claim to cultural power and epistemological privilege, it seems that relocating its location cannot be accomplished by increasing and redirecting the gaze of the "other" or by provoking the "return" of the repressed or the subordinate subject.[84] Therefore, how to escape, dismantle, deconstruct, challenge, and resist white privilege while avoiding revamping the logics of white supremacy, are necessary concerns of "whiteness studies."[85] Yet to study whiteness does not resolve America's oldest problem, which is white supremacy. White supremacy is a structure, which for Alexis de Tocqueville is so "immovable,"[86] it "cannot be willed away."[87] As result, white supremacy remains a system of privileges and advantages, norms, and rights; a site of power that benefits whites individually and collectively; a mode of discernment of the "other" when measured against the "self."[88]

Whiteness, as a system of domination, will not disappear because whiteness is studied. In some ways, studying whiteness can develop into "white studies," which, for good reason, makes Dyer's "blood [run] cold at the thought that talking about whiteness could lead to the development of something called 'White Studies.'"[89] This path has been explored by Michele Fine and her colleagues who extended Dyer's concerns in *Off White: Readings on Race, Power and Society.* They point out,

> In our desire to create spaces to speak, intellectually and empirically, about whiteness, we may have reified whiteness as a fixed category of experience and identity; that we have allowed it to be treated as a monolith, in the singular, as an "essential something." We despair that a terrifying academic flight towards something called white studies could eclipse the important work being done across the range of race, postcolonialism, ethnicity, and "people of color"; that research funds should shift categories; [that] the understanding of whiteness could surface as the new intellectual fetish, leaving questions of power, privilege, and race/ethnic political minorities behind as an intellectual "fad" of the past.[90]

In terms of power and privilege, "whiteness studies" has failed miserably to unravel the manifestation of the cultural hierarchy endemic to white dominance.

Is whiteness as a category of historical analysis in any way a type of a transformative project? How effective is whiteness as an analytic category in promoting social changes? Is whiteness, when analyzed as a racialized position, a form of deracialization?[91] In other words, is the evidence self-evident?

I am concerned with the focus put by many well-meaning whiteness scholars on what Arnesen calls the "materiality, privilege, and rewards of whiteness."[92] In a thoroughgoing way, I do not think that "white studies" is equipped to challenge the power relation that is embedded within norms that are systematic and institutionalized. Arnesen rightfully draws our attention to the synchronizing of whiteness and power. He writes, "Whiteness is, variously, a metaphor for power, a proxy for racially distributed material benefits, a synonym for 'white supremacy,' an epistemological stance defined by power, a position of invisibility or ignorance, and a set of beliefs about racial 'Others' and oneself that can be rejected through 'treason' to a racial category. For those seeking to interrogate the concept critically, it is nothing less than a moving target."[93]

There is no doubt that studying whiteness is important for any antiracist projects and politics especially on college and university campuses. The complexity may arise from the very desire of making whiteness visible for those for whom whiteness is invisible. For blacks and other racialized ethnic groups whiteness has always been visible. Nothing was invisible about Jim Crow South, Japanese internment camps, or the Chinese Exclusion Act. Richard Wright clearly saw what was happening around him. In *Black Boy*, he chronicles the lessons about white supremacy that blacks and other nonwhites had to rapidly learn, growing up during that era. Blacks would be rewarded handsomely if blacks, as Wright notes, made whites "feel safe and superior."[94] Today, there is nothing invisible about black ghettoes, superghettoes, and the prisons; racial profiling; poor schools in black neighborhoods and other ethnic enclaves; the high rate of high school dropouts of blacks, Mexicans, First Nations, and other nonwhites; and increasing poverty in First Nations, black, and Mexican communities.

In a single phrase, white supremacy represents white domination. And despite the argument presented by Steve Martinot and Jared Sexton that "white supremacy is nothing more than what we perceive of it,"[95] the sociology professor Eric M. Dyson uncovers and reminds us how white supremacist ideology brought together poor whites "in the hood of the Ku Klux Klan and sophisticated scholars in robes in the halls of academe."[96] In other words, all whites do not need to occupy the same class and social position for white supremacy and its horrible predispositions to be effective. It is certainly a mistake to reverse such an observation of white supremacy.

George Lipsitz argues that the policies of the government further the political agenda of white supremacy. He shows how the Federal Housing Act (FHA) of 1934 funneled money to white urban spaces (the suburbs) instead of communities occupied by blacks and other racialized groups.[97] A great emphasis is placed on maintaining such policies and their corollary discriminatory practices. Even though race is the modality in which class and other forms of inequalities are experienced, racialized practices are often explained in terms of a class stratification system. In the end, racialized spaces continue to be blighted by crime, underdevelopment, and poverty.[98]

Whites, blinded by their sense of superiority, "behave in accordance with a neurotic orientation," to borrow the words of Fanon, and this becomes a huge part of the psychological violence that they commit against themselves and the "other," which Fanon describes in *The Wretched of the Earth*. Is Mab Segrest's suggestion, in "The Souls of White Folks," that white suffer emotionally and spiritually from living in a society marred by white supremacy merely sagacious?[99] In many ways, feminists and other theorists have appropriated white supremacy. For feminists, patriarchy is where every avenue of power in America is contained, which subordinates women for the benefits of men. This particular logic of sexism is appropriate for racism in the sense that not all white people are racist, but all whites benefit from racism. Another example of how white supremacy manifests itself is found in the seminal works of Karl Marx. Marx's analysis about state–society interaction is not merely about rich and poor, but, more thoroughly, about the ownership of the means of production (the price makers). In both examples the signifier is whiteness with a specific emphasis on gender relations.[100]

Critical studies of whiteness call for multifaceted approaches "to both epistemology and ontology in order to prevent the subject areas from solidifying into a homogenous, institutionalized subject area, an outcome that would thus only serve to reinforce the hegemony of whiteness."[101] Therefore, any critical genealogy of "whiteness studies" must begin largely with the works of such scholars as Morrison (1993), Lorde (1984), and hooks (1992). As Sara Ahmed suggests, the "later work by white academics on representations of whiteness or on how white people experience their whiteness"[102] often ignores the lived daily experiences of nonwhites. Blacks and other nonwhite people have been studying whites for a long time and therefore have a particularly useful set of insights about whiteness. Drawing attention to whiteness and white racism is necessary.

Whiteness as a historical category of analysis is important. Victoria Hattam writes about the contribution of whiteness scholars in "theorizing class and identification, historicizing racial categories, and reexamining questions of the nation and national identity."[103] My concern, however, is ridding whiteness of its presumptive hegemony, "the conditions of its own existence."[104] Hence, the project of stripping whiteness of its hegemony would have to be about making whiteness unmarked by denormalizing whiteness in order to reconstruct a postwhite subject. However, denormalizing whiteness is not an unfinished project. It is constitutive of its everyday logics. I will return to the denormalizing of whiteness in a moment, but for now it is important to pay some attention to the liminality of whiteness. Does the liminality of whiteness signal denormalization?

The "Them" within the "Self": The Liminality of Whiteness

Many whiteness scholars have demonstrated that there is a social distinction among whites. Even though all whites have the same white skin, incorporation, adaptation, and enhancement into the "white club" are not guaranteed for all whites. Whites who are poor may experience "deprivation, stigmatization, and subjugation."[105] In other words, these whites experience the "otherness" of "whiteness within," the liminality of whiteness. They "are not quite white," but are in the process of "becoming white." Neil Foley, in *The White Scourge: Mexicans, Blacks, and Poor Whites in Texas Cotton Culture*, shows how being a poor white person diminishes the benefits of being white. He points to "the ways in which 'whiteness' itself fissured along race and class.... Whiteness also [comes] increasingly to mean a particular kind of white person. Not all whites, in other words, [are] equally white."[106] In Matt Wray, *Not Quite White: White Trash and the Boundaries of Whiteness*, the poor "white trash" is a direct threat to the "symbolic and social order" of whiteness and how white people live their lives.[107] In 1964, Dr. Martin Luther King warns that America "should also be rescuing a large stratum of the forgotten white poor."[108]

Because of gender configuration in society where women are situated differently from men, are white women, then, in a liminal position because they are separated from white men? Are white lesbians and gays liminial whites? White lesbians and gays do experience the stigma of oppression even though they appear to be part of the very whiteness that oppresses them. White lesbians occupy a more precarious subject position than that of white homosexual men. White homosexual men may feel resentful because they expect to be protected and privileged because of their identity as male and white. Without warning, the inaptness of their sexuality puts them in tangible danger. The more pressing question, then, is whether whiteness as a signifier can be resignified because of its liminality? What does liminality of whiteness say about nonwhiteness? In the end, in terms of racial discrimination, poor whites or white homosexuals are still better off than nonwhites because they do not experience racial discrimination. Nonwhites cannot escape from their distinctiveness as racialized bodies. They are, for the most part, situated on the fringe of a white power structure, making it hard for them to free themselves from such constructions.

The liminality of whiteness is a position of avoidance, a pressure to conform to whiteness. And poor whites, "with nothing but whiteness," are more than willing to hold on to their "property right in whiteness."[109] In fact, we should not be fooled into believing that the hierarchy among whites substitutes for the racist structure that is in place, from which all whites benefit. Unlike blacks, and other nonwhites, whose class position is always assumed as lower, poor whites can avoid such stigmatization by shifting their appearances and passing for middle-class whites. Race disrupts the possible potentiality for such liminality when whiteness is juxtapositioned against nonwhiteness. For the most part, race gets configured and reconfigured as a powerful stratifying practice in the United States of America. In the end, the liminality of whiteness only serves to produce a new kind of whiteness that is consistent with the logic of colorblindness. It does not signal denormalized whiteness.

Then, there is the "white Negro" or the "hipster" whom Norman Mailer describes in "The White Negro: Superficial Reflections on the Hipster."[110] There is also the "white Negro" whom Kobena Mercer describes in "Skin Head Sex Thing: Racial Difference and the Homoerotic Imaginary." In this article, Mercer explains that the white Negro is "like a photographic negative, . . . an inverted image of otherness, in which attributes devalorised by the dominant culture [are] simply revalorised or hypervalorised as emblems of alienation and otherness, a kind of strategic self-othering in relation to the dominant cultural norms."[111] The concept of the white Negro raises a fundamental question: What is it about whiteness that makes white people want to "cross over" to "blackness"? Does this crossing over to blackness signal denormalization? Christian Lander, in *Stuff White People Like*, draws our attention to the identity crisis facing young white kids.[112] Is whiteness at present a "cultural liability"? Do whites have a place in black popular culture? What ambivalence arises when white subjects appropriate signs from the other side of the "morphological equation"? In fact, the white Negro "encodes an antagonistic subject position on the part of the white subject in relation to the normative codes of [whiteness]."[113] However, race still confers on the white Negro bona fide privileges; their marginality is different because it is based on a self-conscious choice and was not forced on them by a society that is racist.[114] Many white youths are adopting markers of black self-empowerment, including dress, hairstyle, and music, which give whiteness some kind of meaning by appropriating signs that are considered "black."[115] It is "hip" for white persons to "act" black because they can always revert back to their whiteness. This form of "race trading" is temporary and it should not be taken seriously. In the end, there is no transcendence of whiteness.

Another Look at the Denormalization of Whiteness

In "whiteness studies," a good starting point is that whites are coming to terms with their whiteness.[116] To this end, the first task for the denormalization of whiteness is for whites to recognize that they belong to a race that enjoys unearned racial privilege because of institutionalized racism. In fact, whiteness gained its preeminence from the construction of race and its overwhelmingly determined whites' color-blind perspective on race.[117] For this reason, there is a dire need to critically reject whiteness as unique and consider it as a special ideological marker separate from race. Race, in this case, is rendered implicit and hence surreptitiously positioned in such a way that it is viewed as something outside the structure of whites' daily experiences and immediate consideration unless it is constructed and linked with blacks, First Nations, Chinese, Mexicans, and other racialized groups. It remains an unmentioned racial identity.[118] Nonetheless, we have to be careful in associating race with identity and attributing it to white people. If whiteness is looked at as a racial identity, it is not interrogated as a form of power and privilege that is unavoidably associated with being white.[119] Moreover, we fail to critically analyze the dialogical and also hierarchical relation between whites and nonwhites and its questionable binarism of domination and subordination, which serves as a precursor in determining power relations. In the end, "whiteness studies" should not be understood as what Professor Arnold Farr terms *racialized consciousness*, which is shaped by "racist social structures,"[120] where well-meaning whites "may perpetuate a form of racism unintentionally."[121]

Seemingly, we cannot move beyond this binarism because it is this very binarism that determines the ultimate social conditions of whites and nonwhites in the United States. It is for good reason that philosopher Charles Mills speaks for many when he views whiteness as "a political commitment to white supremacy."[122] Since white supremacy is pathological, we have to analyze and reveal it for what it truly is. It is an obligation that we all share, especially white people.[123] It will be awkward for many whites to engage in the elimination of their rights as whites (their rights in whiteness) that are apparently unquestionable and to which they have become accustomed. Rights, as Michel Foucault says about power, cannot be given up without transforming itself into new forms. This transformation needs to entail a focus on the white "self" instead of the racialized "other." It needs to place an emphasis on the postwhite subject.

Many scholars, including Ahmed (2004), Fields (2001), Aanerud (1997), hooks (1992), and Morrison (1993) have maintained that whiteness is shaped by the exercise of white power and privilege, which determines one's place in America. Making whiteness "visible" through "whiteness studies" merely serves to reconstitute, strengthen, authorize, sanctify, and concretize its power, or, in other words, it rehegemonizes its power. It is less straightforward how whiteness can free itself from its presumptive hegemony without its denormalization. A good starting point is "to interrogate its ontology, its being, as expressed through its imperial and hegemonic gaze."[124] How to insert a different gaze and conceive it as not simply a reversal of the hegemonic gaze but as another kind of exchange becomes quite a challenge. Whites reinventing themselves through self-reflection and counterhegemonic actions would challenge and oppose all forms of domination and oppression. It would call for a repositioning of the denormalized whiteness because, as hooks explains, "this process of repositioning has the power to deconstruct practices of racism and make possible the disassociation of whiteness with terror in the [nonwhites] imagination. As a critical intervention, it allows for the recognition that progressive anti-racist white people might be able to understand the way in which their cultural practice reinscribes white supremacy."[125] White supremacy positions cultural homogeneity against cultural heterogeneity and a normalized whiteness against an abnormal nonwhiteness. In this way, cultural and racial hierarchy is justifiable, and whiteness remains hegemonic.

The dehegemonized positionality of whiteness would create a shift, not in the way that Gayatri C. Spivak envisions the white self as "the subject position of the other,"[126] but as a postwhite subject, not aiming at decentering itself. This raises the following question: What would the postwhite subject look like? The postwhite subject would now have "to speak its name, and acknowledge its role as an organizing principle in social and cultural relations"[127] rather than positing itself external to America's racialized process and practice; the postwhite subject would have to constantly work to decenter itself from such a practice without homogenizing the "self." In fact, there is a form of hierarchical thinking about the "other" in relation to the self. However, can the new location of whiteness be more of a reflective position, a delicate balance between the white self and the nonwhite "other"? We would have to be careful that this new "self-other" is not heading in the direction of a "third self," a merging of the self and "other." For sure, the third self would enable a movement beyond bounded identities and binary oppositions; however, again we have to be careful about the third self, being positioned between the two identities, self and "other," a form of liminality, an in-between sameness and difference. I am the same, but yet I am different. In Chapter 4, I asked whether the very status of the "other" could be reinscribed in a different way. Can the "other" be transformed into the self? As I see it, reinscribing the self as the "other" without addressing power relations would be a disaster. I suppose what is more important is not a "third self," but a postwhite self. The postwhite self would work against the binary opposition of the white self and the nonwhite "other" in which the very status of the white self is already dehegemonized.

Since a white identification requires an internalization of white superiority, it can, for the most part, lead to self-loathing and hatred. In her dialogues with some white women, Ruth Frankenberg draws our attention to the ways in which these women see "white culture" as unlike nonwhite cultures. For them, nonwhite culture is better than their own. It is more "interesting," "natural," and "spiritual." Because of white women's privileged position within the cultural hierarchy, it permits dichotomized thinking of self and "other," which has created anxiety about "white culture." For them, to be a member of a racialized group is a form of "cultural capital" because members of a cultural group can recognize and construct a cultural bond with each other. Whiteness, on the other hand, appears as deficient; it is repeatedly, as Dyer suggests, exposed for its "emptiness, absence, denial, or even a kind of death."[128] Through the maintenance of cultural hierarchy, whiteness responds to its deficiency by asserting its privilege. The postwhite subject would view whiteness in a positive light, not in terms of whiteness as in some kind of "crisis," which is creating anxiety, a "me-too-ism" of white victimhood.

Given that the construction of racial identity is correlated with cultural hierarchy and significant for white supremacist goals, it would be more helpful, I think, to reconstruct racial and cultural identity.[129] But we have to begin with a constructive analysis that takes into account the consequences of racist contamination on the white subject. With the denormalization of whiteness, where whiteness is no longer the unmarked norm, whites would be repositioned within the territory of whiteness as privileged so that whites are now raced. The postwhite self, where whiteness would remain as the signifier, would be imagined differently. It would now be seen in a positive light. As a starting point, whiteness would no longer be hidden to those whites having a "possessive investment in whiteness."[130] With the denormalization of whiteness and the transformation of America's monocultural state into a multicultural state, postmulticulturalism would be the new possibility.

Conclusion

Reflections

In the United States, the focus on an American cultural identity can be traced back to the American Revolution or the War of Independence from the British rule. In many of the extant documents and debates on the Revolution and the formation of the Union, there were hardly any references to racialized ethnic groups, who would later be identified as racial minorities. The white population, at that time, mostly claimed a Protestant identity that developed from the Great Awakening of the 1740s and traced its origins to the British Isles and primarily to England. The founding fathers and the framers of the American Constitution were British. As I have pointed out in Chapter 2, the founders were open to the idea of homogeneity among American citizens. Fearing that racial and cultural differences—stemming from the presence of First Nations, blacks, and later Chinese and other racialized groups—would interrupt and undermine their commitment to a homogenous America, the founders had to find ways to suppress racial and cultural diversity. Hence, in their minds, the dehumanization of First Nations, blacks, Chinese, and other racialized groups were unmistakably warranted. Eventually, the 1790 Naturalization Act would be one of the greatest resources for the confirmation of an American identity as white by allowing only white men to be citizens of the United States of America. In the end, the United States successfully managed to forge a single American cultural identity among its diverse multicultural and multiracial population. The need to exclude racialized ethnic groups from such an identity was not without signification. The Americanization of America's cultural identity had a firm grip on America's foundations and traditions; its policies, "laws and economy; [its] institutionalized structures and discourses, and [its] epistemologies and every day customs."[1] It constitutes the most distinct form of America's racism and brings about, to employ the words of Justice Oliver Wendell Holmes, "the most substantive evils."[2] Even though contemporary racism comes in all guises, it continues to be demonstrable and continues to subvert the very premise of "one America." First Nations, blacks, Chinese, Mexicans, and other racialized groups are never looked on as Americans.

An American cultural identity is the product of a past development involving elements such as common ancestors, ethnic backgrounds, languages, religion, and, more importantly, a common culture. Since an American cultural formation is monocultural in character, it does not emphasize varied factors such as religion, nationality, customs, and language. By downgrading bilingual education and linguistic variety, the English language, as a source of cultural capital, was the language that was established. Language had to be made apparent as a way for the state to ascertain linguistic compliance. Having a common language was important because communication would create a widespread cultural atmosphere and "transform the popular mentality through the imposition of a national language."[3] Whether America should become a bilingual society, with Spanish on an equal footing with English, has been a continuing debate in Congress. In 1849, California's Constitution required the publication of all laws in English and Spanish. However, the emphasis on promoting English as the official language was tied to the broader question of what entails an American identity. Samuel Huntington notes that "three hundred years of history had selected English as the language for Americans."[4] Speaking Spanish is looked on as disloyal to America or un-American. In order to promote "the national consciousness of an American," to use the words of Justice Louis Brandeis,[5] immigrants arriving in America have to suppress their mother tongue and use English as their prevalent language. English as a second language classes are supported and sponsored by governments and are made available to immigrants to help in the transition. By the end of the nineteenth century, testing in English, as a part of the naturalization process, was implemented. For several years, there have been debates about making English language the official language in the United States. Today, in most of the States, English has been championed as the official language.

Speaking another language besides English should not represent a threat to America's cultural homogeneity. Instead, it should be looked on as embracing America's cultural multiplicity. In Louisiana, for most of the nineteenth century, the state legislature and the court functioned in both English and French. Also, it was debated whether German should be the official language in Pennsylvania. When people are exposed to various languages besides English, it equips them with new ways of appreciating and broadening their understanding of the non-dominant cultures. This is not to say that all Japanese Americans can and do speak Japanese or all Mexican Americans can and do speak Spanish. As Sonia Sotomayor explains, being Hispanic in America does not mean speaking Spanish. Most Hispanics "born and bred" in the United States speak Spanish poorly.[6] In America,

English has a hegemonic position. However, I think that it is important to encourage and promote bilingualism in the United States. Spanish speakers should be able to identify as Americans.

In addition to English language, American cultural identity is infused by the protestant religion and British culture. It is exactly what John Jay, in his writing of the *Federalist Papers No.2* had labeled the "band of brethrens."[7] It signifies the adherence to a single way of life, the rite of passage into normative Americaness, the supposedly unitary common culture that is at the heart of the notion of America as the melting pot.[8] What Will Kymlicka identifies as the "Anglo-conformity model" focuses on cultural assimilation, or what Huntington recognizes as "the Anglo-Saxon cultural patterns,"[9] in which all whites were melted into America's cultural oneness. The educational system is a huge part in promoting the Anglo-conformity model. Public schools were instrumental in creating a homogeneous society out of America's heterogeneous population. It undermined the desire of nonwhites's cultures to be incorporated into the school curriculum. All students had to accept the norms and values of the dominant culture. Today, even if you attend a private Muslim school, for example, and are taught in Arabic, you have to adhere to a public culture where English remains dominant. This dominance is manifested through standardized testing such as the New York State Board of Regents exams.

The serious impact of the Americanization of America's cultural identity, as I have shown in Chapter 2, has created a dominant cultural identity as the natural and the most important basis for securing the place of whites in America's historical memory. Also, it is important to define who is an American and to associate Americanness with whiteness. Whiteness, as I have argued, is an unmarked and implicit norm, informing America's dominant cultural identity and is thus taken for granted. Nonwhites' cultural identities are antithetic to the dominant culture. Yet the dominant culture is not self-sustaining. It depends on a nonwhite presence to give it shape and meaning. For this reason, nonwhites' cultural identities have to be recognized and celebrated while the hegemonic culture remains in place as unmarked. Whites are situated within the hegemonic culture and their authority is based on their unmarkedness or unracedness, that is, a position of power that is the source of their privilege.

However, cultural hegemony is on no account a zero-sum cultural fixture; it is constantly about changing the balance of power in relation to culture, which remains complex and unregulated; it is always about changing the outlooks and layout of cultural power, not getting out of it.[10] Since the understanding is that marginalized groups are not powerless and devoid of agency, it is important for racialized ethnics groups to develop cultural strategies that can destabilize the hegemonic culture. First

Nations developed the Ghost Dance; African Americans focused on music and dance. Like African Americans and First Nations, Mexicans developed popular music and dance. Chinese Americans created Chinatowns as safe spaces for Chinese cultural expression.

In addition to specific cultural forms of expression, several move-ments arose out of disgruntlement with the dominant culture. Some of these movements include the Asian American Movement of the 1960s and 1970s; the Chicano Movement of the 1960s, an extension of the Mexican American civil rights movement, which began in the 1940s; the Black Power Movement; Black Nationalism; and Pan-Africanism. Black Nationalism and Pan-Africanism's discourse and actions have centered on promoting the idea of the superiority of blacks. They have pushed forward the idea of separate political representation or region.[11] These groups presented a much-needed challenge to the dominant culture, which had to resort to strategies and processes that aimed at restraining and defusing them.

While some whites are certainly obsessed with appropriating the non-dominant cultures—and there are several reasons for such appropriation that I have already discussed in Chapter 5—and embrace "race trading," whether through hip-hop culture and rap music or through First Nations culture as part of the New Age movement, many whites remain deeply devoted and committed to promoting an American cultural identity as white. Many whites automatically assume that nonwhites are alien to American culture, they do not speak English, and they are from places out-side of the United States. In fact, debates about America's cultural identity and belonging are everywhere present in scholarly writings and the media. The war on terrorism seems to have united Americans from every camp— from left-wing activists to right-wing nationalists, politicians, academes, artists, writers, and even ordinary Americans. What America is and what America should be remains at the forefront. It is too often openly declared that racialized groups are a threat to American cultural identity, which is one form of the de-Americanization of racialized ethnic groups. In this sense, they must be constantly policed, dehumanized, and be reminded of their status as second class Americans.

Even though 9/11 signals to Americans that they are one people with a common culture, and African Americans, Mexican Americans, and the other hyphenated Americans were swinging their American flags in the boundedness of American patriotism, the reality is that unless there are some changes in the very structuring of America's society, racialized groups can never be a part of the majority culture. To understand this point fully, Huntington's tomato soup metaphor is important. For Huntington, America's cultural history is like tomato soup. With a tomato soup, many ingredients are blended together to add flavor without compromising the indispensable makeup of the soup.[12] Racialized ethnic groups, in this sense, are important for adding flavor to the tomato soup, or America's otherwise dull society, but they can never change the very soup itself. Another metaphor that also captures fully the exclusion of racialized ethnic group from an American cultural identity is the tossed salad that I have already examined and described in Chapter 4. Racialized groups have to continue to be a part of the minority cultures that are measured against the majority culture and are reduced to otherness. It is in the same way that maleness or heterosexuality is used as the norms against which women or homosexuals are measured and reduced to otherness. Otherness serves as a foundation for legitimizing exclusion and subordination.

Later on, Horace Kallen, in *Culture and Democracy in America* (1924), would reject the notion of the melting pot and replace it with cultural pluralism. With the development of identity politics and the politics of recognition whose present phase is multiculturalism, multiculturalism is incorrectly viewed by the antimulticulturalists as a threat to America's cultural homogeneity. To keep America's cultural homogeneity intact, there has to be a way of excluding racialized ethnic groups from America's cultural identity. Multiculturalism, in spite of being put down by the antimulticulturalists, serves the very purpose of maintaining America's cultural homogeneity.

In 1997, when President Clinton suggested that the United States needed a "third great revolution" in order to rid itself of whiteness as the core of American culture, his remark was crucial.[13] However, if multiculturalism is the tool used to carve out a new American cultural identity, it is bound to fail. A close examination of multiculturalism shows that its concern is not about incorporating racialized ethnic groups into America's cultural oneness, but to recognize and celebrate cultural manyness. America's cultural manyness should be recognized and celebrated. However, when cultural manyness is looked on as un-Americanness, the racialized implications that un-Americanness entails and assumes are brought to the forefront. It is not surprising, then, that multiculturalism is limited in dealing with America's problematic race relations. As the late feminist theorist Audre Lorde reminded us, "The master's tools would never dismantle the master's house."[14] In other words, the subaltern does not speak through multiculturalism's policy of cultural recognition and celebration. It would be difficult to argue that multiculturalism can free itself from the racialist ontology from which it has evolved. In this sense, it cannot extend itself to incorporate the nondominant cultures into America's cultural oneness. Instead, these cultures are looked as alien to the dominant culture. Cultural borders remains intact, and there are dire consequences for the border crossers.

While multiculturalism runs the risk of promoting cultural solipsism and treats different cultures as fixed and homogeneous in nature, cultures are constantly changing, internally varied, and are subject to their own distinctive logics. Crosscutting cleavages stemming from race, ethnicity, gender, class, sexuality, age, geography, religion and politics, physical and mental ability, and other identities seek some form of cultural expression, and members of each given cultural group tends to disagree on how cultural traditions and practices are expressed. In other words, culture speaks in numerous voices both internally and externally, and no cultural group is freed of the process. What happens to individuals within a cultural group that are torn between the traditions of their nondominant culture and that of the dominant culture? In some cases, they can cope with such conflicts; in other cases these conflicts are not easily resolved. Unresolved conflicts can lead to "confusion, and schizophrenia and even self-destruction."[15]

In other cases, there are individuals who do not feel attached to any culture and as such drifts among or between different cultures. Since each culture acts as a system of regulation that governs our daily activities and relations, being culturally fluid can motivate and channel us into different choices that do not coincide with the prescribed behavioral norms, which are the prerequisites for self-identification and self-actualization. Cultural fluidity can dismantle cultural borders that are intransigent and suffocating. It can open up new and creative possibilities by constructing an alternative space for a different form of cultural expression to flourish. At the same time, cultural fluidity would destabilize and challenge Frantz Fanon's notion of cultural hierarchy.

Hindu, Chinese, and some black communities have particular rituals, practices, and social conventions that are alien to members within and outside these cultural groups. For instance, Chinese New Year is celebrated by the Chinese; Diwali, the festival of light, is celebrated by Hindus; Kwanzaa is an African American Christmas tradition. Yet not all African Americans celebrate Kwanzaa. Also, for the most part, cultural beliefs and practices are subject to constrictions and changes. Religion, in some cases, can play an important role in how we are situated within these given cultural groups. Even if there are some commonalties that link religious groups, religious beliefs are, for the most part, interpreted in different ways. Depending on the geographical influence on the group, Islam or Christianity is perceived and expressed in different forms. Since culture and religion influence each other in various ways,[16] as Bhikhu Parekh puts it, "No culture is ever a fully consistent and coherent whole."[17]

Women's situatedness within culture differs from that of men's. Based on the sanctity of marriage and gender relations, women are not allowed to have more than one husband. Many women have to put up with sexual harassment and abuse from their bosses in order to keep or be promoted in their jobs. Even though the weaving of head scarves by traditional Muslim women is a complicated process and lends itself to much controversy, Muslim women are expected to wear them. I present this example only to show that it is the otherness of the "other" that is located in all cultures that multiculturalism cannot account for. In this sense, we would have to agree with Susan Moller Okin's conclusion that "multiculturalism is bad for women,"[18] and I would add that it is bad for homosexuals as well.

How people conduct themselves at funerals and births varies from one cultural group to another. Our values are not matters of impulse and coincidence. Culture has given us norms and values according to which we behave in private and in public. Each culture relies on developing, defining, regulating, and legitimizing its cultural norms and practices. The fact that we observe the practices of our given cultural group does not mean that we do so for reasons that are necessarily premised on the survival of its practices. In some cases, it is more for our own survival. Each culture has its own system of sanctions for those who do not adhere to the common norms; these sanctions take the form of exclusion, or what Nancy Fraser terms misrecognition, leading to social and psychological harms. On the other hand, even though the misrecognized members are viewed as outsiders, they are very much the insiders "in that [they] have a full understanding of the complexities and perplexities of the culture to which [they] are denied admittance."[19]

In some cases, in order to be a member of a cultural group, we are inclined to go along with the normative practices of the group even if these norms coincide with who we are as individuals. Even though these practices are not realistic options for us, because we do not want to be positioned outside the parameters of normativity and be excluded, we passively accept these constraining cultural norms that can have dire consequences for our spiritual as well as physical growth. For this reason, we have a duty to ourselves to live our lives in the best way we see fit as long as we do not infringe on the rights and duties of others. We have a right to celebrate our differences. Differences in this sense mean identities that do not conform to the cultural norms.

Differences within cultures are inescapable as well as important because they encourage and promote diversification within a cultural group. We should never be ambivalent about embracing differences within ourselves and outside of ourselves. We can learn and grow from the interaction with people who are different from us. At the expense of being misrecognized, as individuals, it is important to live with, and celebrate the differences—or, to use the words of Julia Kristeva in *Stranger to Ourselves*, the "foreignness in ourselves."[20] It is only when we recognize the differences in ourselves that we can be more eager to embrace differences of other individuals and groups. In the words of Arthur M. Schlesinger, "Freedom to differ, Justice Jackson wrote for the Court, is not limited to things that do not matter much. That would be a mere shadow of freedom. The test of its substance is the right to differ as to things that touch the heart of the existing order."[21]

Lately, "whiteness studies" scholars have argued that race is not something that only nonwhites acquire, but a distinctive feature of whites as well that has led to a close study of race and racial identity. The problem is, if we associate race with identity and attribute race to whites, whiteness seems to disengage with the troubling asymmetric power relations that is the fundamental nature of structural as well as ideological racism. Racism is not a matter of impulse and a twist of fate. America's history has proven to promote discriminatory practices that are racially instigated. Hence, we have to be careful that focusing on whiteness would not inevitably recenter rather than decenter whiteness.

Given that whiteness determines membership into the group that is positioned as dominant, nonwhites are excluded from that group. Whereas whites are raceless, nonwhites are conceived of in racial terms, and it is precisely for this reason that nonwhites cannot be racist. Labeling Judge Sotomayor, a Hispanic woman, a racist for her comments in 2001 at a conference at the University of California at Berkeley appears to me as a non sequitur. In her speech, she suggested that even though Oliver Wendell Homes and Justice Cardozo are wise men, they "voted on cases that upheld both sex and race discrimination in our society."[22] In this context, it is Sotomayor's hope that "a wise Latina woman with the richness of her experiences would more often than not reach a better conclusion than a white male who hasn't lived that life."[23] Judging from Newt Gingrich's and the other public figures' malapropic use of the word racist and their preoccupation with Sotomayor's comment about "a wise Latina woman," it is clear to me that the new Supreme Court justice's speech "A Latina Judge's Voice," which appeared in the spring 2002 edition of the *Berkeley La Raza Law Journal*, was not read carefully by Gingrich and his colleagues. Nonetheless, I think that Sotomayor is making a mere elemental point reiterating that we are all products of our socialization. Indeed, we interpret and give meanings to the world around us, for the most part, based on our situatedness whether it is our race, gender, class, sexual preferences, age, locationality, religion or political affiliations. In other words, all these identities do shape and "affect our decision."[24] However, as Sotomayor acknowledges, "we should not be so myopic as to believe that others of different experiences or backgrounds are incapable of understanding the values and needs of people from a different group."[25] By unlearning our socialization, we can strive not to be sexist, racist, classist, homophobic, or ageist.

Women, unless they are in total denial, know what it is to experience sexism; nonwhites, if they are not "dangling dolls on the strings of white puppeteers,"[26] know what it is to experience racial discrimination. It would make sense, then, that women and nonwhites, having legislative power, would work against upholding laws that are sexually and racially discriminatory. In many instances, this is not the case because of the many ways in which power functions in our society. As I have showed throughout this book, power shapes the subject and co-opts it to such an extent that it adheres and defends the discriminatory practice of the very power within which it becomes embedded. In order to appease the racist, sexist, and homophobic structures that are in place, many people from marginalized groups are elected to positions of power. In some cases, it becomes a privilege to serve and protect the interests of the power structures that are in place by becoming compliant agents of racism, sexism, homophobia, classism, and xenophobia. On the contrary, it happens that some people acquiring positions of power are dedicated to challenge the power structures and promote substantial changes that are beneficial to society as a whole.

In the end, for Clinton's "great revolution" to be envisioned, we would have to transcend multiculturalism and move in the direction of post-multiculturalism. As I have previously explicated, for postmulticulturalism to be a possibility, America's monocultural state has to be transformed into a multicultural state. Also, whiteness would have to be denormalized. Instead of focusing on the "other" and ways to incorporate the "other" into America's cultural identity, the white gaze needs to be redirected from the "other" to the self, the "them" to the "us," and the nondominant cultures to the dominant culture. This new emphasis is important if a truthful picture of America's past is to be repainted and the present reframed in which whiteness becomes denormalized. In fact, the unmarkedness of whiteness, would promote an antiracist discourse that would come along as the decentering of whiteness in order to free whiteness from its normalization. The denormalization of whiteness would present, for the most part, some challenges to America's cultural oneness by recognizing and celebrating America's cultural manyness. A careful scrutiny of America's history shows that America's cultural manyness, unlike most countries in Western Europe, is a huge part of its cultural exceptionalism. Yet this exceptionalism, in the making of America, is a neglected part of its history.

In spite of the Americanization of American culture and the de-Americanization of racialized ethnic groups, the reality of America as a diverse and multifaceted society composed of culturally and physically different groups has not disappeared, and thus America cannot be magically transformed into a homogeneous society. America continues to be, inevitably, a pluralistic society in which a variety of racial and cultural identities will continue to coexist. The media has pointed to the growth of America's racial population. A growing number of Americans do not trace their origins to Europe. In California, a multicultural and multiracial population is growing. This cultural mosaic is flourishing in America's largest cities, including New York, Los Angeles, San Francisco, Atlanta, Philadelphia, and Detroit.

Each culture, in its own way, has influenced and contributed to America's cultural identity. And at the expense of promoting America's cultural homogeneity, it would be irresponsible not to recognize America's cultural mosaic. According to Schlesinger, "The great American asylum, as Crèvecoeur called it, open, as Washington said, to the oppressed and the persecuted of all nations, has been from the start an experience in multiethnic society."[27] Also, when the Europeans landed in America, First Nations were already in America. Blacks, Chinese, and other racialized groups were in America when America became this new nation. Given that America, from its birth, is a multicultural mosaic, America needs to confess its cultural manyness, to own up to it and "deal with it."[28] Instead of promoting America's cultural oneness as multiculturalism does, this form of realization of its cultural manyness is where an American identity should begin. It was W. E. B. Du Bois who asked once what would America would be without blacks, First Nations, and other racialized groups: "Will America be poorer if she replaces brutal dyspeptic blundering with light-hearted but determined Negro humanity? Or her coarse and cruel wit with loving jovial good-humor? Or her vulgar music with the souls of the Sorrow Songs?" In the end, he tells us that "there is no true American music but the wild sweet melodies of the Negro slave; the American fairy tales and folklore are Indian and African."[29] In this sense, Schlesinger's conclusion that "to deny the essentially European origins of American culture is to falsify history"[30] is wrong. For this precise reason, we need to look at America's cultural identity through, to borrow from Ronald Takaki's book title, "a different mirror," and focus on the multiracial and multicultural influence in shaping and constructing America's cultural homogeneity. All Americans, of whatever gender, race, color, or creed, should take pride in their contribution to America's cultural makeup. However, given the present climate in America where race continues to be salient, the saliency of race has given new urgency to an old question: Can Americans be ever united? I think the greatest challenge that America faces, and will continue to face, is the problem of race. Sadly, race affects all aspects of American life—the social, political, economical, philosophical, psychological, metaphysical, and the practical. Countless examples—racial profiling, race riots, police brutality against blacks and other nonwhites, and job discrimination based on race—show that the problem of race is not going to be settled anytime soon. Yet the neoconservatives insist that we are living in a colorblind society, concluding from the election of African American president Barack Obama that America has become a postracial society.

In spite of many antiracist and antidiscrimination laws that have been successfully implemented to promote, in principle, racial equality, America continues to be overwhelmed by its race problems. On July 20, 2009, Professor Henry Louis Gates Jr. of Harvard University who is also the director of the W. E. B. Du Bois Institute for African and African American Research at Harvard was arrested by a white police officer, Sergeant James Crowley, outside of Gates's home in Cambridge after Lucia Whalen, a white woman, had notified the police that she saw two black men—one of the black men being Gates—on the porch of Gates's house. In this sense, the model minority and honorary whiteness must be seen for what they truly are: discourses for appeasing members of the nondominant groups and the pretext for setting nonwhites apart from each other. Honorary whiteness, in this sense, where the notion is that racialized groups, especially blacks, having a good economic status, allows for their more just and civil treatment by the law enforcement officers and those in power is not without significance. Blacks and other nonwhites cannot rely on their social and economic standing in their community to pilot their ways through life. Constant policing is especially hard for nonwhites as they make an effort to resolve the cognitive dissonance between their belief of "becoming white" and the reality of being nonwhite in America, especially blacks. And even if some nonwhites are eager to trace their ancestry to Europe instead of Africa, Asia, or the Middle East, the fact of the matter is that their physical appearances as nonwhite cannot be discarded. Their identities are shaped by their racialized subjectivities and are constantly contested, never settled, and never free from the surveillance of the white gaze. Nonwhites' racial identity is not a choice, but a reality that produces their cultural identity and replicates their unequal position in American society. Gates's arrest brought, once again, to the forefront the problematics of America's race relations.

With the nomination of Sotomayor as a Supreme Court judge on May 26, 2009, racism and sexism have once again, without any remorse, shown their ugly faces. The Republic Right, especially, by employing a racist discourse, has defended why Sotomayor should not have been nominated. In October 2007, a noose was found hanging on the office door of Professor Modonna Constantine, an African American Professor at Columbia University. On December 4, 2006, nooses were hanging from a tree in the school yard of Jena High School in Jena, Louisiana. These examples, and more, show that Americans continue to be divided along racial lines. Instead of the Jim Crow South, what we are seeing now are ghettoes and superghettoes located in urban spaces that are populated mostly by blacks,

Mexicans, and other racialized groups. The impact of Hurricane Katrina on the poor black population in New Orleans is more than telling of the interconnectedness of race, class, and power in America, and how this interconnectedness has shaped the daily lives of people located in these racialized enclaves.

Given that nonwhites are racialized and whites remain raceless, white Americans experience the power and privileges, "the property rights in whiteness," that are inseparable from their whiteness. Hence, the self-evident truth is that whiteness remains intact. It is a "valuable asset," a "treasured property," which, as Cheryl I. Harris points out, is protected by American law.[31] It is for this precise reason that I am calling for the denormalization of whiteness, a dislocation of its claims to ascendancy. It is only then that a multiethnic and multiracial American identity can be truly recognized and made possible. For America to celebrate a common culture that is multicultural, its monocultural state has to be transformed into a multicultural state.

Notes

Introduction

1. Michael Walzer begins his essay, "What Does It Mean to Be an 'American'?" by reminding us that there is no country called America. It is the United States of America. See Walzer 1990, 591. Also, see Richard Mayo-Smith, "Assimilation of Nationalities in the United States" (1894, 427).

2. Jim Sleeper has pointed to the "apparent sense of self-contradiction" in the term *Native American*. See Sleeper 2001, 311. In this book, I am using the term *First Nations* to mean Native Americans. First Nations is a contemporary term referring to persons registered as Indians in Canada. It also refers to the communities of Indians in Canada. In the United States, First Nations have continued to identify themselves in terms of Mohawks, Cree, Oneida, Kiowa, Navajo, Comanche, Apache, and Wichita, for example. See Martin E. Spencer, "Multiculturalism, 'Political Correctness,' and the Politics of Identity" (1994, 557–58).

3. Takaki 1993, 11.

4. Davis 1974, 34.

5. Seshadri-Crooks 1998, 357.

6. Wendy Brown 1995, 41.

7. In December 1997, at the meeting of the Modern Language Association held in Toronto, Canada, a panel titled "Frantz Fanon and/as Cultural Studies" was presented on Fanon's work. In 1999, an edited volume, *Frantz Fanon: Critical Perspectives*, was published by Routledge.

8. Mirón 1999, 85.

9. See Judith Butler, *The Psychic Life of Power*, 1997b.

10. Here, I am thinking about the hiring in American universities of nonwhite professors to teach classes in Ethnic Studies or Women's Studies. However, according to Manning Marable, education in the United States "remains a character of elitism and cultural exclusivity" (2004, 164). Also, see Laura A. Harris, "Notes from a Welfare Queen in the Ivory Tower" (2002).

11. Hurtado 1999, 227.

12. Bhabha 1998, 21.

13. Foucault 1980, 11.

14. Ibid., 142.

15. Butler, 1997b, 2.

16. Scholars include Roediger 1991, Dyer 1997, Frankenberg 1997, and Gallagher 1995. For a good overview of the ways in which whiteness is discussed by

whiteness scholars, see Eric Arnesen, "Scholarly Controversy: Whiteness and the Historians' Imagination" (2001, 6–9).

17. Hartigan 1999, 184. In addition, Cheryl I. Harris's sophisticated concept of "whiteness as property" is useful. See Harris, "Whiteness as Property" (1993).

18. Huntington 2004a, 4.

19. Osajima 2007, 140.

20. Osajima gives an example of Asian Pacific American students who confessed that they wanted to be white. One student confessed that all through his childhood, he wanted to be white. See Osajima, "Internalized Racism" (2007, 142).

21. There is a resistance that cannot bring to the forefront its resistance. In Toni Morrison's *Beloved*, a slave woman, instead of resisting the master's brand, claims it as her own, so that her child can identify her when they are separated. This means of resistance is powerful because it becomes a quiet force of empowerment. See Toni Morrison, *Beloved* (1987).

22. The major precursor of multiculturalism is cultural pluralism. Multiculturalism seeking to address the marginalization of racialized minorities cannot escape its relation with the majority.

23. Bonilla-Silva 2007, 131.

24. Intersectionality is an alternative to identity politics. See Avtar Brah and Ann Phoenix, "Ain't I a Woman? Revisiting Intersectionality" (2004). The term was first developed in 1989 by critical race theorist and legal scholar Kimberlé Crenshaw, in *Demarginalizing the Intersection of Race and Sex: A Black Feminist Critique of Antidiscrimination Doctrine, Feminist Theory and Antiracist Politics.* Crenshaw points "to the tendency of treating race and gender as mutually exclusive categories of experience and analysis . . . thus casting aside the multidimensionality of Black women's experience" by employing "a single-axis analysis" (1989, 139). Also, see Patricia Hill Collins, *Black Feminist Thought: Knowledge, Consciousness, and the Politics of Empowerment* (1999).

25. Gressgård 2008.

26. Spelman 1988, 136.

27. The employment of the term *Mexican Americans* is problematic for many scholars. For a more comprehensive reading, see Halford Fairchild 1981. Also, Alfredo Mirandé, for good reasons, has objected to the use of the term *Mexican American*. He writes: "The pervasive use of 'Mexican American' fails to recognize that 'Chicanos' is a word self-consciously selected by many persons as a symbolic positive identification with a unique cultural heritage. Many have not realized that Mexican American is analogous to Negro, or colored, whereas Chicano is analogous to black" (1985, 2–3). Chicanos materialized out of the ardent U.S. colonial policies in the Southwest. Chicanos function as a political stance against U.S. history of "internal colonialism."

28. Wendy Brown 1998, 314.

29. See Homi Bhabha, *The Location of Culture* (1994, 3).

30. Jack Miles 1992.

31. Hall 2004, 257.

32. Takaki 1979, xiv.

33. Mohanty 2004.
34. Mouffe 2005, 85.
35. Young 1990, 302.
36. Mouffe 2005, 85.
37. Laura A. Harris, 2002, 379.

Chapter 1

1. Fanon 1964, 31.
2. I am not contesting the fact that gender and race are not closely interconnected and that gender and race define nonwhite women's position in society and their access to "true womanhood." True womanhood is only accessible to white women, and despite its problematics, white women are the beneficiary of "true womanhood" and the cult of femininity.
3. Caputo and Yount 1993, 6.
4. Knowledge is applied power in the Foucauldian sense.
5. Hall 1997a, 243.
6. Claude Lévi-Strauss introduced this term in 1950.
7. Hall 1997b, 8.
8. For a more detailed reading, see Carolyn Martindale's *The White Press and Black America* (1986); Clint Wilson and Felix Gutierrez's *Race, Multiculturalism and the Media: From Mass to Class Communication* (1995); Robert M. Entman and Andrew Rojecki's *The Black Image in the White Mind: Media and Race in America* (2001); and Ian Law's *Race in the News* (2002).
9. Pinder 2007, 27.
10. Hartigan Jr. 2005, 547.
11. Jefferson 1999, 6.
12. Ibid., 11.
13. The Pioneer Fund was the foundation that gave a grant to Herrnstein and Murray for the research that produced *The Bell Curve*. One of the foundation's missions is to promote eugenics, a view that deems "genetically unfit" certain individuals or races seen as threatening the very fabric of society.
14. Hernandez 1997, 7.
15. Eitzen and Zinn 1991, 47.
16. West 1992, 24.
17. Gilroy 2000a, 12. In the end, he calls for a "deliberate and self-conscious renunciation of race as a means to categorize and divide humanity." See Gilroy, *Against Race: Imagining Political Culture Beyond the Color Line* (2000b, 17).
18. Also, see John Hartigan Jr., "Culture Against Race: Reworking the Basis for Racial Analysis" (2005). In this study, Hartigan shows how and why race matters.
19. West 2001, 155–56.
20. Torres, Mirón, and Xavier 1999, 4.
21. Miles and Torres 1999, 20. Nonetheless, to argue that races derive from particular kinds of classificatory practices is dangerous. Many eighteenth- and

nineteenth-century thinkers, that is, the founding fathers of racial classification and racial theory, including Francois Bernier (1625–1688), Carl Linnaeus (1707–1778), Comte de Buffon (1707–1788), Johann Friedrich Blumenbach (1752–1840), Georges Cuvier (1769–1832), and Arthur de Gobineau (1816–1882), attempted to classify humans by race based on physical attributes. These classifications have been totally discredited. They initiated the significance of black skin and white skin by "inventing" white and black people. For a more broad reading, see S. T. Joshi's *Documents of American Prejudice: An Anthology of Writings on Race from Thomas Jefferson to David Duke* (1999), 51–52. In a frequently cited passage, Anthony A. Appiah, in "The Uncompleted Argument: Du Bois and the Illusion of Race," (1985), takes on a different approach to the understanding of race. He argues, quite persuasively, that race has no real meaning and reference. "Race, we all assume, is, like all other concepts, constructed by metaphors and metonymy; it stands in, metonymically, for Other; it bears the weight, metaphorically, of other kinds of difference.... The truth is that there are no races: there is nothing in the world that can do all we ask 'race' to do for us" (1985, 35). Walter Benn Michaels points to the fact that some scholars refuse to recognize race altogether, claiming that race has no meaning if it is not a scientific fact. See Michaels, "Autobiography of an Ex-White Man," 1998; "Posthistoricism: The End of History" (1996); and "Race into Culture: A Critical Genealogy of Cultural Identity" (1992).

22. Wheeler 1995: A8. See also Miles and Torres 1999, 20.
23. Roediger 2002.
24. Even though racism has some negative ramifications that impact everyone, it does not mean that its impact on whites is the same as on nonwhites. Beverly Daniel Tatum draws our attention to the regrets that white students sometimes experience because of being unable to develop and maintain relationships with people of color because of social segregation (2004, 391). In other words, it is about how the privileges associated with whiteness hinder their unlived identities. I think that Mab Segrest's question, in "The Souls of White Folks," is important: "Why should anyone give up such privilege?" (2001, 43).
25. Robert Miles 1989; Sivanandan 1982.
26. Ahmed 2004.
27. Cheryl Harris 1993, 1711.
28. Frankenberg 1994, 66.
29. Recently, what is referred to as "reverse passing," happens when whites are attempting to be reclassified as blacks or Mexicans to take advantage of affirmative action programs. See Cheryl Harris 1993, n6.
30. The George W. Bush administration was one of the most diverse administrations in United States history.
31. Allen 1994, 27.
32. Wilson 1980.
33. Lott 2001, 231.
34. Hartman 2004.
35. Wilson 1980.

36. See Fausto-Sterling 2000.
37. Various forms of social exclusion included the intimidation by physical force and the threat of death that was used by the Ku Klux Klan. Today, the police officers are employing this kind of control. They are constantly socially and institutionally policing poor and colored neighborhoods. Other forms of social control exist including economical and psychological control. For a more complete reading on social control, see William H. Chafe's *Women and Equality*. In the chapter "Sex and Race: The Analogy of Social Control," he lists several concrete forms of social control (1977, 43–78).
38. van Dijk 1993, 254.
39. Some of the studies on white skin privilege include Ruth Frankenberg's *White Women, Race Matters: The Social Construction of Whiteness* (1993); Douglas S. Massey and Nancy A. Denton's *American Apartheid: Segregation and the Making of the Underclass* (1993); David R. Roediger's *The Wages of Whiteness: Race and the Making of the American Working Class* (1991); Peggy McIntosh's "White Privilege: Unpacking the Invisible Knapsack" (2007); and Michael Tonry's *Malign Neglect: Race, Crime, and Punishment in America* (1995). On a different note, the liminality of whiteness is beginning to surface. See Matt Wray, *Not Quite White: White Trash and the Boundaries of Whiteness* (2006); Neil Foley, *The White Scourge: Mexicans, Blacks, and Poor Whites in Texas Cotton Culture* (1997). Cherríe Moraga points to the fact that being a lesbian or a gay man denies access to white skin privilege. See "La Güera," in her book *Loving in the War Years* (1983). Also, Paula M. L. Moya, in "Postmodernism, 'Realism,' and the Politics of Identity: Cherríe Moraga and Chicana Feminism" (1997) has shown how whiteness functions as "contaminated privilege" for white women who are "reclaiming" their lesbianism. Homosexuals, as the unwelcome "others," most of the time, fall outside the parameters of whiteness.
40. Jacobson 1998, 21.
41. Prashad 2001, 4.
42. Aanerud 2002, 71.
43. Benjamin Franklin, in his 1751 statement, declared the Swedes and Germans to be nonwhites. The shifting notion of race is well articulated in Noel Ignatiev's 1995 book, *How the Irish Became White;* see also *The Invention of the White Race*, Vol. 1, *Racial Oppression and Social Control* (1994), by Theodore W. Allen. Also see Karen Brodkin, *How Jews Became White Folks and What That Says about Race in America* (1999). Fields reminds us that how African and Caribbean immigrants are transformed into black people is not a question with which scholars have concerned themselves. She points to the dialogic relationship between the questions of becoming black and becoming white. She writes: "The question of Afro-immigrants becoming black is the only context in which that of Euro-immigrants becoming white makes any sense at all. Blacks from the Caribbean became oriented because of racism" (2001, 51–52). However, David Roediger, in his books *Working Towards Whiteness: How America's Immigrants Became White, The Strange Journey from Ellis Island to the Suburbs* (2005) and *Towards the Abolition of Whiteness: Essays*

on Race, Politics, and Working Class History (1994), claims that immigrants distance themselves from African Americans in their effort to avoid the damages of American racism. The story is far more complicated. In 1969, Ira De Augustine Reid, in her book *The Negro Immigrant, His Background, Characteristics, and Social Adjustment, 1899–1937* (1969), shows how racism as well as cultural differences between African Americans and West Indians materialized in the conflict in Harlem, New York. Also, as Milton Vickerman notes, for West Indian immigrants, "blackness carries a certain stigma in the United States than in the West Indies." The petrifying, social reality is that West Indian immigrants deal with the realities of race, rather than an abstract notion of race (1998, x). The problematic is noteworthy here. Black immigrants cannot escape, as Fields puts it, "the consequences of the imposed identification by assertion or manipulation of their sense of self" (2001). For a more meticulous reading on Caribbean and West Indian immigrants in the United States, see Mary C. Waters, *Black Identities: West Indian Immigrant Dreams and American Realities* (2000); and Milton Vickerman, *Crosscurrents: West Indian Immigrants and Race* (1998).

44. The Phipps case was filed as *Jane Doe v. the State of Louisiana* in 1983. The *San Francisco Chronicle*, on June 23, 1983, reported that one of the results of the Phipps case was a legislative effort, which culminated in the repealing of the "one drop rule" law.

45. Piper 1992, 10.

46. Hage 2005, 186. Hage also gives an example of a Lebanese migrant already living in Australia who objected to his classification as Asian based on the "White Australia Policy" since the 1880s. The migrant, in 1911, made an argument in a letter addressed to the Australian prime minister about his whiteness/Europeanness. See Ghassan Hage, "White Self-racialization as Identity Fetishism: Capitalism and the Experience of Colonial Whiteness" (2005, 185). According to the U.S. Department of Immigration Directive Number 15, commonly known as the Race and Ethnic Standards for Federal Statistics and Administrative Reporting, "people of European, Northern African, and Middle Eastern origin are collectively designated 'White.'" Mostafa Hefty, an Egyptian living in the United States, in an article in the November 1990 issue of *Jet Magazine* ("Black 'White' Man Challenges Federal Race Identity Law"), contested the U.S. Department of Immigration directive. He stated: "My complexion is as dark as most Black Americans. My features are clearly African. . . . Classification as it is done by the United States government provides Whites with legal ground to claim Egypt as a White Civilization. . . . We are fools if we allow them to take this legacy from us." See Sohier A. Morsy, "Beyond the Honorary 'White' Classification of Egyptians: Societal Identity in Historical Context" (1994, 178). Besides, this classification is especially troubling in post-9/11 America. While many people of Northern African and Middle Eastern backgrounds are victims of discriminatory practices at airports, many reports have pointed out that more white people are victims of these practices.

47. Seshadri-Crooks 1998, 354.

48. For more on the "wages of whiteness" as more than economical, see Charles
    W. Mills, "Racial Exploitation and the Wages of Whiteness" (2004, 43–45).
49. At the beginning, when passing was introduced, it was about blacks who
    looked white who had decided to integrate into the white community. What
    this meant was a break, either temporary or permanent, from the African
    American community "in order to enjoy the privileges of the dominant
    white community." See G. Reginald Daniel's chapter 3, "White by Definition:
    Multiracial Identity and the Binary Racial Project" (2002). In James Weldon
    Johnson's *The Autobiography of an Ex-Colored Man* (1990), Johnson plays
    a Negro who is passing. Incapable of convincing himself that he is white,
    unwilling to accept the harsh consequences of being black in a racist society,
    he rather, or so it seems, relegates himself to moving between racial spaces.
    He becomes what Everett V. Stonequest, borrowing Robert E. Park's phrase,
    calls "the marginal man." The marginal man is "living and sharing intimately
    in the cultural life and traditions of two distinct people" (1935, 3). He feels
    rejected by both cultures. For Merrill Horton, nonetheless, "passers seem to
    return to a culture which they knew in childhood" (1994, 42). See also Nella
    Larsen, *Passing* (1929).
50. Mullen 1994, 72.
51. Harris 1993, 1711.
52. Fields 2003, 1404.
53. Omi and Winant 1994, 72.
54. Alcoff 1998, 12.
55. hooks 1995, 152–53.
56. Roediger 1991, 5.
57. For a Marxist approach to race and ethnicity, which emerged in the 1970s and
    1980s, see Robert Miles, "Racism, Marxism, and British Politics" (1988); and
    Racism and Migrant Labour (1982).
58. Fields 2001, 48.
59. Eitzen and Zinn 1991, 6.
60. Brah 1996, 18.
61. The dichotomization of the superior and the inferior frequently forms the
    basis for racial, gender, and sexual categorizations to be instituted within
    America's society.
62. The work of Fanon's *The Wretched of the Earth* (1963) and Paulo Freire's *The
    Pedagogy of the Oppressed* (2000) both represent a significant case in point in
    such an intertext, for both authors, in their dissimilar ways, are concerned with
    how the oppressed class can free itself of oppression. For Fanon, decolonization
    was the answer. Samia Nehrez, extrapolating from Fanon's concept of decoloni-
    zation, explains it succinctly. The following quote is extracted from *Black Looks:
    Race and Representation*, by bell hooks: "Decolonization . . . continues to be an
    act of confrontation with a hegemonic system of thought; it is hence a process of
    considerable historical and cultural liberation. As such, decolonization becomes
    the contestation of all dominant forms and structures, whether they be linguis-
    tic, discursive, or ideological. Moreover, decolonization comes to be understood

as an act of exorcism for both the colonized and the colonizer. For both parties it must be a process of liberation: from dependency, in the case of the colonized, and from imperialist, racist perceptions, representations, and institutions which, unfortunately, remain with us to this very day. . . . Decolonization can only be complete when it is understood as a complex process that involves both the colonizer and the colonized" (1992, 1).

For Friere, "the oppressors[/colonizers], who oppress, exploit, and rape by virtue of their power, cannot find in this power the strength to liberate either the oppressed[/colonized] or themselves. Only power that springs from the weakness of the oppressed will be sufficiently strong to free both" (2000, 44).

63. In New York City, for example, according to a New York Police Department internal study, 90 percent of their stops involve nonwhites. See Bonilla-Silva and Ray 2009, 177.

64. Fields 2001, 48.

65. See Sanford F. Schram, "Putting a Black Face on Welfare: The Good and the Bad" (2003); Kenneth J. Neubeck and Noel A. Cazenave, *Welfare Racism: Playing the Race Card Against America's Poor* (2001); and Jill Quadagno, *The Color of Welfare: How Racism Undermined the War on Poverty* (1994). Welfare racism is dated back to the implementation of mothers' pensions. For a more thorough reading on mothers' pensions, see Mimi Abramovitz's *Regulating the Lives of Women: Social Welfare Policy from Colonial Times to the Present* (1996).

66. Higginbotham 1996, 185.

67. Clinton 1996.

68. On the other hand, the persistence of race as a social construct "can translate rapidly into more-digestible claims that race is false consciousness; this insistence has worked well for conservative rhetoricians. Turning constructivism into voluntarism, these conservatives attack ameliorative strategies and social programs for racially disadvantaged groups." See Seshadri-Crooks 1998, 354.

69. Dyer 1997, 3.

70. Fanon 1963, 88.

71. Hamilton 1996.

72. Hattam 2007, 9.

73. Robert Miles traces the origin of the term *racialization* to Fanon's *The Wretched of the Earth*, which helps to shape and influence his own development of the concept of racialization. For Fanon, racialization is linked to colonialism and European domination. Michael Banton's influential book *The Idea of Race* (1978) also was instrumental in Miles's development of the concept. For an in-depth understanding of the development of the concept of racialization, see Robert Miles, *Racism* (1989, 73–77).

74. Two interrelated problems faced Jews. They had the advantage of being white and not only white but Jewish. For a good discussion of how Jews became white, see Eric L. Goldstein, *The Price of Whiteness: Jews, Race, and American Identity* (2006); and Karen Brodkin, *How Jews Became White Folks and What That Says about Race in America* (1999).

75. For a good reading of how immigrants became white, see David R. Roediger's *Working Towards Whiteness: How America's Immigrants Became White* (2005). Also, Ruth Frankenberg, in *White Women, Race Matters: The Social Construction of Whiteness*, points out that in various times in United States history, Jews, Italians, and Latinos "have been viewed as both "white" and "nonwhite"(1993, 11).

76. Jacobson 1998, 14.

77. Nayak 2005, 142.

78. Omi 1996, 179.

79. Nayak 2005, 144.

80. Omi 1996, 180.

81. Takaki 1993, 204.

82. For a more detailed discussion of these institutions and their basis, see Loïc Wacquant, "From Slavery to Mass Incarceration: Rethinking the 'Race Question' in the US" (2002).

83. Wacquant 2002.

84. Bhattacharyya, Gabriel, and Small 2002, 17.

85. Anthias and Yuval-Davis explain at length why second-wave feminism, including liberal, Marxist, socialist, and radical feminists, did not deal with the issues stemming from racism (1993, 105). In the end, feminists sought to concentrate on women's own experience and explicitly avoided any claims of being what Judith Butler views as "objective, abstract or universal" (1999, 87). Butler's glaring criticism in her pathbreaking work *Gender Trouble, Feminism and the Subversion of Identity* shows that the necessity to base feminist generalized action on women's identities has detoured the need for an analysis of the "multiplicity of cultural, social, and political intersections in which the concrete array of 'women' are constructed" (1999, 14). What is important is what constitutes an identity as a "woman"? It was an unrelenting attempt by second-wave feminists to give context and legitimacy to the category "woman" and its programmed set of normative idealizations instead of accounting for the various lived experiences of women in these social locations. More recently, many feminists analyze gender oppression in the same way they do race, ethnicity, class, and sexuality.

86. Anthias and Yuval-Davis 1993, 80.

87. Higginbotham 1996, 255.

88. Ibid., 185.

89. Hammonds 2004, 301.

90. Butler 1993, 2.

91. Mohanty 1991, 12–13.

92. Brah and Phoenix 2004, 82.

93. Nayak 2005, 145.

94. Foucault 1978, 96.

95. Fanon 1964. Also, see Horace M. Kallen, *Cultural Pluralism and the American Idea: An Essay in Social Philosophy* (1956).

96. Derbyshire 2000.

97. Fields 2001, 48.
98. Ibid., 50.
99. The Muslims as the "problem" can also be interpreted as a racial problem and with this racialization follows an emphasis on lookism, "the Middle Eastern look."
100. Miles 1989, 43.
101. Given the modalities of these discursively constituted identities, a concern, I think, is whether, as some scholars have argued, one's class transcends these identities. What comes to mind is the work carried out by William Julius Wilson, an African American sociologist, in *The Declining Significance of Race*. Wilson contends that racial oppression of African Americans was a central characteristic of preindustrial America. Because of civil rights legislation and expanded economic opportunities for blacks, the contemporary system of stratification today can be best questioned from the vantage point of class relations. Even though Wilson omits, by default, to mention that, to use the words of Higginbotham, "capital and labor agree sufficiently to exclude blacks from union membership and from more than a marginal place within the emerging industrial working force" (Higginbotham 1996, 190). Nonetheless, a further contextualized reading of Wilson, I think, reveals that he does not disprove of the soundness of race as a determining factor of social outcomes. Yet he makes clear that the inequalities that blacks are facing reflect their working class status rather than racial chauvinism and unfairness. How valid is Wilson's argument? Is there a coupling of blacks' working class status and their race? Higginbotham in her penetrating discussion of the metalanguage of race reminds us that in a society such as the United States where "racial demarcation is endemic to [its] laws and economy. . . . [Class] identity is inextricably linked to and even determined by racial identity" (1996, 234). In her analysis lies the nub of the subject matter I am emphasizing, which is the synchronizing of race and class. Job ceilings and discriminatory practices recruit blacks into "black job ghettoes" characterized by low-paid, poor working conditions, and little or no opportunity for advancement. In other words, as Michael Omi and Howard Winant put it, "when boom became bust and liberal welfare statism moved rightwards the majority of blacks came to be seen, increasingly as the 'underclass' and 'welfare dependent'" (1994, 12). Thus, explanations of blacks' poverty "that invoke a culture of poverty have allowed [many social scientists] to ignore poverty's institutional causes." See Newfield and Gordon 1996b, 79.
102. Hall 2004, 258.
103. Nayak makes this observation in reference to contemporary British popular culture, as evident in "Zadie Smith's novel *White Teeth*, the music of Talvin Singh, or Keith Piper's artistic installations of Black-British cultural identity" (2005, 144).
104. Aronowitz 1999, 308.
105. For a careful reading of what Hall calls the "fundamental mapping of culture between high and low, [which] has been charted into four symbolic domains"

(2004, 258), Hall directs us to Peter Stallybrass and Allon White's book *The Politics and Poetics of Transgression* (1986).

106. Nayak 2005, 144.
107. Stallybrass and White 1986, 2.
108. McDowell 2001, 24. The poetry of Shelley, the plays of Samuel Beckett, and the writing of Jean-Claude Germain "have all been examined in recent criticism with a Bakhtimian frame and with a straightforward and unproblematical enthusiasm for his conceptual schema" (Stallybrass and White 1986, 12).
109. Nayak 2005, 143.
110. Ibid., 146.
111. Ibid., 144.
112. Hall 2004, 260.
113. Cohen 1992, 62.
114. Seshadri-Crooks 1998, 353.
115. Bonnett 1999, 201.
116. Lorde 1984.
117. Liz MacMillan, in "Lifting the Veil of Whiteness: Growing Body of Scholarship Challenges Racial 'Norm,'" 1995, writes about "the new whiteness studies." For various essays on whiteness studies, see Michele Fine et al., *Off White: Readings On Race, Power, and Society* (1997).
118. For good discussions of white racial identity, see Andrew Hacker's *Two Nations: Black and White, Separate, Hostile, Unequal* (2003); and David Roediger's *Towards the Abolition of Whiteness: Essays on Race, Politics, and Working Class History* (1994), and *The Wages of Whiteness: Race and the Making of the American Working Class* (1991).
119. Fields 2001, 49.
120. Ibid.
121. See Omi and Winant, *Racial Formation in the United States from the 1960s to the 1990s* (1994).
122. Kallen 1956. See also Myrdal 1962.
123. Kallen 1915, 220.
124. In the midst of Nazism and a heightened form of racism in Germany, as early as 1942 Ashley Montagu, in his classical book *Man's Most Dangerous Myths: The Fallacy of Race*, points out that "like Buffon, Blumenbach recognized, as did Linnaeus, that all human beings belong to a single species and considered it merely convenient to distinguish between certain geographically localized groups of humankind. Thus, when, in the eighteenth century, the term assumed a classificatory value, it was understood that that value was purely arbitrary and no more than a simple convenience" (1997, 100). "Two centuries later, most Americans, nevertheless, continue to think, speak, and act as if 'race' were the basis of a meaningful taxonomy" (David Goldstein 2007, xvi).
125. In 1976, black Muslims are either members of the American Muslim Mission or the Nation of Islam. Those belonging to the latter group follow in the footsteps of Elijah Muhammad.
126. Omi and Winant 1994, 55.

127. The other paradigms of race as "unstable and politically contested" and occurring in multiple social contexts that Omi and Winant talk about are class and nation. See Omi and Winant 1994, 24–47.
128. Frankenberg 1994, 64.
129. Post 2001b, 14.
130. For a complete account of Proposition 209, see Birgit Brander Rasmussen et al., "Introduction" (2001b, 4–7). Several other states have passed legislation similar to Proposition 209.
131. Sadly so, Dr. Martin Luther King's observation that we should "be judged by the content of [our] character rather than the color of [our] skin" is conveniently misconstrued to mean the promotion of a meritocracy. Dr. King himself understood, quite well, how race is adversative to the notions of meritocracy in the United States. What precisely concerns me, among other things, is that a meritocracy is far from equipped to take on the transforming and reshaping of racial or sexual hierarchy, for example. Many advocates for blindness passionately assert that America, from the beginning of its history, has been based on colorblindness to ascriptive and signifying categories including race, gender, and sexuality. For example, the Declaration of Independence states, "We hold these truths to be self-evident, that all men are created equal, that they are endowed by their Creator with certain unalienable rights that among these are Life, Liberty, and the pursuit of Happiness." The Fourteenth Amendment to America's Constitution extended this view by stating, "No State shall deprive any American citizen of the right to Life, Liberty, and Property without due process of the law." The law, it is argued, is based on blindness. The law forbids discriminatory practices based on immutable distinctiveness including race, gender, and physical handicap. For example, Title VII of the Civil Rights Act of 1964 prohibits employment discrimination on the basis of "race, color, religion, sex, or national origins," which is to say, not judging the worth of a person based on superficial characteristics like race, gender, or religion. For the blindness advocates, the point of rendering such factors irrelevant is to "target" and eliminate "stubborn but irrational prejudice." Some blindness advocates even postulate that Dr. Martin Luther King Jr.'s speech "I have a dream" envisions a color-blind United States of America, and he, in his multicolored speech, wholeheartedly looked forward to the day when race, for example, would not determine one's fate, "when one is evaluated by the content of one's character rather than the color of one's skin." And within the blindness discourse, King's vision of a colorblind society is extrapolated and extended to include gender as well as sexuality and the physical disability of a person.
132. Butler 2001, 79.
133. Foucault 1991, 75.
134. Butler 1995a, 137.
135. Hartigan 1999, 186.
136. duCille 1994, 607.
137. Hartigan 1999, 184.

138. Foley 1997, 5.
139. Ibid., 7.
140. See Derrick A. Bell, "Property Rights in Whiteness—Their Legal Legacy, Their Economic Costs" (1995); and Cheryl I. Harris, "Whiteness as Property" (1993).
141. Morrison 1993, 59. Whiteness and nonwhiteness are codeterminant and cannot exist without each other. The idea is appropriated from Ralph Ellison's *Invisible Man*, in which he draws our attention to the dialogic relations between blackness and whiteness in America.
142. Multiculturalism was developed in the middle of 1970s to diversify the education system. See Newfield and Gordon 1996b, 77.
143. Newfield and Gordon 1996b, 77.
144. Schlesinger 1998, 72.
145. Ibid., 80–81.
146. Nathan Glazer signed the controversial New York State Sobol Report in 1991. Thomas Sobol, who was then New York State's Commissioner of Education, in 1991, issued the ninety-seven-page report, which was written by a task force comprised of twenty-four educators and distinguished scholars. For a more in depth understanding of the report, see "Mr. Sobol's Planet," in *The New Republic*, July 15 and 22, 1991.
147. Glazer 1991, 22.
148. D'Souza 1991b.
149. Schlesinger 2002, 258.
150. Kymlicka 2007, 99.
151. Prashad 2000, 6. Also, on the development of the model minority thesis, see Dana Y. Takagi, *The Retreat From Race: Asian-Americans Admissions and Racial Politics* (1992, 58–59).
152. Eller 1997, 251.
153. hooks 1992, 1.
154. Some "Asian Americans" have accepted the model minority thesis and are hopeful that eventually they will be accepted by the white majority. Others are suspicious of the model minority thesis and tie it to an analysis of systematic racism. See Mia Tuan, *Forever Foreigners or Honorary Whites? The Asian ethnic Experience Today* (1998, 8).
155. Prashad 2000, 6
156. Bhabha 1994, 64.
157. Mullen 1994, 74.
158. I am not arguing here that racial category is fixed and stable. In fact, Omi and Winant point to the instability of racial categorization. Japanese Americans, according to the U.S. census, are no longer within the group "Oriental"; they are now included in the category of "Asian and Pacific Islanders." See Omi and Winant 1994, 14–15.
159. Essed 2005, 229.
160. Gunew 1997, 26.

Chapter 2

1. Vaughan 1989, 317.
2. Ibid.
3. Ramsay 1809, 22.
4. Nelson examined the writings of white authors including Cotton Mather, James Fenimore Cooper, William Gilmore Simms, and Catherine Maria Sedgwick. See Dana Nelson, *The World in Black and White: Reading "Race" in American Literature, 1638–1862* (1994); and Shelley Fisher Fishkin, "Interrogating 'Whiteness,' Complicating 'Blackness': Remapping American Culture" (1995, 432).
5. Huntington 2004b, 53.
6. Harris 1993, 1716.
7. Jacobson 1998, 21.
8. Gouverneur Morris's remarks before the Constitutional Convention posed the essential question whether slaves were men or property. He asks, "Upon what principle is it that slaves shall be computed in the representation? Are they men? Then make them Citizens & let them vote? Are they property? Why then is no other property included?" See George Washington Williams, *History of the Negro Race in America from 1619 to 1880* (1885, 419). In the end, southern delegates held that slaves should be computed in determining a state's share of the direct tax burden. The northern delegates' point of view was exactly the opposite. In order to attend to the problem that chattel slavery posed, the slaves had to be partly humanized. A compromise was reached whereby three-fifths of the slaves were to be counted in apportionment of representation and in direct taxes among the states. The contradictory character of slaves as property and persons was exemplified in the Representation Clause, Article 1, Section 2, of the Constitution. See Cheryl I. Harris, "Whiteness as Property" (1993). While slaves were three-fifths of a person, First Nations were excluded from representation.
9. Later on, Mexicans, enclosed by America's expanding border, would become foreigners in their own land.
10. Patterson 1982, 176.
11. Harris 1993.
12. When cases were brought against slaves in court, slaves were treated as people. In *State v. Cynthia Simmons and Laurence Kitchen*, the court stated that "Negroes are under the protection of the laws, and have personal rights, and cannot be considered on a footing only with domestic animals." Cases against crimes committed by slaves were tried, which challenged the concept of slaves as chattels. A Georgia court in 1854, in *Baker v. State*, stated, "It is not true that slaves are only chattels, . . . and therefore, it is not true that it is possible for them to be prisoners . . . the Penal Code has them in contemplation . . . in the first division . . . as persons capable of committing crimes; and as a . . . consequence . . . as capable of being prisoners." For if a slave was indicted and was killed or thrown in prison, the master was compensated for the loss of his property. For a more thorough discussion of the ambivalence pertaining to

slaves as chattels and as persons and the many cases of the trials of slaves, see Arnold A. Sio, "Interpretations of Slavery: The Slave Status in the America" (1965, 301–2). For example, in Virginia, the May 1723 Act is titled "An Act directing the trials of Slaves, committing capital crimes; and for the more effectual punishing conspiracies and insurrections of them; and for the better government of Negros, Mulattoes, and Indians, bond or free."

13. Fields 2003, 1398.
14. Patterson 1982, 173.
15. Ibid.
16. Fields 1990, 201.
17. A profound discussion of race and racial slavery can be found in Lerone Bennett's *The Shaping of Black America: The Struggles and Triumphs of African-Americans, 1619–1990s* (1975); see also Theodore W. Allen, *The Invention of the White Race*, Vol. 1: *Racial Oppression and Social Control* (1994).
18. Gossett 1963, 31.
19. Cox 1948, 104.
20. Eric Williams 1944, 7.
21. This book was republished by Cambridge University Press in 2004. For other alternative views on the issues of slavery and racism, see Joseph Boskin, *Into Slavery: Racial Decisions in the Virginia Colony* (1976); Alden T. Vaughan, "The Origins Debate: Slavery and Racism in Seventeenth-Century Virginia" (1989); and Daniel L. Noel, ed., *The Origins of American Slavery and Racism* (1972).
22. Jordan 1968, 75.
23. Degler 1959, 58.
24. Degler 1959.
25. Handlin and Handlin 1950. Also see Thomas F. Gossett, *Race: The History of an Idea in America* (1963).
26. Degler 1959, 50.
27. Fields 1990, 104.
28. Degler 1959, 51.
29. Edmund S. Morgan has argued that whites in seventeenth-century Virginia, for example, had a more flexible understanding of race and did not equate race with slavery. In many instances, whites and blacks would join together to oppose the rules of the plantation owners. See Morgan, *American Slavery, American Freedom: The Ordeal of Colonial Virginia* (1975).
30. Takaki 1998, 35.
31. Allen 1994, 17.
32. Allen 1997, 178.
33. Fields 1990, 104.
34. Degler 1959, 49.
35. Handlin and Handlin 1950, 199.
36. Degler 1959, 52.
37. Sio 1965, 304.
38. Eric Williams 1944, 20.
39. Goodell 1968, 10.

40. Vaughan 1989, 315.
41. Jordan 1968, 91.
42. Ibid., 599. In Jordan's introductory chapter, "First Impressions: Initial English Confrontation with Africans," he offers an in-depth analysis of the English prejudice against blacks before 1619 (1968, 5–43). In the end, Jordan concluded, "Rather than slavery causing 'prejudice,' or vice versa, they seemed rather to have generated each other. Both were, after all twin aspects of a general debasement of the Negro. Slavery and 'prejudice' may have been equally cause and effect" (1968, 80).
43. See Alden T. Vaughan, "The Origins Debate: Slavery and Racism in Seventeenth-Century Virginia" (1989, 323).
44. See David Brion Davis, "Constructing Race: A Reflection" (1997, 12).
45. Degler 1959, 52.
46. Outlaw 2004, 165.
47. Butler 1993, 2.
48. Degler 1959, 56.
49. Bennett 1975, 73–74.
50. Ibid.
51. Gossett 1963, 30. See Richard Mayo-Smith, "Assimilation of Nationalities in the United States" (1894, 429–32).
52. The assumption of whites' racial purity gave rise to Nazi Germany.
53. Takaki 1993, 205.
54. Morrison 1993, 47.
55. Gilman 1985, 30.
56. Yancy 2004b, 7.
57. Takaki 1979, xiv.
58. See Frederick Douglass, *Narrative of the Life of Frederick Douglass, an American Slave* (1982); see also Harriet Jocobs, *Incidents in the Life of a Slave Girl* (1973).
59. For further reading on *Hudgins v. Wright*, see Adrienne D. Davis, "Identity Notes, Part One: Playing in the Light" (1997, 232–37); and Robert Cover, *Justice Accused, Anti-Slavery and the Judicial Process* (1975, 51–55).
60. For a further discussion of the enslavement of First Nations, see chapter 4 of Almon Lauber's *Indian Slavery in Colonial Times Within the Present Limits of the United States* (1969).
61. Boskin 1976, 4.
62. Degler 1959, 61.
63. See Michel Foucault, *Discipline and Punish: The Birth of the Prison* (1979).
64. Foucault 1982, 212.
65. Moore and Williams 1942, 351.
66. Also, with the signing of the Treaty of Guadalupe Hidalgo in 1848, after the Mexican-American War (1846–1848), the people who occupied Mexico at that time found themselves "foreigners" in their "native land."
67. Cheryl I. Harris 1993, 1716.
68. Ibid.

69. Cheryl I. Harris 1993.
70. Bell, Higgins, and Suh 1997, 107.
71. Kallen 1915a, 191.
72. Ibid., 191. America, for Kallen in 1915, was no longer a homogeneous society as it had been in colonial times. Thanks to immigration, it is now a "commonwealth of nationalities—Irish, Germans, Scandinavians, Jews, Poles, and Bohemians." For Kallen, the problem that America faced, then, was "how to get order out of this cacophony." In other words, how would America govern these diverse groups of people with "a chorus of many voices singing a different tune." See Kallen 1915c, 217.

    We would see later, in Kallen's *Culture and Democracy in America*, published in 1924, that blacks' presence in constructing America's culture, for sure, was furthermost from Kallen's mind, let alone First Nations, Chinese, Mexicans, or other racialized groups. John Higham, in *Send These to Me: Jews and Other Immigrants in Urban America* (chapter 10, 1975) offers a good critique of Kallen's failure to recognize the impact of African Americans on America's culture as a whole.
73. Jordan 1968, 339.
74. In 1944, Gunnar Myrdal would point to America's dilemma, where the exclusion of nonwhites, especially blacks, from the American creed would have serious repercussions for America. Eventually, the creed would have to extend to include nonwhites, especially blacks. Myrdal was optimistic that this would pave the way for racial equality and the integration of blacks and other racial minorities into the mainstream of American life. See his *An American Dilemma: The Negro Problem and Modern Democracy* (1962). Integration is one thing, but equality is quite another thing.
75. Myrdal 1962, xliii.
76. Kim 2000, 179.
77. See Claire Jean Kim, "Clinton's Race Initiative: Recasting the American Dilemma" (2000, 182).
78. Tocqueville 1999, 192.
79. Kallen 1915a, 192.
80. Arnesen 2001, 7.
81. Goldberg 1994b, 5.
82. Franklin 1961, 234.
83. Ibid.
84. Ronald Takaki has drawn our attention to the racism of Benjamin Franklin. See Takaki, *A Different Mirror: A History of Multicultural America* (1993); *Iron Cages: Race and Culture in Nineteenth-Century America* (1979); *From Different Shores: Perspectives on Race and Ethnicity in America* (1987).
85. Ford 1904–5, 317.
86. Bergh 1905.
87. Ibid.
88. Tocqueville 1945, 374.
89. Yancy 2004b, 14.

90. Taylor 1994, 138.
91. Takaki 1993, 47.
92. Ibid., 88.
93. Morrison 1993, 38.
94. Until 1722, in South Carolina, slave masters were required by law to have their female slaves running away for the fourth time "severely whipped, . . . branded on the left cheek with the letter R, and her left ear cut off." See Winthrop D. Jordan, *White Over Black: American Attitudes Toward the Negro, 1550–1812* (1968, 112).
95. Davis 1983; Cannon 2004, 415.The status of children depended on the mothers' condition, according to the law of 1662.
96. Davis 1983, 7.
97. Patterson 1982, 176.
98. Fields 2003, 1398.
99. Heideking 1997, 104.
100. Jacoby 2004b, 298.
101. The sociologist David Riesman is credited with introducing the word *ethnicity*. See Roediger's *Working Towards Whiteness* (2005, 26).
102. Crèvecoeur 1926, 43. Michel-Guillaume Jean de Crèvecoeur wrote *Letters from an American Framer* under the name J. Hector St. John de Crèvecoeur.
103. In *The History of South Carolina*, David Ramsay's views about the American people contrasted greatly with those of Crèvecoeur. Ramsay writes, "So many and so various have been the sources from which Carolina has derived her population, that a considerable period must elapse, before the people amalgamate into a mass possessing an uniform national character. This event daily draws nearer; for each successive generation drops a part of the peculiarities of its immediate predecessors. The influence of climate and government will have a similar effect. The different languages and dialects, introduced by the settlers from different countries, are gradually giving place to the English. So much similarity prevails among the descendants of the early emigrants from the Old World, that strangers cannot ascertain the original country of the ancestors of the present race" (1809, 22–23).
104. Kallen 1924, 218.
105. Gleason 1980, 32.
106. Ibid.
107. Lipsitz 1995. This period is extremely important in chronicling how Jews, for example, became white. Even before then, various groups were defined as white through historical, political, and economic conditions. See Michael Omi and Howard Winant, *Racial Formation in the United States from the 1960s to the 1990s* (1994).
108. Huntington 2004a, 46.
109. Smith 1988, 236.
110. See *Newsweek*, March 4, 1985, 25.
111. Schlesinger 1998, 34.
112. Ibid.

113. Huntington 2004a, 53.
114. Takaki 1993, 7.
115. Kerber 1997, 834.
116. See Annals of Congress, *Abridgements of Debates of Congress, 1789–1856* (1857, 184).
117. Ibid., 553–58.
118. Jacobson 1998, 25.
119. This clearly contradicted George Washington's idea of America being open to all immigrants. He wrote in 1783, "The bosom of America is open to receive not only the Opulent and respectable Stranger, but the oppressed and persecuted of all Nations and Religions." In 1870, the law of naturalization was extended to "aliens of African nativity, and to persons of African descent." Quoted in Arthur Mann, "From Immigration to Acculturation" (1992, 75).
120. "A foreign miners' tax of $20 monthly was in practice a 'Mexican Miners' Tax.'" Miners who came from Mexico as well as Mexicans living in America (American citizens) had to pay the taxes. See Ronald Takaki, *A Different Mirror: A History of Multicultural America* (1993, 178).
121. Jacobson 1998, 31.
122. Cheryl I. Harris 1993, 1776. The Naturalization Act of 1795, which continued to deny American citizenship to white women and all nonwhite people, superseded this act. Naturalization was not extended to blacks until 1870. East Asians and Filipinos could not naturalize until 1952, with the passage of the McCarran-Walter Act, which restricted immigration into the United States.
123. Yet, free blacks were only free in the sense that they were not slaves. Many free blacks were not allowed to live in certain states. Slaves who were emancipated had to move to other states and could never return. Many restrictions were placed on free blacks exercising their rights. See Leon F. Litwack, *North of Slavery: The Negro in the Free States, 1790–1860* (1965).
124. Blacks could not obtain citizenship until 1870; First Nations until 1924; Chinese after 1943, and Japanese after 1952. However, whites were never barred from claiming citizenship.
125. The Missouri Compromise, which outlawed slavery in the territories, was looked at by the court as unconstitutional. Because Congress had dishonored "property rights and substantive due process rights" of citizens, the Missouri law had to be upheld. For a more in-depth reading of the Dred Scott case, see Benjamin C. Howard, Report of the Decision of the Supreme Court of the United States *and the opinions of the judges thereof* in the Case Dred Scott versus John F. A. Stanford (1857, 9, 13–14, 15–17, 60). The ruling in this case led, to a great extent, to the Fourteenth Amendment in 1868. "All persons born or naturalized in the United States and subject to the jurisdiction thereof, are citizens of the United States and of the States wherein they reside." Nonetheless, as Thomas F. Gossett observed, "the Negro would not be allowed to be a citizen" (1963, 277).
126. Van Evrie 1863, 91.
127. Ibid., 90.

128. Dr. J. H. Van Evrie popularized the scientific basis of white supremacy. In his 1863 book, *Negroes and Negro Slavery*, he drew on such human attributes as skin color, hair, physique (figure), features, and brain as "facts that separate the races" (1863, 132) and would, in the bitter end, determine power relations. In the end, he asked "what are [blacks'] natural relations to whites? He wrote, "if the natural relations that men bear to each other are thus misunderstood in Europe, it may well be supposed that they are wholly ignorant of the natural relations of races, and without even the remotest conception of the relations that naturally exist between white men and negroes [in America]" (187). And if scientific evidence was not enough, he turned his attention to Christianity and blazingly claimed, "God has made the negro different from, and inferior to the white man" (189).

129. Many critics have taken on the responsibility of analyzing the embedded nature of race, and lately the discussion of whiteness, in literary texts. See Toni Morrison, *Playing in the Dark: Whiteness and the Literary Imagination* (1993); and Rebecca Aanerud, "Fictions of Whiteness: Speaking the Names of Whiteness in U.S. Literature" (1997). For example, Aanerud draws from Kate Chopin's *The Awakening* to show how, for white women, whiteness is often expressed as vulnerability, innocence, and purity. In this novel, purity is associated with "the rebirth of her true self." See Aanerud 1997, 34.

130. See Mark Train, *The Adventures of Huckleberry Finn* (1962, chapter 32).

131. See Hemingway 1990.

132. Ellison 1989, 101.

133. For a detailed reading of Section I–IV of Article XIX, see Section 95 in the *Congressional Quarterly's Guide to the U.S. Supreme Court* (1979, 631).

134. For a thorough reading of the Chinese Exclusion Act of 1882 see Sucheng Chan, *Asian Americans: An Interpretive History* (1991b); see also Sucheng Chan, *Entry Denied: Exclusion and the Chinese American Community in America, 1882–1943* (1991a). With the implementation of the Page Law, in 1875, Chinese women were barred from entering the United States.

135. The Scott Act of 1888 allowed Chinese officials, teachers, students, merchants, or travelers for pleasure or curiosity to enter the United States. See Wu Ting-fang, *America Through the Spectacles of an Oriental Diplomat* (1914, 48).

136. Higham 1994, 25.

137. See Dan Caldwell, "The Negroization of the Chinese Stereotype in California" (1971).

138. Roediger 1994, 75.

139. Morrison 1993, 85.

140. Ibid. Ann Pellegrini, in *Performance Anxieties: Staging Psychoanalysis, Staging Race*, puts Fanon's *Black Skin, White Mask* to task in that "the femininity" he "puts into play is white femininity" (1997, 109).

141. See Alexis de Tocqueville, "Democracy in America" (1999).

142. It is from this very basis that American democracy was later looked on by scholars, including Gunnar Myrdal, as compromising America's creed: liberty, equality, and property for all, because of the way nonwhites, especially

blacks, were treated in America. See Myrdal's masterpiece, *An American Dilemma: The Negro Problem and Modern Democracy* (1962). In 1968, the Kerner Commission Report would point to the fact of institutionalized racism. This was old news. Frederick Douglass, already, had observed the inconsistency that existed between America's democratic values and its racial practices. One of the main tasks of a democratic government is to make sure that all members of a society are protected from harsh treatment from individuals, groups, or even the state.

143. Jordan 1968, 169.
144. Allen 1994, 14.
145. Daniel 2002, 400.
146. Ibid., 41.
147. Other readings include Gerald Early's edited volume, *Lure and Loathing: Essays on Race, Identity, and the Ambivalence of Assimilation* (1993).
148. Cheryl I. Harris 1993, 119.
149. The Codes authorized blacks to acquire and own properties, marry, make contracts, sue and be sued, and testify in courts in cases involving only blacks. However, some of the more severe features of the Codes included written evidence of employment and being subjected to arrest by any white person. For a detailed reading of the implementation of the Black Codes during Reconstruction, see Eric Foner, *Reconstruction: America's Unfinished Revolution, 1863–1877* (1988, 199–201).
150. Katz 1986, 19.
151. The former confederate states are Alabama, Arizona, Arkansas, Florida, Georgia, Kentucky, Louisiana, Maryland, Mississippi, Missouri, North Carolina, South Carolina, Tennessee, Texas, Virginia, and West Virginia.
152. Smith 1999, 329.
153. Foner 1988, xx.
154. Bailey 1982.
155. Wacquant 2002, 45.
156. Bailey 1982.
157. Surely, Bailey must have been aware that on August 22, 1831, it was the slave Nat Turner who, for two days in Virginia, led seventy other slaves in a ferocious insurrection where sixty whites were found dead. Also, about 189,000 black men were recruited from the slave states to fight in the Civil War. Abolitionists including Frederick Douglass (himself a slave), David Walker, and Henry Highland were black men and some of the most forceful opposing voices against the conditions of the slaves. In addition, black women who were ex-slaves fought to improve the conditions of black women in America. Anna Julia Cooper published *A Voice from the South by a Black Woman of the South*, and Sojourner Truth, an ex-slave, famous for her speech, *Ain't I a Woman*. I suppose, then, that Bailey's claim about blacks, masquerading as "truth," is astonishingly numb to the otherwise countless evidence. In sum, Bailey's valorization of the Black Codes as tools to curb the capriciousness of ex-slaves is precisely what Nancy Fraser refers to as a "false antithesis." The Black Codes

were in place to circumscribe blacks' freedom, to paralyze them from upward socioeconomic mobility, and to reinforce oppressive ideologies.

158. Casey 2003, 51.There were two conditions by which slaves were freed. The first was that a slave had to prove that he or she had a maternal ancestor who was First Nations, because, in the United States, slavery "descended matrilineally," freeing white men from their responsibilities for children borne by black women. Second, the slave had to provide proof that the maternal ancestor was not enslaved between 1679 and 1705 because during this period First Nations were slaves. See Adrienne D. Davis 1997, 232.

159. Takaki 1993, 163. Also, quoted in Stephen Spencer, "The Discourse of Whiteness: Chinese-American History, Pearl S. Buck, and the Good Earth" (2002).

160. Litwack 1965, 234.

161. Wacquant 2002, 49.

162. Massey and Denton 1993, 30.

163. Litwack 1965, 120.

164. Takaki 1993, 110.

165. Homer Plessy was a mulatto. On June 7, 1892, he bought a first class ticket on the East Louisiana Railway for a trip from New Orleans to Covington, Louisiana. The first class tickets provided seats in the "white section" of the train. Plessy was convicted of violating the 1890 statute. His appeal was useless. The Supreme Court of Louisiana upheld the conviction.

166. George Washington Cable draws our attention to the state of the public accommodations for Negroes. He said that "the negroes compartment on a train was in every instance and without recourse, the most uncomfortable, uncleanest, and unsafest place . . . [and these conditions] are a shame to any community pretending to practice public justice" (quoted in Gossett 1963, 275).

167. Harlan 1997, 34.

168. Ibid., 58.

169. Wu Tingfang, *America Through the Spectacles of an Oriental Diplomat*, recounted in his 1914 memoir how he was treated at the Washington, DC, train station. Although a porter led him to the "white area" of the station, he was not sure whether he belonged in the "white area."

170. Du Bois 2003, 113.

171. Ibid., 115.

172. Kymlicka 2007, 116.

173. Wu 2002, 19. African American film maker Spike Lee, in his 1989 movie *Do the Right Thing*, used the same scenario in the film. See Wu, *Yellow: Race in America Beyond Black and White* (2002, 19).

174. See Kobena Mercer, "'1968': Periodizing Postmodern Politics and Identity" (1991, 426–27).

175. Allen 1994, 32.

Chapter 3

1. Keating 1995, 904.
2. In America, we know that to be black or nonwhite amounts to a specific place in the society, where nonwhites are deemed as inferior. It is "natural" for whites to be dominant and "natural" for nonwhites to be subordinate. Reinforcing these distinctive categories was once achieved by grounding social and cultural differentiation of whites and nonwhites within a scientific fact-based approach to racial "truths." Today the focus is on "culture," which has become a metonym for "race."
3. Lane 1998b, 12.
4. Dyer 1988, 46.
5. For an in-depth reading of whiteness invisibility, see Dyer 1997 and Frankenberg 1993. Recently, many scholars have engaged in "whiteness studies." For a detailed discussion on "whiteness studies," see Chapter 5 in this book.
6. Frankenberg 1997, 1.
7. Ahmed 2004.
8. Butler 1990, 140.
9. hooks 1992, 170.
10. Barthes 1972, 11.
11. Also, see W. E. B. Du Bois's *Darkwater: Voices from Within the Veil*, in the chapter titled "The Souls of White Folk," where he draws our attention to how the visibility of whiteness is played out when whites become aware of how very visible they are to blacks and other people of color. This knowledge, Du Bois points out, makes whites feel "embarrassed" and in the end "furious" (1969, 29).
12. See Loïc Wacquant, "Slavery to Mass Incarceration" (2002).
13. Stephanson 1989, 276.
14. West 2001, 28.
15. Frankenberg 2001.
16. Dyer 1997, 44.
17. For a good analysis of otherness, see Henry Louis Gates, *"Race," Writing, and Difference* (1985); and Kwame Anthony Appiah and Henry Louis Gates, *Identities* (1985).
18. Roediger 1991.
19. Devos and Banaji 2005, 449.
20. Mann 1992, 68.
21. Constance Perin, in her book *Belonging in America: Reading Between the Lines* (1988), chooses to interview white women whom she kept referring to as "Americans."
22. Schlesinger 1945.
23. Handlin 1951.
24. Devos and Banaji 2005, 449.
25. Roosevelt 1915.
26. Schlesinger 1998, 41.

27. See Marcela Sanchez, "Demonizing Dual Citizenship" (2005).
28. Cheryan and Monin 2005, 720.
29. Fanon writes about the various stages of resistance by the subordinate groups. In the end, armed resistance through violence may be the only solution. This is in fact the only way in which the oppressed groups can be liberated. For a careful reading see Fanon, "On Violence," in his book, *The Wretched of the Earth* (1963). Also, Freire, in *The Pedagogy of the Oppressed*, writes about liberation. For him, if the oppressed group is to be liberated, it would have to be liberated by itself because the oppressor cannot find it in himself to liberate the oppressed.
30. Harris 1993, 1714. For an additional reading on white supremacy, see George M. Fredrickson, *White Supremacy: A Comparative Study in American and South African History* (1982).
31. Fields 2001, 49. Theorists of American political culture, from Alexis de Tocqueville to Louis Hartz, have perceived racism as an anomaly. See Rogers M. Smith, *Civic Ideals: Conflicting Visions of Citizenship in U.S. History* (1997, 15–27).
32. Bell 1995, 75.
33. Hacker 2003, 4.
34. Roediger 1994, 13.
35. Dyer 1988, 45.
36. See Aanerud, "The Legacy of White Supremacy and the Challenge of White Antiracist Mothering" (2007).
37. Seshadri-Crooks 1998, 358.
38. Ibid.
39. Ingram 2001, 161.
40. Sáenz 1997, 94.
41. Crèvecoeur 1926, 41.
42. Gleason 1980, 33.
43. Schwarz 1995, 65.
44. McLaren 1994, 61.
45. Devos and Banaji 2005, 449.
46. Fine et al., 1997, xi.
47. See Thierry Devos and Mahzarin R. Banaji, "American = White?" 2005; Sapna Cheryan and Bonît Monin, "Where are you *really* from? Asian Americans and Identity Denial" (2005); Frank H. Wu, *Yellow: Race in America Beyond Black and White* (2002); Ronald Takaki, *A Different Mirror: A History of Multicultural America* (1993).
48. Devos and Banaji 2005, 462.
49. Ibid., 463.
50. Ibid., 451.
51. Takaki 1993, 1.
52. See Takaki 1993.
53. Ibid., 66.
54. Goldberg 1994b, 4.

55. Huntington 2004b, 40.
56. Schwarz 1995, 62.
57. Montgomery 2000, 15.
58. Wu 2002, 20.
59. The question, can there be a black European? is important in the sense that "black European" is considered paradoxical.
60. Mullen 1994, 71–72. Eduardo Bonilla-Silva points to the fact that the United States "is evolving into a complex tri-racial stratification system" (2002, 4). In the 2000 census, people were allowed to check more than one race for themselves or family members, further obscuring the social practice of racial identification. See G. Reginald Daniel, *More than Black? Multiracial Identity and the New Racial Order* (2002); David Parker and Miri Song, *Rethinking "Mixed Race"* (2001). A report presented by the U.S. Census Bureau, in August 2008, shows that racialized ethnic groups who are now classified as racial minorities would, by 2042, count for the majority of the population in the United States. What does this mean for whiteness? In South Africa, there was a small white population who were invested with power to implement an apartheid premised on the institutionalization of whiteness.
61. Cheryan and Monin 2005, 717.
62. West 1992, 24.
63. Wu 2002, 80.
64. McLennan 2001, 397.
65. Deaux 2008, 938.
66. The Pulitzer Prize–winning novel *The Good Earth* was written by Pearl S. Buck in 1931. The review in the *New York Times Book Review* claimed that "one tends to forget, after the first few pages, that the persons of the story are Chinese and hence foreign." What is more daunting, according to Stephen Spencer, is that the book, in itself, was never criticized for its racist contents—"how the Chinese as a racial 'other' in opposition to whiteness" was constructed. See Spencer, "The Discourse of Whiteness: Chinese-American History, Pearl S. Buck, and the Good Earth" (2002).
67. Wu 2002, 79.
68. Ibid.
69. A sign of not belonging or a feeling of belonging in another country is a form of "prescribed otherness." See Rey Chow, *Women and Chinese Modernity: The Politics of Reading Between West and East* (1991).
70. Fanon 1967, 109.
71. Pellegrini 1997, 111.
72. Mileczarek-Desai 2002, 127.
73. Fanon 1967, 111.
74. Du Bois 2003. The various meanings of the double consciousness have energized many scholars. Most recently, Paul Gilroy, in "Multiculture, Double Consciousness and the 'War on Terror,'" states that W. E. B. Du Bois drew the idea of the double consciousness "from Hegel and refined it during his life-changing time as a student in Germany. It was shaped, I think by his sociological

reading of the problem of assimilation as it arose there during the nineteenth century. In his hands, the concept was tailored both to specific U.S. conditions and to a deeply Hegelian view that presented black American consciousness of freedom as a world-historic force: a precious gift to the whole world from the descendants of the modern slave" (2005, 439).

75. See Franz Fanon's *Black Skin, White Mask* (1967).
76. Du Bois 2003, 5.
77. Citrin 2001, 294.
78. See Devos and Banaji 2005; and Cheryan and Monin 2005.
79. Dyson 1999, 220.
80. Yuval-Davis 1999, 112.
81. Hall 1989, 16.
82. Parry 1987, 29.
83. Schlesinger 1998, 18.
84. Moreton-Robinson 2008, 85.
85. Schlesinger 1998, 20.
86. In 1997, Connerly, a conservative, criticized President Clinton's advisory panel on race for not including him in the discussion on affirmative action. See Steven A. Homes, "Race Panel Excludes Critics of Affirmative Action Plans" (1997a).
87. Connerly 1998, 3. Also quoted in Samuel Huntington, *Who Are We: The Challenges to America's National Identity* (2004, 6).
88. Connerly 1998, 3.
89. For a detailed reading of whiteness as property that one possesses, see also George Lipsitz, *The Possessive Investment in Whiteness: How White People Profit from Identity Politics* (1998); Thomas K. Nakayama and Judith N. Martin, eds., *Whiteness: The Communication of Social Identity* (1999).
90. The Hispanic identity is quite ambiguous. Hispanics are classified as an ethnic group instead of a race, with "cultural designators: a person of Mexican, Puerto Rican, Cuban, Central or South American or other Spanish culture origin. In this definition, Hispanics can be of any race" (Powell 1999, 144). "In the 1990 Census, half of all Hispanics reported themselves as white, a little under half as 'other,' and a few as black, native, or Asian" (Bonnett 1999, 211).
91. Citrin 2001, 294.
92. Broder 1998, A21.
93. Sáenz 1997, 69.
94. Fanon 1963, 203.
95. Bhabha 1987, 120.
96. Eller 1997, 251.
97. Du Bois 2003, 5.
98. Yamada 1992.
99. Anzaldúa 1987, 194.
100. McLaren 1994, 60.
101. Bhabha 1994.
102. Ahmed 2008, 13.

103. Giroux 1994, 335.
104. Johnson 1990, 14.
105. Fanon 1967, 8.
106. In some cases, the marginalized groups are able to refuse to go along with some of the obligatory norms and values of the dominant group. These resistances may take the form of Black Nationalism, for example. In addition, many black women, including Sojourner Truth and Ida B. Wells-Barnett, were not silent. In spite of the physical as well as psychological violence experienced by those who spoke against the status quo, Truth, in 1851, spoke at the Women's Rights Convention in Akron, Ohio, about equal rights for women. On May 2, 1892, Wells-Barnett's editorial in the *Memphis Free Speech* exposed the cult of the chaste southern white women by suggesting that white women willingly engaged in sexual entanglement with black men. See Wells-Barnett, *The Red Record* (2005, 8). Also, Wells-Barnett, Angelina Weld Grimké, and Church Terrell spoke out against lynching albeit they were threatened on several occasions by the KKK for refusing to remain silent. Wells-Barnett traveled throughout the United States and went to Britain twice to speak about anti-lynching activities.
107. King 1964, 93.
108. See Bonilla-Silva and Ray 2009, 177.
109. Cheryan and Monin 2005, 728.
110. McKinney 2003, 47.
111. Glazer 1997, 86.
112. Morrison 1993, 9.
113. Hacker 2003, 4.
114. Morrison 1993, 47.
115. Frankenberg 1994, 64.
116. Frankenberg 1993, 202.
117. Frankenberg 1994, 64.
118. Haney-López 1996, 3.
119. McKinney 2003, 42.
120. Kantrowitz and Wingert 2003, 35.
121. Hamilton 1996, 173.
122. See Roediger, *Colored White: Transcending the Racial Past* (2002, 10).
123. McLaren 1994, 59.
124. Griffin and McFarland 2007, 122.
125. Agamben 1998, 8.
126. Morrison 1993, 47.
127. I must add without pausing that a formidable reality for racialized ethnic groups is that democratic citizenship encompasses only political rights, the right to vote and to hold office, but its wider unease is its fundamental failure to extend itself to include social and economic equalities that strengthen individual/group autonomy.
128. Bonilla-Silva 2000, 188.
129. Fishkin 1995, 431.

130. Chafe, Gavins, and Korstad 2001, xxiii–xxiv.
131. Fishkin 1995, 432.
132. See Moreton-Robinson, "Writing Off Treaties: White Possession in the United States Critical Whiteness Studies Literature" (2008); Mills, "Racial Exploitation and the Wages of Whiteness" (2004); Outlaw, "Rehabilitate Racial *Whiteness?*" (2004); Baldwin, *Collective Essays* (1998); Morrison, *Playing in the Dark: Whiteness and the Literary Imagination* (1993); Mullen, "Optie White: Blackness and the Production of Whiteness" (1994); Cheryl I. Harris, "Whiteness as Property" (1993); hooks, *Black Looks: Race and Representation* (1992).
133. For further discussion, see Roediger, *Colored White: Transcending the Racial Past* (2002, 5).
134. Auster 1994, 61.
135. Gates 1992, 174.
136. Clinton 1992, 64–65. Clinton was criticized for lacking opponents on affirmative action. See three of Steven A. Homes's articles in the *New York Times*: "Race Panel Excludes Critics of Affirmative Action Plans" (1997a, A24); "Clinton Panels on Race Relations Is Itself Biased, Gingrich Says" (1997b, A30); and "Conservative Voices Enter Clinton's Dialogue on Race" (1997c, A24).
137. Obama 2004.
138. Giroux 1994, 339.
139. Thernstrom and Thernstrom 1997, 10.
140. See the *New York Times*, "Barack Obama's View on Race" (2008).
141. For a detailed discussion of whiteness as one of the reasons for the persistence of racism, see Bhabha, "The White Stuff" (1998); Dyer, *White* (1997); Bonnett, "'White Studies': The Problems and Projects of a New Research Agenda" (1996); Ignatiev and Garvey, *Race Traitor* (1996); Frankenberg, *White Women, Race Matters: The Social Construction of Whiteness* (1993); and Roediger, *The Wages of Whiteness: Race and the Making of the American Working Class* (1991).
142. The colonial model of white domination was carried out, in part, by its cultural reproduction in the minds of both the colonizers and the colonized, even though the colonized, in many ways, resisted their subordinate position forced and imposed on them by the oppressive structures. See Fanon, *The Wretched of the Earth* (1963).
143. Freire 2000, 49.
144. Fanon 1967, 16.
145. See *Bill Clay: A Political Voice at the Grass Roots* (2004).
146. Du Bois 2003, 5.
147. The "double consciousness," on the other hand, provides valuable insights into knowing "the ways" of the oppressor.
148. Fanon 1967, 110.
149. Yancy 2004c, 111.
150. Patterson 2000, 6. Also, see William Julius Wilson, *The Declining Significance of Race* (1980); and Richard J. Payne, *Getting Beyond Race: The Changing American Culture* (1998).

151. See Orlando Patterson, *Slavery and Social Death: A Comparative Study* (1982).
152. See Milton Friedman, *Capitalism and Freedom* (1962, 108–10).
153. Bhabha 1987, 123.
154. Angelou 1993.
155. Bonilla-Silva 2007, 135.
156. Pinder 2007, 29.
157. Austin 1963. The other type of performative act is the illocutionary act, which brings into being certain effects as its results; by saying something, a certain effect follows. See Judith Butler's *Excitable Speech: A Politics of the Performative* (1997a, 3). When speeches do not do what they say, they are nonperformative. For a good discussion on nonperformative speech acts, see Sara Ahmed, "The Non-Performativity of Anti-racism" (2005).
158. Hurtado 1999, 226.
159. For a detailed reading on the Patriot Act, see Vijay Sekhon, "The Civil Rights of 'Others': Antiterrorism, the Patriot Act, and Arab and South Asian Americans Rights in Post 9/11 American Society" (2003).
160. Bonnett 1996, 147.
161. Omi and Winant 1994, 72.
162. Frankenberg 1993, 6.
163. Bonilla-Silva and Ray 2009, 177.
164. Cox 1948, 336.
165. Seshadri-Crooks 1998, 355.
166. For a good discussion, see Bonilla-Silva, *White Supremacy and Racism in the Post Civil Rights Era* (2001).
167. Gilroy 2000b, 34.
168. Hartigan 2005, 548.
169. Mills 1997.
170. Lewis Mumford Center 2001.
171. See Payne 2001, 149.
172. Wilson 1980. Also, see Thernstrom and Thernstrom, *America in Black and White: One Nation, Indivisible* (1997); and Patterson, "Race Over" (2000).
173. See D'Souza, *The End of Racism: Principles for a Multiracial Society* (1995).
174. Bonilla-Silva and Ray 2009, 177.
175. Hartigan 2005, 545. Hartigan, in "Culture Against Race: Reworking the Basis for Racial Analysis," points to the dialectic interplay "between race and culture" (2005, 544).
176. Giroux 1994, 335.
177. Culturalism is based on biological determinism that constructs and shapes the racialized subject positions. Historically, biological determinism was used to explain nonwhites' inferiority.
178. Mamdani 2004, 32.
179. Gilroy 2005, 439.
180. The latest rendition of white superiority is propagated in Richard J. Herrnstein and Charles Murray's bell curve theory. There are other similar studies

that also generated similar notions of racial superiority and the "genetics" of intelligence. See Robert Wright, *The Moral Animal: Evolutionary Psychology and Everyday Life* (1994, 345–63); Thomas Sowell, *Race and Culture: A World View* (1994, 156–85); and Rushton J. Philippe, *Race Evaluation and Behavior: A Life History Perspective* (1995).

181. González Casanova 1965, 33.
182. Fanon 1967.
183. Gressgård 2008.
184. Giroux 1994, 340.
185. Parry 1987, 31.
186. Bhabha 1987, 122.
187. Cornell 1995, 155.
188. Morrison 1987, 216. Quoted also in Cornell 1995, 155.
189. Giroux 1994, 336.
190. Schlesinger 1998.
191. Huntington 2004a, 19.
192. For writings on the new racism, see Étienne Balibar, "Is There a Neo-Racism?" in *Race, Nation, Class: Ambiguous Identities,* by Étienne Balibar and Immanuel Wallerstein (1992); see also Penelope Ingram, "Racializing Babylon: Settlers' Whiteness and the New Racism" (2001). For various explanations of the new racism, see Eduardo Bonilla-Silva, "This Is a White Country": The Racial Ideology of the Western Nations of the World-System" (2000, 189–91). This new racism is also referred to as color-blind racism.

Chapter 4

1. For commentaries on interculturalism, see Bhikhu Parekh, "Multiculturalism" (2007); Paul Gilroy, *After Empire: Melancholia or Convivial Culture* (2004); and Avtar Brah, *Cartographies of Diaspora: Contesting Identities* (1996).
2. Phillips 2007, 15.
3. Kymlicka 2007, 98.
4. Goldberg 1994a, 24.
5. Phillips 2007, 71.
6. Miller 2004, 15.
7. Taylor 1994.
8. Nancy Fraser tells us that the "identity model starts from the Hegelian idea that identity is constructed dialogically, through a process of mutual recognition. According to Hegel, recognition designates an ideal reciprocal relation between subjects, in which each sees the other both as its equal and also as separate from it" (2000, 109). In the end, for Fraser, this model denies its Hegelian premise by "assuming that identity is dialogical, constructed via interaction with another subject, it ends by valorizing monologism—supposing that misrecognized people can and should construct their identity on their own" (112). Walter Benn Michaels, in "Race into Culture: A Critical Genealogy of Cultural Identity," does not completely reject the Hegelian notion of identity

and allows for the very possibility that identity construction bears the mark of one's social relation to others, who are "in some respects like us and other respects different," and shapes our commitment to the ontology of the "other," "to the identity of 'we' and 'they' and the primacy of race" (1992, 682). However, for Michaels, in the end, racialized identity presents some challenge to Fraser's "identity model" because cultural identity is viewed through race.

9. Because of the way in which gender is constructed, a woman's situatedness is different depending on class, sexuality, age, religion, geographical location, and physical and mental abilities within each of these cultures. In the end, women experience subordination because of patriarchy's horrible predisposition.

10. Taylor 1994, 32.

11. For some, diversity is an irritation rather than a positive addition to their lives. See Karyn D. McKinney, "'I feel "Whiteness" When I Hear People Blaming Whites': White as Cultural Victimization" (2003, 51–52).

12. Glazer 1997, 12.

13. For further reading on affirmative action, see *Dissent*, "Affirmative Action Under Fire" (1995, 461–76).

14. Benhabib 1996, 17. In Seyla Benhabib's edited volume published in 1996, *Democracy and Difference: Contesting the Boundaries of the Political*, according to Benhabib, the contributors have not employed the term *multiculturalism* for the precise reason that it has lost its meaning. See note 9.

15. Okin 1999, 10.

16. Gilroy 2005, 432.

17. Wieviorka 1998, 881.

18. Fanon 1967, 31.

19. Sechi 1980, 444.

20. Michaels 1992, 683.

21. Fanon 1967, 36.

22. Michaels 1992, 684–85.

23. Newfield and Gordon 1996b, 77.

24. See Nathan Glazer, *We Are All Multiculturalists Now* (1997); and "In Defense of Multiculturalism" (1991); Todd Gitlin, *The Twilight of Common Dreams: Why America Is Wracked by Culture Wars* (1995); Arthur M. Schlesinger, *The Disuniting of America: Reflections on a Multicultural Society* (1998); Dinesh D'Souza, *Illiberal Education: The Politics of Race and Sex on Campus* (1991b); Allan Bloom, *The Closing of the American Mind* (1987); and Eric D. Hirsch Jr., *Cultural Literacy: What Every American Needs to Know* (1987).

25. Alarcón 1996, 139–40.

26. Because Canada is recognized as a bilingual nation, multiculturalism has for a long time existed in Canada. In 1965, the Royal Commission on Bilingualism and Biculturalism made some recommendations that multiculturalism replace the bicultural policy and take into account the ethnic diversity in Canada instead of focusing on only the two main groups, the British and the French. Multiculturalism became an official policy in Canada in 1971. About ten years later, in 1982, it was incorporated into Canada's Constitution in the form *Canada's*

Charter of Rights and Freedom. Language, culture, education, and equality of opportunities to employment and promotions were now protected from any discriminatory practices. The idea was to envision Canada as a mosaic, which makes it comparatively different from the United States whose emphasis was on the melting pot. See Joseph Garcea, "Provincial Multiculturalism Policies in Canada, 1974–2004: A Content Analysis" (2006); and Michel Wieviorka, "Is Multiculturalism the Solution?" (1998, 884). Charles Taylor, the Canadian philosopher, for one, saw the fundaments of multiculturalism as building on the established liberal principles of equal respect, "as a logical extension of the politics of dignity" (1994, 68) as the prerequisites for individual freedom. According to political theorist Will Kymlicka, in *Multicultural Citizenship: A Liberal Theory of Minority Rights*, freedom "provides its members with a meaningful way of life across the full range of human activities, including social, educational, religious, and economic life" (1995, 76). Is this freedom that Kymlicka talks about attainable and sustainable for every member of a democratic society? Are there any preconditions? Are the preconditions achievable for every individual? Since "men" are not angels, as James Madison warns in his Federalist Paper number 10, can individual rights be respected and defended juridically?

27. Multiculturalism as a policy was implemented in Australia in the 1970s. For a more detailed reading, see Michel Wieviorka, "Is Multiculturalism the Solution?" 1998.

28. McLennan 2001, 396.

29. In 1992, the United Nations adopted a Declaration on the Rights of Persons Belonging to National or Ethnic, Religious and Linguistic Minorities. International organizations including the United Nations Educational, Scientific and Cultural Organization (UNESCO), the International Labor Organization, and the World Bank have developed norms on the rights of minorities. See Will Kymlicka, *Multicultural Odysseys: Navigating the New International Politics of Diversity* (2007, 4).

30. Kymlicka 1995, 6.

31. hooks 1992, 167.

32. Cultural authenticity has gone too far. For instance, a young Laotian American was abducted from California State University, Fresno where she was employed, and was raped. Her assailant, a Hmong immigrant, declared to the court that he did nothing wrong because what he did is a part of his custom for choosing a bride. The court agreed that the man has to be judged according to his custom. Accordingly, the man was sentenced to only 120 days in jail. Also, in California, a Japanese American woman was abandoned by her husband. Consequently, she drowned her two children and was rescued from drowning herself. Later, she explained that in Japan her action would be acceptable because of the "time-honored custom of parent-child suicide." She was acquitted of murder charges. In New York, a Chinese man murdered his wife because she was unfaithful. According to him, the murder of his wife is an acceptable "Chinese custom that has the function of removing the shame brought upon him by an unfaithful spouse." He was acquitted of murder

charges. See Seyla Benhabib, *The Claims of Culture: Equality and Diversity in the Global Era* (2002, 87). In instances of domestic violence, whereas a white woman is directed to get an injunction in order to keep her violent husband away from her, in the case of a Chinese woman, for example, the social worker, or police officer, silently tells her "it is your culture."

33. Minh-ha 1989, 89.
34. See Nathan Glazer, *We Are All Multiculturalists Now* (1997); Todd Gitlin, *The Twilight of Common Dreams: Why America Is Wracked by Culture Wars* (1995); and Ronald Takaki, *A Different Mirror: A History of Multicultural America* (1993).
35. McLaren 2001, 411.
36. Marcuse 1965.
37. Hage 1994, 21.
38. Derrida 2003, 27.
39. Hage 1994, 24.
40. The Nation of Islam is condemned for its "un-American" activities and is viewed especially by the power elite as a threat to America's culture where Protestantism is antonymic to Islamism. Black Muslims' capacity to unlearn voluntary obedience and to engender resistance to the inexpressible oppressive and despotic status quo is making the mainstream nervous. This was clear when in 1957, Hinton Johnson, a member of the Nation of Islam, was beaten and then arrested by a police officer. Malcolm X and other members of the Nation of Islam demanded proper medical attention for Johnson, and as a result the black Muslims were viewed by the police departments and federal investigators as dangerous. Even though structural, societal oppression is dehumanizing because the oppressed can lose the ability to see themselves as individual human beings, the black Muslims find widespread expression in a long history of political oppression and unequal practice toward blacks. See Frederick Knight, "Justifiable Homicide, Police Brutality, or Governmental Repression? The 1962 Los Angeles Police Shooting of Seven Members of the Nation of Islam" (2004).
41. The regime change is supposed to bring about and promote democracy. Other nations, including Britain, France, and Australia, have positioned themselves globally as the defenders of democracy. Muslim nations are conceived as opposed to Western democracy and freedom.
42. Glazer 2004, 64.
43. Turner 2004, 465.
44. Wendy Brown 2006, 2.
45. The post September 11 era has unmasked the tolerance discourse in many ways. Tolerance is upfront in its many efforts to regulate ethnic, racial, gender, sexual, and religious identities.
46. Fields 2003, 1402.
47. Žižek 1993, 223.
48. Young 1990, 33.
49. See Bhabha, *The Location of Culture* (1994, 53–56).
50. McLennan 2001, 395.

51. Hacker 2003, 9.
52. Angela Y. Davis 1996, 41.
53. And even if we think of America as no longer a melting pot, but as a tossed salad, it is important that we examine its components. A salad, which comprises several ingredients, is colorful and beautiful, and it is to be consumed. However, certain ingredients have been demonstrated to be indigestive. Blacks and other racialized ethnic groups represent the indigestive ingredients within America's cultural identity in this culinary metaphor. See Angela Y. Davis, "Gender, Class, and Multiculturalism: Rethinking 'Race' Politics" (1996, 45).
54. Mandel 2005.
55. Angela Y. Davis 1996, 45.
56. hooks 1992, 61.
57. Bhabha 1994, 34.
58. Minh-ha 1989, 89–90.
59. Raz 1994, 177.
60. Kymlicka 1995, 83.
61. For a good reading, see Gloria E. Anzaldúa, *Borderlands La Frontera: The New Mestiza* (1987).
62. Outlaw 2004, 165.
63. McLaren 1994, 60.
64. Hacker 2003, 9.
65. Kallen 1915b, 192.
66. Kymlicka 1995, 89. See also Kymlicka, *Liberalism, Community, and Culture* (1989). Kymlicka, Okin, and Taylor are more in favor of group rights for First Nations, for example. However, group rights should not be guaranteed to immigrants who have, after all, decided to come to America. In most cases, nonwhites in America are viewed as immigrants, as new comers. Bhikhu Parekh is more in favor of group rights for immigrants. See Parekh, *Rethinking Multiculturalism: Cultural Diversity and Political Theory* (2000, 102–3).
67. Antiessentialist usage of cultural identity has been expressed within race and postcolonial studies. See Gayatri C. Spivak, "Can the Subaltern Speak?" 1988; Stuart Hall, "Ethnicity: Identity and Difference" (1989); Homi K. Bhabha, *The Location of Culture* (1994); and Chandra Talpade Mohanty, "Cartographies of Struggle" (1991). Other studies that have employed antiessentialist usage of identity include feminist studies and gay and lesbian studies. See Judith Butler, "Collected and Fractured: Response to Identities" (1995b); Kobena Mercer, "'1968': Periodizing Postmodern Politics and Identity" (1991); and Gloria E. Anzaldúa, *Borderlands La Frontera: The New Mestiza* (1987). Jean-Luc Nancy, in "Cut Throat Sun," has suspected Anzaldúa of essentializing Mexican culture in her employment of *mestizaje* on the basis of race (1994, 123). Cited also in Norma Alarcón, "Conjugating Subjects in the Age of Multiculturalism" (1996, 131). Alarcón's findings contrast with Nancy's. For the former, Anzaldúa is not "essentialist at all" (132). "'Mestiza consciousness' reveals a 'tolerance for contradictions,' paradox, and ambiguity because the term 'mestiza' projects a confluence of

conflicting subject positions that keep 'breaking down the unitary aspect of each new paradigm'" (134).

68. The "minorities within minorities" point to the many ways in which internal oppression is practiced within groups where not only women are oppressed, but other groups as well, such as homosexuals and the poor. For a more thorough reading, see Anne Phillips, *Multiculturalism without Culture* (2007).

69. McLennan 2001, 402.

70. Okin 1999.

71. Harding 1991, 179.

72. This phrase is extracted from Sebastian Poulter's writing, "Ethnic Minority Customs, English Law, and Human Rights." He uses "clash of culture" to explain nonwhite women immigrants' experiences working and living within the urban British culture (1987, 590).

73. Michaels 1992, 684.

74. For a good summation of the main elements of the "new racism" that permeates the globe, see Eduardo Bonilla-Silva, "'This is a White Country': The Racial Ideology of the Western Nations of the World-System" (2000, 189–90).

75. D'Souza 1995.

76. Wilson 1980.

77. Hurtado 1999, 226.

78. In term of cultures, Will Kymlicka has drawn a distinction between assimilation and integration where what he calls minority cultures becomes a part of a particular society in a very distinct manner. This is an example of "liberal multiculturalism" where there is public recognition of minority cultures. See Kymlicka, *Multicultural Citizenship: A Liberal Theory of Minority Rights* (1995). Also, see Joseph Raz, "Multiculturalism: A Liberal Perspective," in his *Ethics in the Public Domain: Essays in the Morality of Law and Politics* (1994, 170–92). Because minority cultures are distinct from the dominant culture, individual rights within these cultures are not adequately protected. Hence, there is an emphasis on group rights or privileges that are not necessarily granted to individuals within the groups. Susan Moller Okin argues that group rights are cultural rights (1999); therefore, group rights are necessary if individuals are to stand up against assimilation that undermines the sense of identity they derive from being members of a respected racialized community. In the end, because rights are based on a male prerogative, women are overwhelmingly disadvantaged. Okin shows the tension between feminism and multiculturalism. She suggests that multiculturalism has created a measurable backlash for feminism in the sense that it threatens women's rights which feminists have worked so hard to accrue. In many ways, she argues, group rights are antifeminist. See Susan Moller Okin, *Is Multiculturalism Bad for Woman* (1999); see also Raz, "Multiculturalism: A Liberal Perspective," in his 1994 book, *Ethics in the Public Domain*. The emphasis on group rights clearly contrasts with the liberal theory that focuses on individual rights, which Charles Taylor labels "procedural liberalism," a notion which, he says, is "inhospitable to differences because it insists on uniform application to rules defining those rights . . . and

is suspicious of collective goals" (1994, 60). Also, see Raz, "Multiculturalism: A Liberal Perspective" (1994).

79. Later on assimilation was looked on as a response to the racial problems imposed by racism. E. Franklin Frazier, Gunnar Myrdal, and Daniel Patrick Moynihan would suggest that only assimilation would rid blacks of the "pathological" part of their culture. See Frazier, *The Negro in the United States* (1969); Myrdal, *An American Dilemma: The Negro Problem and Modern Democracy* (1962); and Glazer and Moynihan, *Beyond the Melting Pot* (1970).

80. Myrdal 1962.

81. Sowell 1981, 184.

82. Park 1930, 282.

83. Yuval-Davis 1999, 118.

84. Parekh 2000, 338.

85. Powell 1999, 151.

86. Gates 1992, 109.

87. Laura A. Harris 2002, 372.

88. Wilkins 2000, 338.

89. Aanerud 2007, 22. A report was published in 1992 by the federal education panel, which provided some ideas on how to organize the history. See Parekh, *Rethinking Multiculturalism* (2000, 228).

90. McKinney 2003, 44.

91. Gates 1992, 80.

92. Martin and Neal 2001, 5.

93. Schlesinger 1998, 122.

94. Huntington 1996, 307.

95. Sáenz 1997, 75.

96. Joppke 2004, 249.

97. Newfield and Gordon 1996b, 83.

98. Smith 1993.

99. For a more detailed reading on the main tenets of American culture, see Deborah J. Schildkraut, "Defining American Identity in the Twenty-first Century: How Much 'There' Is There?" (2007, 599–601); Smith, "The 'American Creed' and American Identity: The Limits of Liberal Citizenship in the United States" (1988).

100. Smith 1988, 229–30.

101. Ibid., 228. See, for example, the landmark cases, *Dred Scott v. Sandford* (1857); *Bradwell v. Illinois* (1882); *Chae Chan Ping v. U.S.* (1889); *Plessy v. Ferguson* (1896).

102. See John Higham, *Strangers in the Land: Patterns of American Nativism, 1860–1925* (1994); David Walker Howe, *The Political Culture of American Whigs* (1979); and George M. Fredrickson, *The Black Image in the White Mind* (1971). Both Howe and Fredrickson disagree with Higham who sees biological inferiority of nonwhites as a minor strand in America's cultural identity in the late nineteenth century. Howe and Fredrickson show that the notion of biological inferiority became a part of the political discourse by the 1840s, and it was openly defended by the intellectual and political elites. And we would

see that these ideas helped in the creation of de jure racial segregation. It was not until *Brown v. Board of Education* that the schools were desegregated.

103. However, it is cheering to know that in 1856, in *English Traits*, Ralph Waldo Emerson, a transcendental American poet and essayist, recognized that societal and environmental factors, more or less, could be used as explanations for people's accomplishments.

104. See Myrdal, *An American Dilemma* (1962); and Moynihan, *The Negro Family* (1965).

105. Huntington 1996, 305.

106. Schlesinger 1998, 133.

107. W. E. B. Du Bois, on the other hand, was not impressed by Europe. He stated: "This is Europe; this seemingly terrible is the real soul of white culture— back of all culture,—stripped and visible today. This is where the world has arrived,—these dark and awful depths and not the shining and ineffable heights of which it had boasted" (1969, 28). Also Frantz Fanon begs us to discard Europe's history and turn to "a history which will have some regard to the sometime prodigious theses which Europe has put forward, but which will not forget Europe's crimes of which the most horrible was committed in the heart of man" (1963, 315).

108. Schlesinger 1998, 133.

109. Glazer 1997, 147.

110. Huntington 2004a, 390. Nonetheless, a larger question, which is ignored, is the notion of cosmopolitanism's dedication to hybridization where homosexuals or women, for example, exist inside of these bounded cultural groups, and consequently challenge, as they must, the so-called authenticity or purity of these groups. For more readings on cosmopolitanism, see Anthony Appiah, *Cosmopolitanism Ethics in a World of Strangers* (2006); Paul Gilroy, *After Empire: Melancholia or Convivial Culture* (2004); Carol A. Breckenridge et al., *Cosmopolitanism* (2002); Martha C. Nussbaum, "Patriotism and Cosmopolitanism" (1996); Bruce Ackerman, "Rooted Cosmopolitanism" (1994); and Jeremy Waldron, "Minority Cultures and the Cosmopolitan Alternative" (1992). For a good critique of the problematics of cosmopolitanism, see Anne Phillips, "Between Culture and Cosmos," in *Multiculturalism without Culture* (2007, 67–72).

111. Phyllis Schlafly, a political activist, warns that immigrants are the ones threatening America's culture, which is based on a good work ethic and the rule of law. See John Farmer, "The Nation's Melting Pot Is Showing Huge Cracks" (2006); and Patrick Buchanan, *State of Emergency: The Third World Invasion and State of America* (2006).

112. For an in-depth reading see Manning Marable, "Multicultural Democracy: The Emerging Majority for Justice and Peace" (1992, 249–59).

113. Huntington 2004a, 158.

114. Citrin et al. 2007, 32.

115. Huntington 2004a, 20.

116. A recent survey, conducted by Alejandro Portes and Rubén Rumbaut, shows that about "40 percent of the children of Mexican-born parents prefer using

English rather than Spanish, and if at least one parent is native-born, the figure rises to 75 percent" (see Massey 2004, 114).

117. Huntington 2004a, 241.
118. Dyson 1999, 220.
119. Kallen 1956, 85.
120. For a similar reading on "cultural racism," see Frantz Fanon's "Racism and Culture," in *Toward the African Revolution: Political Essays* (1964).
121. Huntington 2004a, 142.
122. Auster 1994.
123. McKinney 2003, 50–51.
124. Kymlicka 1995, 104.
125. Bonilla-Silva 2000, 189.
126. Many of the states have declared English to be the official language. States including Oregon, Nevada, Texas, New Mexico, Delaware, Michigan, and Vermont have not decided as yet to make English the official language.
127. See Huntington, *Who Are We? The Challenges to America's National Identity* (2004a).
128. Schlesinger 1998, 135.
129. Ibid., 163.
130. Goldberg 1994b, 5.
131. McLennan 2001, 392.
132. Goldberg 1994b, 3.
133. For a complete reading on Harlan's speech, see John Harlan, *Plessy v. Ferguson: A Brief History with Documents* (1997).
134. Trinh T. Minh-ha, in "An Acoustic Journey," tells us it is important to read between the lines as well as the words (1996).
135. See *People v. Hall* (1854); *Dred Scott v. Sandford* (1857); *Plessy v. Ferguson* (1896); *United States v. Wong Kim Ark* (1898).
136. Fanon 1967, 112.
137. Schelesinger 1998, 15.
138. Ibid., 138.
139. Huntington 1996, 305.
140. Huntington 2004a, 20.
141. Ibid., 315.
142. Ahmed 2008, 1.
143. Glazer 1997, 14.
144. McKinney 2003, 49.
145. Kymlicka 1995, 31.
146. Mohanty 1993, 56.
147. Angela Y. Davis 1996, 42.
148. Taylor 1994, 68.
149. Newfield and Gordon 1996b, 79.
150. Blauner 1972, 2.
151. For a more careful reading on "differential rights," see Kymlicka, *Multicultural Citizenship: A Liberal Theory of Minority Rights* (1995, 6–7, 26–33).

152. Kathleen M. Brown 1996, 2.
153. Hammonds 2004, 301. For a good grasp of the position of women, see Kathleen M. Brown, *Good Wives, Nasty Wenches, and Anxious Patriarchs* (1996: 107–244); and bell hooks, *Ain't I a Woman: Black Woman and Feminism* (1981, 15–51).
154. Johnson 1934, 170.
155. Butler 1995a, 137.
156. Fraser 2000, 109.
157. For a more meticulous reading on the importance of recognition as a member of a group, see Kwame A. Appiah, *The Ethics of Identity* (2005); Charles Taylor, *Multiculturalism and The Politics of Recognition: An Essay* (1992).
158. Taylor 1994, 25.
159. For a comprehensive reading on the importance of communities to determine their own membership, see Peter H. Schuck and Rogers M. Smith, *Citizenship without Consent: Illegal Aliens in the American Polity* (1985).
160. Parekh 2000.
161. Kymlicka 1989, 162.
162. Kymlicka 2007, 101.
163. Alarcón 1996, 139.
164. Stonequest 1935, 2.
165. Ibid.
166. We saw the harmful impact of assimilation on First Nations, for example, destroying First Nations' family units by forcing them to give up their language.
167. For whiteness as a cultural practice, see Ruth Frankenberg, *White Women, Race Matters: The Social Construction of Whiteness* (1993).
168. Schlesinger 1998, 145.
169. Ibid., 132.
170. Fuss 1989, 93.
171. Hurtado 1999, 226.
172. McLaren 2001, 409. Also, see David T. Goldberg, "Introduction: Multicultural Conditions" (1994b).

Chapter 5

1. Fine et al. 1997, x.
2. Conservative whites are now identifying themselves as marginalized and the new oppressed group. This form of white identification is another feature of white privilege because to be oppressed is to experience the difficulties that accompany the oppression.
3. It was President Lyndon Johnson's hope that with the ratification of the 1964 Civil Rights Act, "the last vestiges of injustice in this country" would be eliminated. A year later, on March 15, 1965, Johnson urged Congress to pass the Voting Rights Act, and called on America to "make good [this] promise of America." At Howard University, on June 4, 1965, where he presented his

commencement speech, he claimed that it "is the glorious opportunity of this generation to end the one huge wrong of the American Nations," which was the denial of blacks, other racialized groups, and women their equal rights. Given the Court's decision on cases of affirmative action as reverse discrimination, America has not overcome the promoting and perpetuating of white privilege. On President Johnson's speeches, see Claire Jean Kim, "Imagine Race and Nation in Multiculturalist America" (2004, 990).

4. A notable exception is *Grutter v. Bollinger*. In the Supreme Court ruling on affirmative action at the University of Michigan Law School, Sandra Day O'Connor in her majority decision held diversity as central to the American dream and the legitimacy of the dominant class.

5. In *White Women, Race Matters: The Social Construction of Whiteness*, Ruth Frankenberg saw whiteness as unmarked. In "The Mirage of an Unmarked Whiteness," she changed her mind about whiteness as unmarked. For more on whiteness as unmarked, especially in literature and film, see Toni Morrison, *Playing in the Dark: Whiteness and the Literary Imagination* (1993); and Richard Dyer, *White* (1997).

6. Frankenberg 2001, 73.

7. Assimilation was the basis for the government's policy toward First Nations from the 1880s to the 1930s. The passage by Congress of the General Allotment Act (The Dawes Severalty Act) of 1887 is one example of the assimilation process that was allotted to First Nations.

8. This is in line with "interactive pluralism," which emphasizes "mutual recognition and respect" of differences as opposed to "fractured pluralism." For a more detailed reading on these two forms of pluralism, see Douglas Hartmann and Joseph Gerteis, "Dealing with Diversity: Mapping Multiculturalism in Sociological Terms" (2005, 223, 229–32).

9. Hall 2004, 261.

10. Gilroy 2000a, 29.

11. See Michael Omi and Howard Winant, *Racial Formation in the United States from the 1960s to the 1990s* (1994). In addition, countries including France, Germany, England, and Sweden that were once "white countries" have increasing numbers of racial minorities.

12. Recent work conducted by Tyrone A. Forman, "Color-blind Racism and Racial Indifference: The Role of Racial Apathy in Facilitating Enduring Inequalities," shows that, concerning numerous matters of race, whites who confess they are indifferent to racial issues express traditional racist attitudes toward nonwhites (2006, 23–66). Also, see Eduardo Bonilla-Silva and Victor Ray, "When Whites Love a Black Leader: Race Matter in Obamerica" (2009); Eduardo Bonilla-Silva, "Color-Blind Racism" (2007); Karyn D. McKinney, "'I feel "Whiteness" When I Hear People Blaming Whites': White as Cultural Victimization" (2003); and David R. Roediger, *Colored White: Transcending the Racial Past* (2002).

13. Dyer 1997, 1.

14. Hartigan 2005, 550.

15. Ibid., 549. Also see Eduardo Bonilla-Silva, *Racism without Racists: Color-Blind Racism and the Persistence of Racial Inequality in the United States* (2006).

16. See Paul Gilroy, *Against Race: Imagining Political Culture Beyond the Color Line* (2000b), and *Between Camps: Nations, Culture and the Allure of Race* (2000a).

17. Hartigan 2005, 551.

18. Gilroy 2000a, 12.

19. "It is persuasively argued that the "culture of poverty" creates a subcultural set of values and traits, where expectations have developed as a direct result of the structural constraints associated with living in poverty. There is a range of inaccurate opinions about the decisive consequences of the subculture." See Sherrow O. Pinder, *From Welfare to Workfare* (2007, 42).

20. Du Bois 2003, 5.

21. Fanon 1967, 110.

22. Fanon 1963, 218.

23. Immigrants from different cultural backgrounds have to adhere to the larger American public culture. When immigrants from parts of Southeast Asia, Africa, and the Middle Eastern countries where female circumcision is practiced arrive in the United States, where female circumcision is illegal, they have to abandon such practices.

24. In France, for example, on October 19, 1989, three Muslim girls, Fatima, Leila, and Samaria, attending the college Gabriel-Havez of Creil, were asked by Ernest Chenière, the headmaster of the school, not to attend classes with their head covered. Even though the girls' parents accepted Chenière's recommendation and encouraged the girls not to wear their scarves, the girls expressed their dissent by continuing to wear them. The girls were forced to leave the school. In November 1996, twenty-three Muslim girls faced the same kind of removal from school. See Seyla Benhabib, *The Claims of Culture: Equality and Diversity in the Global Era* (2002, 95–96). This is just one instance that reflects the growing uneasiness with visible differences.

25. McLaren 1999, 36.

26. Ibid., 35–36.

27. Kymlicka 2007, 155.

28. Transculturalism in my mind is just as problematic as assimilation in terms of promoting cultural homogenization. Its motives, values, and expectations are Western. Since nonwestern cultures are seen as backward, underdeveloped, and inferior they must be liberated from their backwardness, and adapt to the civilized and enlightened Western norms and values. Unless they conform to the dominating Western culture they remain alienated. In short, transculturalism is a new form of neocolonialism reinscribing the colonial model of the normal and abnormal, superior and subordinate, as if nothing had changed. It is the code word for cultural intolerance and its racial implications. This is, to borrow from John Hartigan, "the culturalization of differences" (2005, 545) where race is implicated.

29. See Samuel P. Huntington, *Who Are We? The Challenges to America's National Identity* (2004a); Arthur M. Schlesinger, *The Disuniting of America: Reflections on a Multicultural Society* (1998); and Dinesh D'Souza, *Illiberal Education: The Politics of Race and Sex on Campus* (1991b).

30. Kymlicka 2007, 65–66.
31. Ibid., 66.
32. Phillips 2007, 71.
33. See Will Kymlicka, *Multicultural Citizenship: A Liberal Theory of Minority Rights* (1995); Charles Taylor, *Multiculturalism: Examining the Politics of Recognition* (1994); and Iris M. Young, *Justice and the Politics of Difference* (1990).
34. McLaren 2001, 417–18.
35. Dyer 1988, 44.
36. Toni Morrison, in *Playing in the Dark: Whiteness and the Literary Imagination*, calls for an interrogation of whiteness in America's canonic literary text (1993). For AnaLouise Keating, in "Interrogating 'Whiteness,' (De)Constructing 'Race,'" the interrogation of whiteness makes sense. "After all, we examine 'black,' Chicano/a, Native American, and Asian American literacy traditions" (1995, 903). She calls for the deconstructing of whiteness to reflect the dangers of not interrogating whiteness (1995, 902).
37. See Roediger 1991; Dyer 1997; Frankenberg 1997; and Gallagher 2003. Other whiteness studies scholars include Noel Ignatiev (1995); Elizabeth G. Hale (1998); George Lipsitz (1998); Richard Delgado and Jean Stefancic (1997); and Matthew F. Jacobson (1998). Also, many scholars have provided commentaries on the whiteness literature. An entire volume of *International Labor and Working-Class History* (2001) was dedicated to "whiteness." In this volume, Eric Arnesen's critical response to "whiteness studies" has provoked many debates about "whiteness studies" from historians like Barbara Fields and political scientists like Victoria Hattam and Adolph Reid Jr. Also, in a different venue, the British scholar Sara Ahmed has put forward a critical analysis of "whiteness studies" (2004).
38. Dyer 1997, 2. I call it "new" because African American scholars, including W. E. B. Du Bois, in *The Souls of Black Folk* (2003); Toni Morrison, in *Playing in the Dark: Whiteness and the Literary Imagination* (1993); and bell hooks, in *Black Looks: Race and Representation* (1992), have been writing about whiteness and its effects on African Americans and other nonwhite people. To paraphrase bell hooks: Among African Africans, there is an old oral tradition of studying and theorizing whiteness in order to be equipped with the necessary knowledge about how to survive in a white supremacist society. Du Bois, for example, coined the term *the wages of whiteness* in his 1935 classic book, *Black Reconstruction in America: 1860–1880*. See Du Bois 1998. Charles W. Mills offers an excellent account of the "wages of whiteness" in his "Racial Exploitation and the Wages of Whiteness" (2004, 43–48).
39. Fine et al. 1997, xi.
40. See Toni Morrison, *Playing in the Dark: Whiteness and the Literary Imagination* (1993); Rebecca Aanerud, "Fictions of Whiteness: Speaking the Names of Whiteness in U.S. Literature" (1997); Shelley Fisher Fishkin, "Interrogating 'Whiteness,' Complicating 'Blackness': Remapping American Culture" (1995); David Roediger, *Black on White: Black Writers and What It Means to Be White* (1998); and Crispin Sartwell, *Act Like You Know: African American Autobiography and White Identity* (1998).

41. Fishkin 1995, 442.
42. Roediger 1991, Dyer 1997, Frankenberg 1997, and Gallagher 2003.
43. Frankenberg 1997, 1. Although "whiteness may be a new subject of study, there is a tradition of anthropological research that is relevant to its examination." See Hartigan 1999, 193, and endnote 20 on p.195.
44. Roediger 2002, 19.
45. Roediger 2006, 8.
46. Bonnett 1996, 146.
47. hooks 1992, 166.
48. Baldwin 1998, 120–21.
49. hooks 1992, 167
50. Morrison 1993, 90.
51. See David R. Roediger, *The Wages of Whiteness: Race and the Making of the American Working Class* (1991); Neil Foley, *The White Scourge: Mexicans, Blacks, and Poor Whites in Texas Cotton Culture* (1997); Noel Ignatiev, *How the Irish Became White* (1995); and Matthew F. Jacobson, *Whiteness of a Different Color: European Immigrants and the Alchemy of Race* (1998).
52. Bonnett 1996, 146. See Ruth Frankenberg, *White Women, Race Matters: The Social Construction of Whiteness* (1993); Richard Dyer, *White* (1997); and Charles A. Gallagher, "White Reconstruction in the University" (2003).
53. Frankenberg 1993, 234.
54. This unacknowledged privilege assigned to whiteness has always been a problem for postcolonial theorists. This position is well articulated and defended by Edward Said, in *The Politics of Dispossession: The Struggle for Palestinian Self-Determination, 1969–1994* (1994); see also Gayatri C. Spivak, "Can the Subaltern Speak?" (1988).
55. Butler 1999, 12.
56. Frankenberg, 7.
57. Roediger 1991.
58. Rasmussen et al. 2001b, 14.
59. See Lazarre 1996.
60. hooks 1992, 12.
61. See Alastair Bonnett, "From the Crisis of Whiteness to Western Supremacy" (2005); Robyn Wiegman, "Whiteness Studies and the Paradox of Particularity" (1999); Frank Towers, "Projecting Whiteness: Race, and the State of Labor History" (1998); Eric Arnesen, "Scholarly Controversy: Whiteness and the Historians' Imagination" (2001); and Sara Ahmed, "Declaration of Whiteness: The Non-performativity of Antiracism" (2004).
62. Bonnett 1996, 146.
63. Roediger 1993, 132.
64. Arnesen 2001, 3.
65. See, for example, David R. Roediger, *Working Towards Whiteness: How America's Immigrants Became White, The Strange Journey from Ellis Island to the Suburbs* (2005); Karen Brodkin, *How Jews Became White Folks and What That Says about Race in America* (1999); Matthew Frye Jacobson, *Whiteness of a*

Different Color: European Immigrants and the Alchemy of Race (1998); and Noel Ignatiev, *How the Irish Became White* (1995). Also, in Texas, in the early twentieth century, Mexicans were seen as "almost white."

66. For a different reading of hybridity produced by immigration, exile, or existence in the borderlands, and how it can sometimes silence one emergent identity, see Maxine Hong Kingston, *The Woman Warrior: Memoirs of a Girlhood among Ghosts* (1976); and Gloria E. Anzaldúa, *Borderlands La Frontera: The New Mestiza* (1987). For Anzaldúa, "to survive the Borderlands, you live *sin fronteras* [without borders]/by a crossroads" (1987, 135). Also, Hamid Nafficy is dubious about the cultural politics of hybridity. See Nafficy, *The Making of Exile Cultures: Iranian Television in Los Angeles* (1993).

67. Ahmed 2004.

68. Charles A. Gallagher, in "White Racial Formation: Into the Twenty-first Century," notes that "the majority of whites in [his] study have come to understand themselves and their interests as white. Many of my respondents now think of themselves as whites, not as ethnics; they see themselves as individuals who are members of a racial category with its own particular set of interests. They have attached new meanings to being white and have used those meanings as the basis for forging an identity centered on race. They have, to borrow Michael Omi and Howard Winant's term, gone through the process of racialization" (1997, 7). Ruth Frankenberg, in "Whiteness and Americanness: Examining Constructions of Race, Culture, and Nation in White Women's Life Narratives," interviewed nine white women. The women who were "sympathetic to, or involved in, antiracist or promulticultural activity . . . viewed white culture and Americanness as 'bad' because both were seen as definitively linked to domination" (1994, 64).

69. Whites' victimization is a discourse that has emerged as a response to employers' focus on preferential hiring practices to promote cultural diversity in the workplace, for example. Also, see Dyer, *White* (1997, 10); and Gallagher, "White Reconstruction in the University" (2003). Michael Omi speaks to this anxiety. See his "Racialization in the Post–Civil Rights Era" (1996). See also Karyn D. McKinney, "'I feel "Whiteness" When I Hear People Blaming Whites': White as Cultural Victimization" (2003).

70. For the opposite reading of the transparency of whiteness, see Ian F. Haney-López, *White by Law: The Legal Construction of Race* (1996).

71. See James Baldwin, "White Man's Guilt" (1985); Clayborne Carson, *In Struggle: SNCC and the Black Awakening of the 1960s* (1981); and Norman Podhoretz, "My Negro Problem—and Ours" (1997).

72. Gallagher 2003, 302.

73. For further discussion on the abolition of whiteness, see Noel Ignatiev and John Garvey, *Race Traitor* (1996); and David Roediger, *Towards the Abolition of Whiteness: Essays on Race, Politics, and Working Class History* (1994).

74. See Michael Omi, "Racialization in the Post–Civil Rights Era" (1996); and Charles A. Gallagher "White Racial Formation: Into the Twenty-first Century" (1997).

75. Ferguson 1990, 10.
76. Westcott 2004.
77. Dyer 1988, 44.
78. Roediger 1991, 3.
79. Frankenberg 1993, 2.
80. In terms of speaking as the "other" the opposite occurs. The tendency, most of the time, implies a distance from oneself since one's subjectivity is never fully steeped in the modality of the speaking position one inhabits at a particular moment. When one is speaking as the "other," there is an expectation of the "other" to speak as the "other." There is a kind of homogenization of otherness operating from authentic and fixed categories such as race, ethnicity, gender, class, sexuality, location, religion, and so on. See Gayatri C. Spivak, *The Postcolonial Critic, Interviews, Strategies, Dialogues* (1990a, 60).
81. Butler 1995b, 443.
82. Bonnett 1996, 147.
83. Bonnett 2005.
84. Bhabha 1998, 21.
85. Ibid.
86. Tocqueville 1999.
87. Hacker 2003, 4.
88. Yancy 2004b, 7–8.
89. Dyer 1997, 10.
90. Fine et al. 1997, xi–xii.
91. Deracialization is a concept developed as an analytical construct in American urban politics. This "concept is deployed to objectify the degrees of freedom and construct black mayors face as they articulate campaign themes and strategy in a 'postblack' register." Another approach of deracialization is found in the studies on "racelessness" or "acting white" by people of color. See Hartigan 1999, 193. It brings us to an important point about the metaphoric construction of a white identity and whiteness as a structure that is in place in America.
92. Arnesen 2001, 6.
93. Ibid., 9.
94. Wright 1937, 175.
95. Martinot and Sexton 2003, 169.
96. Dyson 1999, 220.
97. Lipsitz 1995, 372.
98. The racialization of space is being reconfigured through the movement of migrant workers, especially from Mexico, legal and illegal immigrants, and refugees from nonwhite nations. These factors are producing more complicated racialized ethnic communities.
99. See Mab Segrest, "The Souls of White Folks" (2001, 44). On the other hand, W. E. B. Du Bois, in "The Souls of White Folk," admits that the souls of white folks intrigue him enormously. He writes, "I know many souls that toss and whirl pass, but none there are that intrigue me than The Soul of White Folk. Of them I am singularly clairvoyant. I see in and through them. . . . I see these

souls undressed from the back and the side. I see the working of their entrails. I know their thoughts and they know that I know. This knowledge now makes them embarrassed, now Furious." (1969, 29).

100. Yancy 2004b, 32.
101. Ahmed 2004.
102. Ibid.
103. Hattam 2001, 62.
104. Rasmussen et al. 2001b, 3.
105. Ibid., 8.
106. Foley 1997, 5.
107. Wray 2006, 2.
108. King 1964, 138.
109. See Derrick A Bell, Tracy Higgins, and Sung-Hee Suh, "Racial Reflections: Dialogues in the Direction of Liberation" (1997, 107–8).
110. Mailer 1957, 278. However, according to Gary T. Marx, the phrase "the white Negro" was popularized by Norman Mailer and did not originate from him. For several centuries, in the West Indies, the term has been used "to describe white men who have become submerged among their Negro servants and concubines." See Marx 1967, 169n3.
111. Mercer 1992, 207–8.
112. Lander 2008.
113. Mercer 1991, 432–33.
114. In Jane Lazarre, in *Beyond the Whiteness of Whiteness: Memoir of a White Mother of Black Sons*, her "crossing over" or "passing over" to blackness is quite different. She draws our attention of the tensions between having a white skin and rejecting whiteness as her social identity. According to Lazarre, her social identity was "hidden" by her white skin. "I am no longer white. However I may appear to others, I am a person of color now" she writes (1996, 135).
115. Mercer 1994, 339.
116. See David R. Roediger, *Colored White: Transcending the Racial Past* (2002); Matthew F. Jacobson, *Whiteness of a Different Color: European Immigrants and the Alchemy of Race* (1998); Noel Ignatiev and John Garvey, *Race Traitor* (1996); and Ruth Frankenberg, *White Women, Race Matters: The Social Construction of Whiteness* (1993).
117. Bonilla-Silva, *Racism without Racists: Color-Blind Racism and the Persistence of Racial Inequality in the United States* (2006); McKinney, "'I feel "Whiteness" When I Hear People Blaming Whites': White as Cultural Victimization" (2003); Frankenberg, *White Women, Race Matters: The Social Construction of Whiteness* (1993).
118. Recently, scholars have explored the construction of white racial identity as an unexamined racial formation and the normativity of a particular set of cultural practices. See Frankenberg, *White Women, Race Matters: The Social Construction of Whiteness* (1993); Roediger, *The Wages of Whiteness: Race and the Making of the American Working Class* (1991); Dyer, *White* (1997); and Ignatiev and Garvey, *Race Traitor* (1996).

119. Fields 2001, 49.
120. Farr 2004, 144.
121. Ibid., 145.
122. Mills 1997, 126–27.
123. Lipsitz 1998, xix.
124. Yancy 2004b, 10.
125. hooks 1992, 177.
126. See Spivak, *The Post-colonial Critic: Interviews, Strategies, Dialogues* (1990a).
127. Lipsitz 1995, 369.
128. Dyer 1988, 44.
129. Many scholars have dismissed the biological and essentialist explanations for race, gender, and sexuality. They have pointed to the historical and cultural facts of race, sexuality, and gender as socially constituted and the ways theoretical and empirical analyses have shifted to demonstrate that race, gender, and sexual formations are context specific and change overtime. See Judith Butler, *Gender Trouble: Feminism and the Subversion of Identity* (1999); Michael Omi and Howard Winant, *Racial Formation in the United States from the 1960s to the 1990s* (1994); Ruth Frankenberg, *White Women, Race Matters: The Social Construction of Whiteness* (1993). Black feminists especially have drawn our attention to the intersectionality of identities. See Kimberlé Crenshaw, "Demarginalizing the Intersection of Race and Sex: A Black Feminist Critique of Antidiscrimination Doctrine, Feminist Theory and Antiracist Politics" (1989); and Patricia Hill Collins, *Black Feminist Thought: Knowledge, Consciousness, and the Politics of Empowerment* (1990). Other feminists who are working on intersectionality include Randi Gressgård, "Mind the Gap: Intersectionality, Complexity and 'the Event,'" 2008; and Avtar Brah and Ann Phoenix, "Ain't I a Woman? Revisiting Intersectionality" (2004).
130. Lipsitz 1995, 372.

Conclusion

1. Higginbotham 1996, 198.
2. See Arthur M. Schlesinger, *The Disuniting of America: Reflections on a Multicultural Society* (1998, 154).
3. Gardiner 1992, 186.
4. Huntington 2004a, 158.
5. See Louis D. Brandeis, *The Words of Justice Brandeis* (1953, 29).
6. Sotomayor 2002, 87.
7. Jay 1787.
8. The melting pot image is found in Crèvecoeur's *Letters from an American Farmer* (1926) and Israel Zangwill's *The Melting Pot, Drama in Four Acts* (1909).
9. Huntington 2004a, 129.
10. Hall 2004, 257.

11. Black Nationalist strategies can be traced back to the repatriation movements of the mid-nineteenth century under the leadership of Martin Delany. In 1854, the National Emigration Convention held in Pittsburgh called for emigration to "places where the black and colored man comprise, by population . . . the ruling element of the body politic." See the edited volume by J. H. Bracey Jr. et al., *Black Nationalism in America* (1970, 93). For an in-depth reading of the development of Black Nationalism from slavery through the early twentieth century, see Wilson Jeremiah Moses, *The Golden Age of Black Nationalism 1850–1925* (1978). Black Nationalism must be tied to internal colonialism in order to avoid reducing it to a militant or separatist group. Many Black Nationalists embrace the language, values, traditions, and culture of Africa through Pan-Africanism. Pan-Africanism focused on mobilizing blacks through the Universal Negro Improvement Association, which was led by Marcus Garvey.
12. Huntington 2004, 129.
13. Francis 1998, 293.
14. Lorde 1984, 123.
15. Parekh 2000, 149.
16. Ibid., 147.
17. Ibid., 146.
18. See Susan Moller Okin, *Is Multiculturalism Bad for Women?* (1999).
19. Benhabib 2002, 102.
20. Kristeva 1991, 191.
21. Schlesinger 1998, 155.
22. Sotomayor 2002, 92.
23. Ibid.
24. Ibid., 91.
25. Ibid., 92.
26. See Bill Clay, *Bill Clay: A Political Voice at the Grass Roots* (2004).
27. Schlesinger 1998, 135.
28. Yancy 2005, 217.
29. Du Bois 2003, 14.
30. Schlesinger 1998, 145.
31. Harris, 1993.

References

Aanerud, Rebecca. 1997. Fictions of whiteness: Speaking the names of whiteness in U.S. literature. In *Displacing whiteness. Essays in social and cultural criticism*, ed. Ruth Frankenberg, 35–59. Durham, NC: Duke University Press.

———. 2002. Thinking again: This bridge called my back and the challenge to whiteness. In Anzaldúa and Keating 2002, 69–76.

———. 2007. The legacy of white supremacy and the challenge of white antiracist mothering. *Hypatia* 22 (2): 20–38.

Abramovitz, Mimi. 1996. *Regulating the lives of women: Social welfare policy from colonial times to the present*. Boston: South End Press.

Ackerman, Bruce. 1994. Rooted cosmopolitanism. *Ethics* 104 (3): 516–35.

Agamben, Giorgio. 1998. *Homo sacer: Sovereign power and bare life*. Stanford, CA: Stanford University Press.

Ahmed, Sara. 2004. Declaration of whiteness: The non-performativity of anti-racism. *Borderlines* 3 (2). http//www.borderlandsejournal.adelaide. edu.au/issues/vol3no2.html.

———. 2005. The non-performativity of anti-racism. *Borderlines* 5 (3). http://www.borderlands.net.au/vol5no3_2006/ahmed_nonperform.htm.

———. 2008. The politics of good feelings. *Australian Critical Race and Whiteness Studies Association* 4 (1): 1–18. http://www.acrawsa.org.au/.

Alarcón, Norma. 1996. Conjugating subjects in the age of multiculturalism. In Newfield and Gordon 1996, 127–48.

Alcoff, Linda Martín. 1998. What should white people do? *Hypatia* 13 (3): 6–23.

Alessandrini, Anthony C., ed. 1999. *Frantz Fanon: Critical perspectives*. New York: Routledge.

Allen, Theodore W. 1994. *Racial oppression and social control*. Vol. 1 of *The invention of the white race*. New York: Verso Press.

———. 1997. *The origin of racial oppression in Anglo-America*. Vol. 2 of *The invention of the white race*. New York: Verso Press.

Angelou, Maya. 1993. The inauguration poem "On the Pulse of the Morning." New York: Random House.

Annals of Congress. 1857. *Abridgements of debates of Congress, 1789–1856*. Vol. 1. New York: D. Appleton and Co.

Anthias, Floya, and Nira Yuval-Davis. 1993. *Racialized boundaries: Race, nation, gender, colour and class and the anti-racist struggles*. London: Routledge.

Anzaldúa, Gloria E. 1987. *Borderlands La Frontera: The new mestiza*. San Francisco: Aunte Lute Book Co.

Anzaldúa, Gloria E., and AnaLouise Keating, eds. 2002. *This bridge we call home.* New York: Routledge.

Appiah, Anthony A. 1985. The uncompleted argument: Du Bois and the illusion of race. In *"Race," writing, and difference,* ed. Henry Louis Gates Jr. Chicago: University of Chicago Press.

———2005. *The ethics of identity.* Princeton, NJ: Princeton University Press.

———. 2006. *Cosmopolitanism ethics in a world of strangers.* New York: Norton.

Appiah, Kwame A., and Henry Louis Gates Jr., eds. 1985. *Identities.* Chicago: University of Chicago Press.

Arnesen, Eric. 2001. Scholarly controversy: Whiteness and the historians' imagination. *International Labor and Working-Class History* (60): 3–32.

Aronowitz, Stanley. 1999. Between nationality and class. In Torres, Mirón, and Inda 1999, 304–21.

Auster, Lawrence. 1994. 1994. The U.S. must restrict immigration to prevent cultural disintegration. In *Culture wars: Opposing viewpoints,* ed. Fred Whitehead, 56–62. San Diego, CA: Greenhaven Press.

Austin, J. L. 1963. *How to do things with words.* Oxford, UK: Oxford University Press.

Bailey, Thomas. 1982. *The American pageant revisited: Recollections of a Stanford Historian.* Stanford: Hoover Institution Press.

Baldwin, James. 1985. White man's guilt. In *The price of the ticket.* New York: St. Martin's Press.

———. 1998. *Collective essays.* New York: Library of America.

Balibar, Étienne, and Immanuel Wallerstein. 1992. *Race, nation, class: Ambiguous identities.* London: Verso.

Banton, Michael P. 1978. *The idea of race.* Boulder, CO: Westview Press.

Barthes, Roland. 1972. *Mythologies.* Trans. Annette Lavers. New York: Hill and Wang.

Bell, Derrick A. 1995. Property rights in whiteness—their legal legacy, their economic costs. In *Critical race theory,* ed. Richard Delgado, 2–8. Philadelphia: Temple University Press.

Bell, Derrick A., Tracy Higgins, and Sung-Hee Suh. 1997. Racial reflections: Dialogues in the direction of liberation. In Delgado and Stefancic 1997, 106–11.

Benhabib, Seyla. 1996. Introduction: The democratic moment and the problem of difference. In *Democracy and difference: Contesting the boundaries of the political,* ed. Seyla Benhabib. Princeton, NJ: Princeton University Press.

———. 2002. *The claims of culture: Equality and diversity in the global era.* Princeton, NJ: Princeton University Press.

Benhabib, Seyla, Fudith Butler, Drucilla Cornell, and Nancy Fraser, eds. 1995. *Feminist contentions: A philosophical exchange.* New York: Routledge.

Bennett, Lerone. 1975. *The shaping of black America: The struggles and triumphs of African-Americans, 1619–1990s.* Chicago: Johnson.

Bergh, Albert E., ed. 1905. *The writings of Thomas Jefferson.* Vol. 2. Washington, DC: Thomas Jefferson Memorial Association.

Bhabha, Homi K. 1987. What does the black man want? *New Formations: A Journal of Culture/Theory/Politics* (1): 118–24.

———. 1998. The white stuff. *Artforum* (36): 21–24.

———, ed. 1990. *Nation and narration*. New York: Routledge.

———. 1994. *The Location of Culture*. New York: Routledge.

Bhattacharyya, Gargia, John Gabriel, and Stephen Small. 2002. *Race and power: Global racism in the twenty-first century*. London: Routledge.

Blauner, Robert. 1972. *Racial oppression in America*. New York: Harper and Row.

Bloom, Allan. 1987. *The closing of the American mind*. New York: Simon and Schuster.

Bobo, Jacqueline, Cynthia Hudley, and Claudine Michel, eds. 2004. *The black studies reader*. New York: Routledge.

Bonilla-Silva, Eduardo. 2000. "This is a white country": The racial ideology of the western nations of the world-system. *Sociological Inquiry* 70 (2): 188–214.

———. 2001. *White supremacy and racism in the post civil rights era*. Boulder, CO: Lynne Rienner.

———. 2002. We are all Americans! The Latin Americanization of racial stratification in the USA. *Race & Society* 5:3–16.

———. 2006. *Racism without racists: Color-blind racism and the persistence of racial inequality in the United States*. Lanham, MD: Rowman and Littlefield.

———. 2007. Color-blind racism. In Rothenberg 2007, 131–38.

Bonilla-Silva, Eduardo, and Victor Ray. 2009. When whites love a black leader: Race matters in Obamerica. *Journal of African American Studies* 13 (2): 176–83.

Bonnett, Alastair. 1996 "White studies": The problems and projects of a new research agenda. *Theory, Culture & Society* 13 (2): 145–55.

———. 1999. Constructions of whiteness in European and American anti-racism. In Torres, Mirón, and Inda 1999, 200–218.

———. 2005. From the crisis of whiteness to western supremacy. *Australia Critical Race and Whiteness Studies Association Journal* 1:8–20.

Boskin, Joseph. 1976. *Into slavery: Racial decisions in the Virginia Colony*. Philadelphia: Lippincott.

Bracey, John H., August Meier, and Elliott Rudwick, eds. 1970. *Black nationalism in America*. Indianapolis: Bobbs-Merrill.

Brah, Avtar. 1996. *Cartographies of diaspora: Contesting identities*. London: Routledge.

Brah, Avtar, and Ann Phoenix. 2004. Ain't I a woman? Revisiting intersectionality. *Journal of International Women's Studies* 5 (3): 75–86.

Brandeis, Louis D. 1953. *The words of Justice Brandeis edited by Solomon Goldman with a Foreword by William O. Douglas*. New York: Henry Schuman.

Breckenridge, Carol A., Sheldon Pollock, Homi K. Bhabha, and Dipesh Chakrabarty, eds. 2002. *Cosmopolitanism*. Durham, NC: Duke University Press.

Broder, David. 1998. The unity among us. *Washington Post*, November 25.

Brodkin, Karen. 1999. *How Jews became white folks and what that says about race in America*. New Brunswick, NJ: Rutgers University Press.

Brown, Kathleen M. 1996. *Good wives, nasty wenches, and anxious patriarchs: Gender, race and power in colonial Virginia*. Chapel Hill: University of North Carolina Press.

Brown, Wendy. 1995. *States of injury*. Princeton, NJ: Princeton University Press.

———. 1998. Freedom's silences. In *Censorship and silencing: Practices of cultural regulation*, ed. Robert Post, 313–26. Los Angeles: Getty Research Institute for the History of Art and the Humanities.

———. 2006. *Regulating aversion tolerance in the age of identity and empire*. Princeton, NJ: Princeton University Press.

Buchanan, Patrick. 2006. *State of emergency: The Third World invasion and state of America*. New York: St. Martin's Press.

Bulbeck, Chilla. 2004. The "white" worrier in South Australia: Attitudes to multiculturalism, immigration and reconciliation. *Journal of Sociology* 40 (4): 341–61.

Butler, Judith. 1990. *Gender trouble, feminism and the subversion of identity*. New York: Routledge.

———. 1993. *Bodies that matter: On the discursive limits of "sex."* London: Routledge.

———. 1995a. For careful reading. In Benhabib, Butler, Cornell, and Fraser 1995, 35–57.

———. 1995b. Collected and fractured: Response to identities. In *Identities*, ed. Kwame Anthony Appiah and Henry Louis Gates Jr., 439–47. Chicago: University of Chicago Press.

———. 1997a. *Excitable speech: A politics of the performative*. New York: Routledge.

———. 1997b. *The psychic life of power*. Stanford, CA: Stanford University Press.

———. 2000. Restaging the universal: Hegemony and the limits of formalism. In *Contingency, hegemony, universality: Contemporary dialogues on the left*, ed. Judith Butler, Ernesto Laclau, and Slavoj Žižek, 11–43. London: Verso Press.

———. 2001. "Appearances aside." In Post 2001a, 73–84.

Caldwell, Dan. 1971. The negroization of the Chinese stereotype in California. *Southern California Quarterly* 33:123–31.

Cannon, Katie Geneva. 2004. Slave ideology and biblical interpretation. In Bobo, Hudley, and Michel 2004, 413–20.

Caputo, John, and Mark Yount. 1993. Institutions, normalization, and power. In *Foucault and the critique of institutions*, ed. John Caputo and Mark Yount, 3–23. University Park: Pennsylvania State University Press.

Cardyn, Lisa. 2002. Sexualized racism/gendered violence: Outraging the body politic in the reconstruction south. *Michigan Law Review* 100 (4): 675–867.

Carmichael, Stokely, and Charles V. Hamilton. 1967. *Black power: The politics of liberation in America*. New York: Random House.

Carson, Clayborne. 1981. *In struggle: SNCC and the black awakening of the 1960s*. Cambridge, MA: Harvard University Press.

Casey, Marion R. 2003. The limits of equality: Racial and ethnic tensions in the new republic, 1989–1836. In *Race and ethnicity in America: A concise history*, ed. Ronald H. Bayor, 41–62. New York: Columbia University Press.

Chafe, William H. 1977. *Women and equality: Changing patterns in American culture*. New York: Oxford University Press.

Chafe, William H., Raymond Gavins, and Robert Korstad. 2001. *Remembering Jim Crow: African Americans tell about life in the segregated south*. New York: New Press.

Chan, Sucheng. 1991a. *Entry denied: Exclusion and the Chinese American community in America, 1882–1943*. Philadelphia: Temple University Press.

———. 1991b. *Asian Americans: An interpretive history*. New York: Twayne.

Cheryan, Sapna, and Bonît Monin. 2005. "Where are you *really* from?": Asian Americans and identity denial. *Journal of Personality and Social Psychology* 89 (5): 717–30.

Chow, Rey. 1991. *Women and Chinese modernity: The politics of reading between west and east*. Minneapolis: University of Minnesota Press.

Citrin, Jack. 2001. The end of American identity? In Renshon 2001, 285–307.

Citrin, Jack, Amy Lerman, Michael Murakami, and Kathryn Pearson. 2007. Testing Huntington: Is Hispanic immigration a threat to American identity? *Perspectives on Politics* 5 (1): 31–48.

Cixous, Helene, Keith Cohen, and Paula Cohen. 1997. The laugh of the Medusa. *Signs* 1 (4): 875–93.

Clay, Bill. 2004. *Bill Clay: A political voice at the grass roots*. Columbia: University of Missouri Press.

Clinton, William Jefferson. 1992. *Putting people first: How we can all change America*. New York: Times Books.

———. 1996, August 22. Statement on signing the Personal Responsibility and Work Opportunity Reconciliation Act of 1996. In *Public papers of the presidents of the United States*. Washington, DC: U.S. Government Printing Office.

Cohen, Philip. 1992. "It's racism what dunnit": Hidden narratives in theories of racism. In *"Race," culture and difference*, ed. James Donald and Ali Rattansi, 62–103.London: Sage.

Collins, Patricia Hill. 1990. *Black feminist thought: Knowledge, consciousness, and the politics of empowerment. London, UK*: HarperCollins.

Connerly, Ward. 1998. Back to equality. *Imprimis* 27 (2).

Cornell, Drucilla. 1995. Rethinking the time of feminism. In Benhabib 1995, 145–56.

Cover, Robert. 1975. *Justice accused, anti-slavery and the judicial process*. New Haven, CT: Yale University Press.

Cox, Oliver C. 1948. *Caste, class & race: A study in social dynamics*. New York: Doubleday.

Crenshaw, Kimberlé. 1989. *Demarginalizing the intersection of race and sex: A black feminist critique of antidiscrimination doctrine, feminist theory and antiracist politics*. University of Chicago Legal Forum, 139–67.

Crèvecoeur, de Hector St. John. 1926. *Letters from an American framer*. Introduction by Warren Barton Blake. New York: E. P. Dutton & CO.

Crouch, Stanley. 1996. Race is over: Black, white, red, yellow—same difference. *New York Times Magazine*, September 29.

Daniel, G. Reginald. 2002. *More than black? Multiracial identity and the new racial order*. Philadelphia: Temple University Press.

Davis, Adrienne D. 1997. Identity notes, Part One: Playing in the light. In Delgado and Stefancic 1997, 231–38.

Davis, Angela Y. 1974. *With my mind on freedom: An autobiography*. New York: Bantam Books.

———. 1983. *Women, race & class*. New York: Vintage Books.

———. 1996. Gender, class, and multiculturalism: Rethinking "race" politics. In Newfield and Gordon 1996, 40–48.

———. 2007. Mashed racism: Reflection on the prison industrial complex. In Rothenberg 2007, 683–88.

Davis, David Brion. 1966. *The problem of slavery in western culture*. Ithaca, NY: Cornell University Press.

———. 1997. Constructing race: A reflection. *William and Mary Quarterly* 54 (1): 7–18.

Deaux, Kay. 2008. To be an American: Immigration, hyphenation, and incorporation. *Journal of Social Issues* 64 (4): 925–43.

Degler, Carl N. 1959. Slavery and the genesis of American race prejudice. *Comparative Studies in Society and History* 2 (1): 49–66.

Delgado, Richard, and Jean Stefancic, eds. 1997. *Critical white studies: Looking behind the mirror*. Philadelphia: Temple University Press.

———. 2001. *Critical race theory: An introduction*. New York: New York University Press.

Derbyshire, John. 2000. Thinking about internment. *Chronicles* January, 42–44. http://www.olimu.com/Journalism/Texts/Commentary/Internment.htm.

Derrida, Jacques. 2003. Autoimmunity: Real and symbolic suicides—a dialogue with Jacques Derrida. In *Philosophy in a time of terror: Dialogues with Jürgen Habermas and Jacques Derrida*, trans. Pascale Ann-Brault and Michael Nass, ed. Giovanna Borradori, 25–44. Chicago: University of Chicago Press.

Devos, Thierry, and Mahzarin R. Banaji. 2005. America = white? *Journal of Personality and Social Psychology* 88 (3): 447–66.

Dissent. 1995. "Affirmative Action Under Fire." *Dissent* (Fall): 461–76.

Douglass, Frederick. 1982. *Narrative of the Life of Frederick Douglass, an American Slave*. New York: Penguin Classics.

D'Souza, Dinesh. 1991a. Multiculturalism 101: Great books of the non-Western world. *Policy Review*, no. 56 (Spring): 22–30.

———. 1991b. *Illiberal education: The politics of race and sex on campus*. New York: Free Press.

———. 1995. *The end of racism: Principles for a multiracial society*. New York: Free Press.

Du Bois, W. E. B. 1969. *Darkwater: Voices from within the veil*. New York: Schocken Books.

———. 1998. *Black reconstruction in America: 1860–1880*. New York: Free Press.

———. 2003. *The souls of black folk*. Introduction by David Levering Lewis. New York: Modern Library.

duCille, Ann. 1994. The occult of true black womanhood: Critical demeanor and black feminist studies. *Signs* 19 (3): 591–629.

Dyer, Richard. 1988. White. *Screen* 29 (4): 44–64.

———. 1997. *White*. London: Routledge.

Dyson, Michael Eric. 1999. The labor of whiteness, the whiteness of labor, and the perils of whitewishing. In Torres, Mirón, and Inda 1999, 219–24.

Early, Gerald, ed. 1994. *Lure and loathing: Essays on race, identity, and the ambivalence of assimilation*. New York: Penguin Books.

Eitzen, D. Stanley, and Maxine Baca Zinn. 1991. *In conflict and order: Understanding society*. Boston: Allyn and Bacon.

Eller, Jack D. 1997 Anti-anti-multiculturalism. *American Anthropologist, New Series* 99 (2): 249–56.

Ellison, Ralph. 1989. *Invisible man*. New York: Vintage Books.

Entman, Robert M., and Andrew Rojecki. 2001. *The black image in the white mind: Media and race in America*. Chicago: University of Chicago Press.

Essed, Philomena. 2005. Gendered preferences in racialized spaces: Cloning the physician. In Murji and Solomos 2005, 227–48.

Evans, Emory G., ed. 1963. A question of complexion: Documents concerning the Negro and the franchise in eighteenth-century Virginia. *Virginia Magazine of History and Biography* 71:411–15.

Fairchild, Halford. 1981. Chicano, Hispanic, or Mexican American: What's in a name. *Hispanic Journal of Behavioral Sciences* 3 (2): 191–98.

Fanon, Frantz. 1963. *The wretched of the earth*. Trans. Constance Farrington. New York: Grove Press.

———. 1964. *Toward the African revolution: Political essays*. Trans. Haakon Chevalier. New York: Grove Press.

———. 1967. *Black skin white masks*. Trans. Charles Lam Markmann. New York: Grove Press.

Farmer, John. 2006. The nation's melting pot is showing huge cracks. http//.www.nj.com/columns/ledger/farmer/index.ssf?/base/columns-/1146590708102300.xml&coll.

Farr, Arnold. 2004. Whiteness visible: Enlightenment racism and the structure of racialized consciousness. In Yancy 2004a, 143–58.

Fausto-Sterling, Anne. 2000. *Sexing the body: Gender politics and the construction of sexuality*. New York: Basic Books.

Feminist Review. 1984. Many voices, one chant: Black feminist perspectives. *Feminist Review*, no.17 (Autumn): 1–118.

Ferguson, Russell. 1990. Introduction to *Out there: Marginalization and contemporary cultures*, ed. Russell Ferguson, Martha Gever, Trinh T. Minh-ha, and Cornel West. New York: New Museum of Contemporary Art.

Fields, Barbara J. 1990. Slavery, race and ideology in the United States of America. *New Left Review*, no. 181 (Summer): 95–118.

———. 2001. Whiteness, racism, and identity. *International Labor and Working-Class History*, no. 60 (Fall): 48–56.

———. 2003. Of rouges and geldings. *American Historical Review* (December): 1397–1405.

Fine, Michele, Linda Powell, Lois Weis, and L. Mun Wong. 1997. *Off white: Readings on race, power, and society.* New York: Routledge.

Fishkin, Shelley Fisher. 1995. Interrogating "whiteness," complicating "blackness": Remapping American culture. *American Quarterly* 47 (3): 428–66.

Fitzgerald, F. Scott. 1999. *The great Gatsby.* Ed. Nicolas Tredell. New York: Columbia University Press.

Foley, Neil. 1997. *The white scourge: Mexicans, blacks, and poor whites in Texas cotton culture.* Berkeley, CA: University of California Press.

Foner, Eric. 1988. *Reconstruction: America's unfinished revolution, 1863–1877.* New York: HarperCollins.

Ford, Paul L. 1904–5. *The works of Thomas Jefferson.* Vol. 9. New York and London: Putnam's Sons.

Forman, Tyrone A. 2006. Color-blind racism and racial indifference: The role of racial apathy in facilitating enduring inequalities. In *The changing terrain of race and ethnicity,* ed. Maria Krysan and Amanda E. Lewis, 43–66. New York: Russell Sage Foundation.

Foucault, Michel. 1978. *The history of sexuality: An introduction.* Trans. Robert Hurley. New York: Random House.

———. 1979. *Discipline and punish: The birth of the prison.* Trans. Alan Sheridan. New York: Vintage Book.

———. 1980. *Power/Knowledge: Selected interviews and other writings, 1972–1977.* Ed. and trans. Colin Gordon. New York: Pantheon Books.

———. 1982. Afterword: The subject and power. In *Michel Foucault: Beyond structuralism and hermeneutics,* ed. Hubert L. Dreyfus and Paul Rabinow, 208–28. Chicago: University of Chicago Press.

———. 1991. Questions of method. In *The Foucault effect: Studies in governmentality with two lectures by and an interview with Michel Foucault,* ed. Graham Burchell, Colin Gordon, and Peter Miller, 73–86. Chicago: University of Chicago Press.

Frankenberg, Ruth. 1993. *White women, race matters: The social construction of whiteness.* Minneapolis: University of Minnesota Press.

———. 1994. Whiteness and Americanness: Examining constructions of race, culture, and nation in white women's life narratives. In Gregory and Sanjek 1994, 62–77.

———. 1997. Introduction: Local whitenesses, localizing whiteness. In *Displacing whiteness: Essays in social and cultural criticism,* ed. Ruth Frankenberg, 1–33. Durham, NC: Duke University Press.

———. 2001. The mirage of an unmarked whiteness. In Rasmussen, Nexica, Klinenberg, and Wray 2001, 72–96.

Francis, Samuel. 1998. Whose future? Projection of a non-white American. *The Social Contract* 8 (4): 293–99.

Franklin, Benjamin. 1961. Observations concerning the increase of mankind. In *The papers of Benjamin Franklin*. Vol. 4. Ed. Leonard W. Labaree. New Haven, CT: Yale University Press.

Fraser, Nancy. 2000. Rethinking identity politics. *New Left Review* 3 (2): 107–20.

Frazier, Edward F. 1969. *The Negro in the United States*. New York: Macmillan.

Fredrickson, George M. 1971. *The black image in the white mind*. New York: Harper and Row.

———. 1982. *White supremacy: A comparative study in American and South African history*. New York: Oxford University Press.

———. 1988. *The arrogance of race: Historical perspective on slavery, racism and social inequality*. Middletown, CT: Wesleyan University Press.

Freire, Paulo. 2000. *Pedagogy of the oppressed*. Trans. Myra Bergman Ramos. New York: Continuum.

Friedman, Milton. 1962. *Capitalism and freedom*. Chicago: University of Chicago Press.

Fuss, Diana. 1989. *Essentially speaking: Feminism, nature and difference*. New York: Routledge.

Gallagher, Charles A. 1997. White racial formation: Into the twenty-first century. In Delgado and Stefancic 1997, 6–11.

———. 2003. White reconstruction in the university. In *Privilege: A reader*, ed. Michael Kimmel and Abby Ferber 2003, 299–318. Boulder, CO: Westview Press.

Garcea, Joseph. 2006. Provincial multiculturalism policies in Canada, 1974–2004: A content analysis. *Canadian Ethnic Studies* 38 (3): 1–20.

Gardiner, Michael. 1992. *The dialogics of critique: M. M. Bakhtin and the theory of ideology*. London: Routledge.

Gates, Henry Louis, ed. 1985. *"Race," writing, and difference*. Chicago: University of Chicago Press.

———. 1992. *Loose cannons: Notes on the culture war*. New York: Oxford University Press.

Gilman, Sander L. 1985. *Difference and pathology: Stereotypes of sexuality, race, and madness*. Ithaca, NY: Cornell University Press.

Gilroy, Paul. 2000a. *Between camps: Nations, culture and the allure of race*. London: Allen Lane.

———. 2000b. *Against race: Imagining political culture beyond the color line*. Cambridge, MA: Harvard University Press.

———. 2004. *After empire: Melancholia or convivial culture*. London: Routledge.

———. 2005. Multiculture, double consciousness and the "war on terror." *Pattern of Prejudice* 39 (4): 431–43.

Giroux, Henry A. 1994. Insurgent multiculturalism and the promise of pedagogy. In Goldberg 1994a, 325–43.

Gitlin, Todd. 1995. *The twilight of common dreams: Why America is wracked by culture wars*. New York: Holt.

Glazer, Nathan. 1991 In defense of multiculturalism. *The New Republic* 205 (1): 18–22.

———. 1997. *We are all multiculturalists now.* Cambridge, MA: Harvard University Press.

———. 2004. Assimilation today: Is one identity enough? In *Reinventing the melting pot: The new immigrants and what it means to be American,* ed. Tamar Jacoby, 61–73. New York: Basic Books.

Glazer, Nathan, and Daniel P. Moynihan. 1970. *Beyond the melting pot: The Negroes, Puerto Ricans, Jews, Italians and Irish of New York City.* Cambridge, MA: MIT Press.

Gleason, Philip. 1980. American identity and Americanization. In *Harvard encyclopedia of American ethnic groups,* ed. Stephen Thernstrom, Ann Orlov, and Oscar Handlin, 31–58 Cambridge, MA: Belknap Press of Harvard University Press.

Goldberg, David T. 1990. The social formation of racist discourse. In *Anatomy of racism,* ed. David T. Goldberg, 295–318. Minneapolis: University of Minnesota Press.

———. 1994a. Multiculturalism: A critical reader. Oxford, UK: Blackwell.

———. 1994b. Introduction: Multicultural conditions. In Goldberg 1994a.

Goldstein, David. 2007. Introduction to *Complicating constructions: Race, ethnicity, and hybridity in American text,* ed. David S. Goldstein and Audrey B. Thacker. Seattle: University of Washington Press.

Goldstein, Eric L. 2006. *The price of whiteness: Jews, race, and American identity.* Princeton, NJ: Princeton University Press.

González Casanova, Pablo. 1965. Internal colonialism and national development. *Studies in Comparative International Development* 1 (4): 27–37.

Goodell, William. 1968. *Slavery and anti-slavery; A history of the great struggle in both hemispheres, with a view of the slavery question in the United States.* New York: Negro Universities Press.

Gossett, Thomas F. 1963. *Race: The history of an idea in America.* Dallas, TX: Southern Methodist University Press.

Gregory, Steven, and Roger Sanjek, eds. 1994. *Race.* New Brunswick, NJ: Rutgers University Press.

Gressgård, Randi. 2008. Mind the gap: Intersectionality, complexity and "the event." *Theory and Science* 10 (1). http://theoryandscience.icaap.org/currentissue.php.

Griffin, Larry F., and Katharine McFarland. 2007. "In my heart I'm an American": Regional attitudes and American identity. *Southern Culture* 13 (4): 119–37.

Gunew, Sneja. 1997. Postcolonialism and multiculturalism: Between race and ethnicity. *Yearbook of English Studies* 27: 22–39.

Hacker, Andrew. 2003. *Two nations: Black and white, separate, hostile, unequal.* New York: Scribner.

Hage, Ghassan. 1994. Locating multiculturalism's other: A critique of practical tolerance. *New Formations* 24 (1): 19–34.

———. 2005. White self-racialization as identity fetishism: Capitalism and the experience of colonial whiteness. In Murji and Solomos 2005, 185–206.

Hale, Elizabeth G. 1998. *Making whiteness: The culture of segregation in the south, 1890–1940.* New York: Vintage Books.

Hall, Stuart.1982. The rediscovery of ideology: Return of the repressed in media studies. In *Culture, society and the media*, ed. Michael Gurevitch, Tony Bennett, James Curran, and Janet Woollacott, 52–86. London: Methuen.

———. 1989. Ethnicity: Identity and difference. *Radical America* (Spring): 9–19.

———. 1997a. The spectacle of the "Other." In *Representation: Cultural representation and signifying practices*, ed. Stuart Hall, 223–90. London: Sage.

———.1997b. *Race, the floating signifier*. Northampton, MA: Media Education Foundation.

———. 2004. What is this "Black" in black popular culture? In Bobo, Hudley, and Michel 2004, 255–64.

Hamilton, Cynthia. 1996. Multiculturalism as political strategy. In Newfield and Gordon 1996, 167–77.

Hammonds, Evelynn M. 2004. Black (w)holes and the geometry of black female sexuality. In Bobo, Hudley, and Michel 2004, 301–14.

Handlin, Oscar. 1951. *The uprooted: The epic story of the great migrations that made the American people*. Boston: Little, Brown.

Handlin, Oscar, and Mary Handlin. 1950. Origins of the southern labor system. *William and Mary Quarterly* 7 (2): 199–222.

Haney-López, Ian F. 1996. *White by law: The legal construction of race*. New York: New York University Press.

Harding, Sandra G. 1991. *Whose science? Whose knowledge? Thinking from women's lives*. Ithaca, NY: Cornell University Press.

Harlan, John M. 1997. *Plessy v. Ferguson: A brief history with documents*, ed. Brook Thomas. Boston: Bedford/St. Martin's.

Harris, Cheryl I. 1993. Whiteness as property. *Harvard Law Review* 106 (8): 1707–91.

Harris, Laura A. 2002. Notes from a welfare queen in the ivory tower. In Anzaldúa and Keating 2002, 372–80.

Hartigan, John, Jr. 1999. Establishing the fact of whiteness. In Torres, Mirón, and Inda 1999, 183–99.

———. 2005. Culture against race: Reworking the basis for racial analysis. *South Atlantic Quarterly* 104 (3): 543–60.

Hartman, Andrew. 2004. The rise and fall of whiteness studies. *Race and Class* 46 (2): 22–38.

Hartmann, Douglas, and Joseph Gerteis. 2005. Dealing with diversity: Mapping multiculturalism in sociological terms. *Sociological Theory* 23 (2): 218–40.

Hartz, Louis. 1991. *The liberal tradition in America*. Harcourt Brace.

Hattam, Victoria. 2001. Theorizing race: Eliding ethnicity. *International Labor and Working-Class History* (60): 61–68.

———. 2007. *In the shadow of race: Jews, Latinos, and immigrant politics in the United States*. Chicago: University of Chicago Press.

Heideking, Jurgen. 1997. The image of the English enemy during the American Revolution. In *Enemy images in American history*, ed. Ragnhild Fiebig-von Hase and Ursula Lehmkuhl, 91–108. Providence, RI: Berghahn Books.

Hemingway, Ernest. 1990. *Green hills of Africa: Decorations by Edward Shenton*. Norwalk, CT: Easton Press.

Henry, Howell Meadoes. 1968. *Police control of the slave in South Carolina*. New York: Negro Universities Press.

Hernandez, Roger. 1997. Racism with good intensions a misguided policy. *The Victoria Advocate*, October 10.

Herrnstein, Richard J., and Charles Murray. 1994. *The bell curve: Intelligence and class structure in American life*. New York: Free Press.

Hewitt, Roger. 2005. *White backlash and the politics of multiculturalism*. Cambridge: Cambridge University Press.

Higginbotham, Evelyn Brooks. 1996. African-American women's history and the metalanguage of race. In *Feminism and history*, ed. Joan Wallach Scott, 183–208. New York: Oxford University Press.

Higham, John. 1975. *Send these to me: Jews and other immigrants in urban America*. New York: Atheneum.

———. 1994. *Strangers in the land: Patterns of American nativism, 1860–1925*. New Brunswick, NJ: Rutgers University Press.

Hirsch, Eric D., Jr. 1987. *Cultural literacy: What every American needs to know*. Boston: Houghton Mifflin.

Hoffmann, Stanley. 1997. More perfect union America. *Harvard International Review* 20 (1): 72–75.

Homes, Steven A. 1997a. Race panel excludes critics of affirmative action plans. *New York Times*, November 20.

———. 1997b. Clinton panels on race relations is itself biased, Gingrich says. *New York Times*, November 21.

———. 1997c. Conservative voices enter Clinton's dialogue on race. *New York Times*, December 18.

hooks, bell. 1981. *Ain't I a woman: Black woman and feminism*. Boston: South End Press.

———. 1990. *Yearning: Race, gender, and cultural politics*. Boston: South End Press.

———. 1992. *Black looks: Race and representation*. Boston: South End Press.

———. 1995. *Killing rage/Ending racism*. New York: Holt.

Horton, Merrill. 1994. Blackness, betrayal, and childhood: Race and identity in Nella Larden's passing. *CLA Journal* 28 (1): 31–45.

Howard, Benjamin C. (1857). Report of the Decision of the Supreme Court of the United States *and the opinions of the judges thereof in* the Case Dred Scott versus John F. A. Stanford. Washington, DC: Cornelius Wendell Printers.

Howe, David Walker. 1979. *The political culture of American Whigs*. Chicago: University of Chicago Press.

Huntington, Samuel P. 1996. *The clash of civilizations and the remaking of world order*. New York: Simon and Schuster.

———. 2004a. *Who are we? The challenges to America's national identity*. New York: Simon and Schuster.

———. 2004b. The Hispanic challenge. *Foreign Policy* 141:30–45.

Hurtado, Aída. 1999. The trickster's play: Whiteness in the subordination and liberation process. In Torres, Mirón, and Inda 1999, 225–43.

Ignatiev, Noel. 1995. *How the Irish became white*. New York: Routledge.

Ignatiev, Noel, and John Garvey. 1996. *Race traitor*. New York: Routledge.

Ingram, Penelope. 2001. Racializing Babylon: Settler whiteness and the "new racism." *New Literary History* 32 (1): 157–76.

Jacobs, Harriet A. 1973. *Incidents in the life of a slave girl*. New York: Harcourt Brace Jovanovich.

Jacobson, Matthew F. 1998. *Whiteness of a different color: European immigrants and the alchemy of race*. Cambridge, MA: Harvard University Press.

Jacoby, Tamar, ed. 2004a. *Reinventing the melting pot: The new immigrants and what it means to be American*. New York: Basic Books.

———. 2004b. What it means to be American in the 21st century. In Jacoby 2004a, 293–314.

Jay, John. 1787. Federalist Papers No. 2. Concerning dangers from foreign force and influence. *Independent Journal*, October 31. http://www.constitution.org/fed/federa02.htm.

Jefferson, Thomas. 1999. Notes on the state of Virginia. In *Documents of American prejudice: An anthology of writings on race from Thomas Jefferson to David Duke*, ed. S. T. Joshi, 3–11. New York: Basic Books.

Johnson, James Weldon. 1934. *Along this way*. New York: Viking.

———. 1990. *The autobiography of an ex-colored man*. New York: Penguin Books.

Joppke, Christian. 2004. The retreat of multiculturalism in the liberal state: Theory and policy. *British Journal of Sociology* 55 (2): 237–57.

Jordan, Winthrop D. 1962. Modern tensions and the origins of American slavery. *Journal of Southern History* 28 (February): 18–30.

———. 1968. *White over black: American attitudes toward the Negro, 1550–1812*. Chapel Hill: University of North Carolina Press.

Joshi, S. T., ed. 1999. *Documents of American prejudice: An anthology of writings on race from Thomas Jefferson to David Duke*. New York: Basic Books.

Kahlenberg, Richard D. 2001. How to achieve one America: Class, race, and the future of politics. In Renshon 2001, 335–43.

Kallen, Horace M. 1915a. Beyond the melting pot: A study of American nationality. *The Nations* 100 (February 18): 190–94.

———. 1915b. Democracy versus the melting pot. *The Nations*. (February 18): 190–98.

———. 1915c. Democracy versus the melting pot. *The Nations*. (February 25): 217–20.

———. 1924. *Culture and democracy in America*. New York: Boni and Liveright.

———. 1956. *Cultural pluralism and the American idea: An essay in social philosophy*. Philadelphia: University of Pennsylvania Press.

Kantrowitz, Barbara, and Pat Wingert. 2003. What's at stake. *Newsweek*, January 27.

Katz, William, L. 1986. *The invisible empire: The Ku Klux Klan's impact on History*. Washington, DC: Open Hand Publications.

Keating, AnaLouise. 1995. Interrogating "whiteness," (de)constructing "race." *College English* 57 (8): 901–18.

Kennedy, Randall. 1997. *Race, crime, and the law.* New York: Vintage Books.

Kerber, Linda K. 1997. The meaning of citizenships. *Journal of African American History* 84 (3): 833–54.

Kim, Claire Jean. 2000. Clinton's race initiative: Recasting the American dilemma. *Polity* 33 (2): 175–97.

———. 2004. Imagine race and nation in multiculturalist America. *Ethnic and Racial Studies* 27 (6): 987–1005.

King, Martin Luther, Jr. 1964. *Why we can't wait.* New York: New American Library.

Kingston, Maxine Hong. 1976. *The woman warrior: Memoirs of a girlhood among ghosts.* New York: Vintage Books.

Kinkead, Gwen. 1992. *Chinatown: A portrait of a closed society.* New York: HarperCollins.

Knight, Frederick. 2004. Justifiable homicide, police brutality, or governmental repression? The 1962 Los Angeles police shooting of seven members of the nation of Islam. In Bobo, Hudley, and Michel 2004, 139–52.

Kristeva, Julia. 1991. *Strangers to ourselves.* Trans. Leon S. Roudiez. New York: Columbia University Press.

Kristol, Irving. 1991. The tragedy of multiculturalism. *Wall Street Journal,* July 31.

Kymlicka, Will. 1989. *Liberalism, community, and culture.* Oxford, UK: Clarendon Press.

———. 1995. *Multicultural citizenship: A liberal theory of minority rights.* Oxford, UK: Clarendon Press.

———. 2007. *Multicultural odysseys: Navigating the new international politics of diversity.* New York: Oxford University Press.

Lander, Christian. 2008. *Stuff white people like.* Prahran, Victoria, Australia: Hardie Grant Books.

Lane, Christopher, ed. 1998a. *The psychoanalysis of race.* New York: Columbia University Press.

———. 1998b. The psychoanalysis of race: An introduction. In Lane 1998a, 1–37.

Larsen, Nella. 1929. *Passing.* New York: Knopf.

Lauber, Almon W. 1969. *Indian slavery in colonial times within the present limits of the United State.* New York: AMS Press.

Law, Ian. 2002. *Race in the news.* Basingstoke, UK: Palgrave Macmillan.

Lazarre, Jane. 1996. *Beyond the whiteness of whiteness: Memoir of a white mother of black sons.* Durham, NC: Duke University Press.

Lee, James Kyung-Jin. 2004. *Urban triage: Race and the fictions of multiculturalism.* Minneapolis: University of Minnesota Press.

Lewis Mumford Center. 2001, April 3. Ethnic diversity grows, neighborhood integration is at a standstill. http://mumford1.dyndns.org/cen2000/WholePop/WPreport/1.html.

Lipsitz, George. 1995. The possessive investment in whiteness: Racialized social democracy and the "white" problem in American studies. *American Quarterly* 47 (3): 369–87.

————. 1998. *The possessive investment in whiteness: How white people profit from identity politics*. Philadelphia: Temple University Press.

Litwack, Leon F. 1965. *North of slavery: The Negro in the free states, 1790–1860*. Chicago: University of Chicago Press.

————. 1998. *Trouble in mind: Black southerners in the age of Jim Crow*. New York: Knopf.

Lorde, Audre. 1984. *Sister outsider: Essays and speeches*. Trumansburg, NY: Crossing Press.

Lott, Eric. 2001. The new liberalism in America: Identity politics in the "vital center." In Rasmussen, Nexica, Klinenberg, and Wray 2001, 214–33.

Loury, Glenn C. 2002. *The anatomy of racial inequality*. Cambridge, MA: Harvard University Press.

Lowndes, Mary. 1913. Slavery. *The Englishwomen* 17 (51): 241–53.

MacMillan, Liz. 1995. Lifting the veil of whiteness: Growing body of scholarship challenges racial "norm." *Chronicle of Higher Education*, September 6, A23.

Mailer, Norman. 1957. The white Negro: Superficial reflections on the hipster. *Dissent* 4 (3): 276–93.

Mamdani, Mahmood. 2004. *Good Muslim, Bad Muslim: America, the cold war, and the roots of terror*. New York: Pantheon Books.

Mandel, Michael J. 2005. The melting pot is still melting. *Business Week*, July 7, 23. http://www.businessweek.com/magazine/content/05_50/b3963121.htm.

Mann, Arthur. 1992. From immigration to acculturation. In *Making America: The society & culture of the United States*, ed. Luther S. Luedtke, 62–82. Chapel Hill: University of North Carolina Press.

Marable, Manning. 1992. Multicultural democracy: The emerging majority for justice and peace. In *The crisis of color and democracy: Essays on race, class and power*, by Manning Marable. Monroe, ME: Common Courage Press.

————. 2000. *Problems in race, political economy, and society: How capitalism underdeveloped black America*. Boston: South End Press.

————. 2004. Racism and sexism. In Rothenberg 2004, 160–65.

Marcuse, Herbert. 1965. Repressive tolerance. In *A critique of pure tolerance*, ed. Robert Paul Wolff, Barrington Moore, and Herbert Marcuse, 81–117. Boston: Beacon Press.

Martin, Jerry L., and Anne D. Neal. 2001. *Defending civilization: How our universities are failing America and what can be done about it*. Washington, DC: American Council of Trustees and Alumni, 2001. http://www.goacta.org.

Martindale, Carolyn. 1986. *The white press and black America*. New York: Greenwood Press.

Martinot, Steve, and Jared Sexton. 2003. The avant-garde of white supremacy. *Social Identity* 9 (2): 169–81.

Marx, Gary T. 1967. The white Negro and the Negro white. *Phylon* 28 (2): 168–77.

Massey, Douglas S. 2004. The American side of the bargain. In Jacoby 2004, 111–22.

Massey, Douglas S., and Nancy A. Denton. 1993. *American apartheid: Segregation and the making of the underclass*. Cambridge, MA: Harvard University Press.

Mayo-Smith, Richard. 1894. Assimilation of nationalities in the United States. *Political Science Quarterly* 9 (3): 426–44.

McDowell, Deborah E. 2001. New directions for black feminist criticism. In *Black feminist cultural criticism*, ed. Jacqueline Bobo, 24–37. Malden, MA: Blackwell.

McIntosh, Peggy. 2007. White privilege: Unpacking the invisible knapsack. In Rothenberg 2007, 177–82.

McKinney, Karyn D. 2003. "I feel 'whiteness' when I hear people blaming whites": White as cultural victimization. *Race and Society* 6: 39–55.

McLaren, Peter. 1994. White terror and oppositional agency: Towards a critical multiculturalism. In Goldberg 1994a, 45–74.

———. 1999. Unthinking whiteness, rethinking democracy: Critical citizenship in gringolandia. In *Becoming and unbecoming white: Owning and disowning a racial identity*, ed. Christine Clark and James O'Donnell, 10–54. Westport, CT: Bergin and Garvey.

———. 2001. Wayward multiculturalists: A reply to Gregor McLennan. *Ethnicities* 1 (3): 408–19.

McLennan, Gregor. 2001. Can there be a "critical" multiculturalism? *Ethnicities* 1 (3): 389–422.

Memmi, Albert. 1965. *The colonizer and the colonized*. Boston: Beacon Press.

Mercer, Kobena. 1991. "1968": Periodizing postmodern politics and identity. In *Cultural studies*, ed. Lawrence Grossberg, Cary Nelson, and Paula Treichler, 424–49. New York: Routledge.

———. 1992. Skin head sex thing: Racial difference and the homoerotic imaginary. In *How do I look?* ed. Bad Object-Choices, 169–222. Seattle, WA: Bay Press.

———. 1994. *Welcome to the jungle: New positions in black cultural studies*. New York: Routledge.

Michaels, Walter Benn. 1992. Race into culture: A critical genealogy of cultural identity. *Critical Inquiry* 18 (4): 655–85.

———. 1996. Posthistoricism: The end of history. *Transition* 70 (2): 4–19.

———. 1998. Autobiography of an ex-white man. *Transition* 73 (1): 122–43.

Mileczarek-Desai, Shefali. 2002. Living fearlessly with and within differences: My search for identity beyond categories and contradictions. In Anzaldúa and Keating 2002, 136–35.

Miles, Jack. 1992. Black vs. brown: African Americans and Latinos. *Atlantic Monthly*, October, 41–47.

Miles, Robert. 1982. *Racism and migrant labour*. London: Routledge and Kegan Paul.

———. 1988. Racism, Marxism, and British politics. *Economy and Society* 17 (3): 428–60.

———. 1989. *Racism*. London: Routledge.

Miles, Robert, and Rodolfo D. Torres. 1999. Does "race" matter? Transatlantic perspectives on racism after "race relations." In Torres, Mirón, and Inda 1999, 19–38.

Miller, Jean Baker. 2004. Domination and subordination. In Rothenberg 2004, 110–16.

Mills, Charles W. 1997. *The racial contract*. Ithaca, NY: Cornell University Press.

———. 2004. Racial exploitation and the wages of whiteness. In Yancy 2004a, 25–54.

Minh-ha, Trinh T. 1989. *Woman, native, other: Writing postcoloniality and feminism*. Bloomington: Indiana University Press.

———. 1996. An acoustic journey. In *Rethinking borders*, ed. John C. Welchman, 1–17. Minneapolis: University of Minnesota Press.

Mirandé, Alfredo. 1985. *The Chicano experience: An alternative perspective*. Notre Dame, IN: University of Notre Dame Press.

Mirón, Louis F. 1999. Postmodernism and the politics of racialized identities. In Torres, Mirón, and Inda 1999, 79–99.

Mohanty, Chandra Talpade. 1991. Introduction: Cartographies of struggle. In *Third world women and the politics of feminism*, ed. Chandra Talpade Mohanty, Ann Russo, and Lourdes Torres, 1–47. Bloomington: Indiana University Press.

———. 1993. On race and voice: Challenges for liberal education in the 1990s. In *Beyond a dream deferred: Multicultural education and the politics of excellence*, ed. Becky W. Thompson and Sangeeta Tyagi, 41–65. Minneapolis: University of Minnesota Press.

———. 2004. *Feminism without borders: Decolonizing theory, practicing solidarity*. Durham, NC: Duke University Press.

Montagu, Ashley. 1997. *Man's most dangerous myths: The fallacy of race*. 6th ed. London: Altamira Press.

Montgomery, David. 2000. Empire, race, and working-class mobilizations. In *Racializing class, classifying race: Labour and difference in Britain, the USA and Africa*, ed. Peter Alexander and Rick Halpern, 1–31. Houndsmill, UK: Palgrave Macmillan.

Moore, Wilbert E., and Robin M. Williams. 1942. Stratification in the ante-bellum south. *American Sociological Review* 7 (3): 343–51.

Moraga, Cherríe. 1983. *Loving in the war years*. Boston: South End Press.

Moreton-Robinson, Aileen. 2008. Writing off treaties: White possession in the United States critical whiteness studies literature. In *Transnational whiteness matters: Mythunderstanding*, ed. Aileen Moreton-Robinson, Maryrose Casey, and Fiona Nicoll, 81–96. New York: Lexington Books.

Morgan, Edmund S. 1975. *American slavery, American freedom: The ordeal of colonial Virginia*. New York: Norton.

Morrison, Toni. 1987. *Beloved*. New York: Penguin Books.

———. 1993. *Playing in the dark: Whiteness and the literary imagination*. Cambridge, MA: Harvard University Press.

Morsy, Sohier A. 1994. Beyond the honorary "white" classification of Egyptians: Societal identity in historical context. In Gregory and Sanjek 1994, 175–98.

Moses, Wilson Jeremiah. 1978. *The golden age of black nationalism, 1850–1925*. New York: Oxford University Press.

Mouffe, Chantal. 2005. *The return of the political*. New York: Verso Press.

Moya, Paula M. L. 1997. Postmodernism, "realism," and the politics of identity: Cherríe Moraga and chicana feminism. In *Feminist genealogies, colonial legacies*, *democratic futures*, ed. Chandra Mohanty and M. Jacqui Alexander, 125–50. New York: Routledge.

Moynihan, Daniel P. 1965. *The Negro family: The case for national action.* Washington, DC: Office of Policy Planning and Research, United States Department of Labor.

Mullen, Harryette. 1994. Optie white: Blackness and the production of whiteness. *Diacritics* 24 (2–3): 71–89.

Murji, Karim, and John Solomos, eds. 2005. *Racialization: Studies in theory and practice.* New York: Oxford University Press.

Myrdal, Gunnar. 1962. *An American dilemma: The Negro problem and modern democracy.* New York: Harper & Row.

Nafficy, Hamid. 1993. *The making of exile cultures: Iranian television in Los Angeles.* Minneapolis: University of Minnesota Press.

Nakayama, Thomas K., and Judith N. Martin, eds. 1999. *Whiteness: The communication of social identity.* Thousand Oaks, CA: Sage.

Nancy, Jean-Luc.1994. Cut throat sun. In *An other tongue: Nation and ethnicity in the linguistic borderlands*, ed. Alfred Arteaga, 113–24. Durham, NC: Duke University Press.

Nayak, Annop. 2005. Whites lives. In Murji and Solomos 2005, 141–62.

Nelson, Dana. 1994. *The world in black and white: Reading "race" in American literature, 1638–1862.* New York: Oxford University Press.

Neubeck, Kenneth J., and Noel A. Cazenave. 2001. *Welfare racism: Playing the race card against America's poor.* New York: Routledge.

Newfield, Christopher, and Avery F. Gordon, eds. 1996a. *Mapping multiculturalism.* Minneapolis: University of Minnesota Press.

———. 1996b. Multiculturalism's unfinished business. In Newfield and Gordon 1996a, 1–16.

New York Times. 2008. Barack Obama's view on race. March 18.

Noel, Daniel L., ed. 1972. *The origins of American slavery and racism.* Columbus, OH: Merrill.

Nussbaum, Martha C. 1996. Patriotism and cosmopolitanism. In *For love of country: Debating the limits of patriotism. Martha C. Nussbaum with respondents*, ed. Joshua Cohen. Boston: Beacon Press.

Obama, Barack. 2004. Remarks to the Democratic National Convention. *New York Times*, July 27.

Okin, Susan Moller. 1999. *Is multiculturalism bad for women.* Princeton, NJ: Princeton University Press.

Omi, Michael. 1996. Racialization in the post–civil rights era. In Newfield and Gordon 1996, 178–86.

Omi, Michael, and Howard Winant. 1994. *Racial formation in the United States from the 1960s to the 1990s.* New York: Routledge.

Osajima, Keith. 2007. Internalized racism. In Rothenberg 2007, 138–43.

Outlaw, Lucius T., Jr. 2004. Rehabilitate racial whiteness? In Yancy 2004, 159–72.

Parekh, Bhikhu. 2000. *Rethinking multiculturalism: Cultural diversity and political theory.* Cambridge, MA: Harvard University Press.

————. 2007. Multiculturalism. In *What more philosophers think*, ed. Julian Baggini and Jeremy Strangroom, 45–56. London: Continuum.

Park, Robert E. 1930. Assimilation. In *Encyclopedia of the Social Sciences*. Vol. 2, ed. Edwin R. Seligman and Alvin Johnson, 282. New York: Macmillan.

————. 1950. *Race and culture*. New York: Free Press.

Parker, David, and Miri Song. 2001. *Rethinking "mixed race."* London: Pluto Press.

Parry, Benita. 1987. Problems in current theories of colonial discourse. *Oxford Literacy Review* 9 (1–2): 27–58.

Patterson, Orlando. 1982. *Slavery and social death: A comparative study*. Cambridge, MA: Harvard University Press.

————. 2000. Race over. *New Republic*, January 10.

Payne, Richard J. 1998. *Getting beyond race: The changing American culture*. Boulder, CO: Westview Press.

————. 2001. Moving beyond racial categories. In Renshon 2001, 143–68.

Pellegrini, Ann. 1997. *Performance anxieties: Staging psychoanalysis, staging race*. New York: Routledge.

Perin, Constance. 1988. *Belonging in America: Reading between the lines*. Madison: University of Wisconsin Press.

Philippe, Rushton J. 1995. *Race evaluation and behavior: A life history perspective*. New Brunswick, NJ: Transaction.

Phillips, Anne. 2007. *Multiculturalism without culture*. Princeton, NJ: Princeton University Press.

Pinder, Sherrow O. 2007. *From welfare to workfare: How capitalist states create a pool of unskilled cheap labor (a Marxist feminist social analysis)*. Lewiston, NY: Edwin Mellen Press.

Piper, Adrian. 1992. Passing for white: Passing for black. *Transition* 58 (Summer): 4–32.

Podhoretz, Norman. 1997. My Negro problem—and ours. In *The essential neoconservative reader*, ed. Mark Gerson and James Q. Wilson, 5–22. New York: Basic Books.

Post, Robert C., with K. Anthony Appiah, Judith Butler, Thomas C. Grey, and Reva B. Siegel. 2001a. *Prejudicial appearances: The logic of American antidiscrimination law*. Durham, NC: Duke University Press.

Post, Robert C. 2001b. Prejudicial appearances: The logic of American antidiscrimination law. In Post 2001a, 1–53.

Poulter, Sebastian. 1987. Ethnic minority customs, English law, and human rights. *International and Comparative Law Quarterly* 36 (3): 589–615.

Powell, John A. 1999. The colorblind multiracial dilemma: Racial categories reconsidered. In Torres, Miron, and Inda 1999, 141–57.

Prashad, Vijay. 2000. *The karma of brown folk*. Minneapolis: University of Minnesota Press.

Quadagno, Jill. 1994. *The color of welfare: How racism undermined the war on poverty*. New York: Oxford University Press.

Rai, Amit S. 1998. "Thus spake the subaltern . . .": Postcolonial criticism and the scene of desire. In Lane 1998a, 91–119.

Ramsay, David. 1809. *The history of South Carolina from its first settlement in 1670 to the year 1808*. Vol. 1. Charleston, SC: David Longworth.

Rasmussen, Birgit Brander, Irene J. Nexica, Eric Klinenberg, and Matt Wray, eds. 2001a. *The Making and unmaking of whiteness*. Durham, NC: Duke University Press.

———. 2001b. Introduction to Rasmussen, Nexica, Klinenberg, and Wray 2001a.

Ravitch, Diane. 1990. Multiculturalism e pluribus plures. *American Scholar* 59 (3): 337–54.

Raz, Joseph. 1994. *Ethics in the public domain: Essays in the morality of law and politics*. Oxford, UK: Clarendon Press.

Reed, Adolph Jr. 2001. Response to Arnesen. *International Labor and Working-Class History*, no. 60: 69–80.

Reid, Ira De Augustine. 1969. *The Negro immigrant, his background, characteristics, and social adjustment, 1899–1937*. New York: Arno Press.

Renshon, Stanley A. 2000. American character and national identity: The dilemmas of cultural diversity. In *Political psychology: Cultural and crosscultural foundations*, ed. Stanley A. Renshon and John Duckitt, 285–308. London: Macmillan.

———, ed. 2001. *One America? Political leadership, national identity, and the dilemmas of diversity*. Washington, DC: Georgetown University Press.

Richardson, Charles F. 2007. *The development of American thought*. Vol. 2 of *American literature, 1607–1885*. Whitefish, MT: Kessinger.

Riggs, Damien W. 2004. "We don't talk about race anymore": Power, privilege and critical whiteness studies. *Borderlines* 3 (2). http//www.borderlandsejournal. Adelaide.edu.au/issues/vol3no2.html.

Roediger, David R. 1991. *The wages of whiteness: Race and the making of the American working class*. New York: Verso Press.

———. 1993. Race and the working-class past in the United States: Multiple identities and the future of labor history. *International Review of Social History*, no. 38:127–43.

———. 1994. *Towards the abolition of whiteness: Essays on race, politics, and working class history*. New York: Verso Press.

———. 1998. *Black on white: Black writers and what it means to be white*. New York: Schocken Books.

———. 2002. *Colored white: Transcending the racial past*. Berkeley and Los Angeles: University of California Press.

———. 2005. *Working towards whiteness: How America's immigrants became white. The strange journey from Ellis Island to the suburbs*. New York: Basic Books.

———. 2006. Whiteness and its complications. *Chronicle of Higher Education*, July 14, 6–8.

Roosevelt, Theodore R. 1915, October 12. Hyphenated Americanism. http://home .comcast/net/ñhprman/tr.htm#top.

Rothenberg, Paula S., ed. 2007. *Race, class, and gender in the United States: An integrated study*. New York: Worth.

Russell, John H. 1913. *Free Negroes in Virginia, 1619–1865*. Baltimore: Johns Hopkins University Press.

Sáenz, Benjamin Alire. 1997. In the borderlands of chicano identity, there are only fragments. In *Border theory: The limits of cultural politics*, ed. Scott Michaelsen and David E. Johnson, 68–96. Minneapolis: University of Minnesota Press.

Said, Edward W. 1993. *Culture and imperialism*. New York: Knopf.

———. 1994. *The politics of dispossession: The struggle for Palestinian self-determination, 1969–1994*. New York: Vintage Books.

Sanchez, Marcela. 2005. Demonizing dual citizenship. *Washington Post*, October 27.

Sartwell, Crispin. 1998. *Act like you know: African American autobiography and white identity*. Chicago: University of Chicago Press.

Schildkraut, Deborah J. 2007. Defining American identity in the twenty-first century: How much "there" is there? *Journal of Politics* 69 (3): 597–616.

Schlesinger, Arthur M., Jr. 1945. *The age of Jackson*. Boston: Little, Brown.

———. 1998. *The disuniting of America: Reflections on a multicultural society*. New York: W. W. Norton.

———. 2002. The return to the melting pot. In *Debating diversity: Clashing perspectives on race and ethnicity in America*, ed. Ronald Takaki, 257–59. New York: Oxford University Press.

Schram, Sanford F. 2003. Putting a black face on welfare: The good and the bad. In *Race and the Politics of Welfare Reform*, ed. Sanford F. Schram, Joe Soss, and Richard C. Fording, 196–221. Ann Arbor: University of Michigan Press.

Schuck, Peter H., and Rogers M. Smith. 1985. *Citizenship without consent: Illegal aliens in the American polity*. New Haven, CT: Yale University Press.

Schwarz, Benjamin. 1995. The diversity myth: America's leading export. *Atlantic Monthly*, May, 57–67.

Sechi, Joanne Harumi. 1980. Being Japanese-American doesn't mean "made in Japan." In *The third woman: Minority women writers of the United States*, ed. Dexter Fisher, 442–49. Boston: Houghton Mifflin.

Segrest, Mab. 2001. The souls of white folks. In Rasmussen, Nexica, Klinenberg, and Wray 2001, 43–71.

Sekhon, Vijay. 2003. The civil rights of "others": Antiterrorism, the Patriot Act, and Arab and South Asian Americans rights in post-9/11 American society. *Texas Forum on Civil Liberties and Civil Rights* 8 (1): 117–48.

Seshadri-Crooks, Kalpana. 1998. The comedy of domination: Psychoanalysis and the conceit of whiteness. In Lane 1998a, 353–79.

Shah, Sonia. 2007. Asian American? In Rothenberg 2007, 221–23.Siegel, Reva B. 2001. Discrimination in the eyes of the law: How "color blindness" discourse disrupts and rationalizes social stratification. In Post 2001a, 99–152.

Silberman, Charles. 1964. *Crisis in black and white*. New York: Random House.

Sio, Arnold T. 1965. Interpretations of slavery: The slave status in the Americas. *Comparative Studies in Society and History* 7 (3): 289–308.

Sivanandan, Ambalavaner. 1982. *A different hunger: Writings on black resistance*. London: Pluto Press.

Sleeper, Jim. 2001. American national identity in a postnational age. In Renshon 2001, 308–34.

Small, Stephen. 1999. The contour of racialization: Structures, representations and resistance in the United States." In Torres, Mirón, and Inda 1999, 47–64.

Smith, Rogers M. 1988. The "American creed" and American identity: The limits of liberal citizenship in the United States. *Western Political Quarterly* 47 (2): 225–51.

———. 1993. Beyond Tocqueville, Myrdal, and Hartz: The multiple traditions. *American Political Science Review* 87 (3): 549–66.

———. 1997. *Civic ideals: Conflicting visions of citizenship in U.S. history*. New Haven, CT: Yale University Press.

———.1999. Toward a More Perfect Union: Beyond Old Liberalism and New Liberalism. In *The new Liberalism and our Retreat from Racial Equality Without Justice for all*, ed. Adolph Reed Jr., 327–52. Boulder, CO: Westview Press.

Sollors, Werner. 1986. A critique of pure pluralism. In *Reconstructing American literary history*, ed. Sacvan Bercovitch, 250–79. Cambridge, MA: Harvard University Press.

Solow, Barbara Lewis, and Stanley L. Engerman, eds. 1987. *British capitalism and Caribbean slavery: The legacy of Eric Williams*. New York: Cambridge University Press.

Sothern, Billy. 2006. New Orleans abandoned its citizens in jail. *The Nation*, January 2.

Sowell, Thomas. 1981. *Ethnic America: A history*. New York: Basic Books.

———. 1994. *Race and culture: A world view*. New York: Basic Books.

Spelman, Elizabeth. 1988. *Inessential women problems of exclusion in feminist thought*. Boston: Beacon Press.

Spencer, Martin E. 1994. Multiculturalism, "political correctness," and the politics of identity. *Sociological Forum* 9 (4): 547–67.

Spencer, Stephen. 2002. The discourse of whiteness: Chinese-American history, Pearl S. Buck, and *The Good Earth*. *Americana: The Journal of American Popular Culture, 1900 to Present* 1 (1). http://www.americanpopularculture.com/journal/index.htm.

Spivak, Gayatri C. 1988. Can the subaltern speak? In *Marxism and the interpretation of culture*, ed. Cary Nelson and Lawrence Grossberg, 271–313. Urbana: University of Illinois Press.

———. 1990a. *The post-colonial critic: Interviews, strategies, dialogues*. Ed. Sarah Harasym. New York: Routledge.

———. 1990b. Gayatri Spivak on the politics of the subaltern. *Socialist Review* 20 (3): 81–97.

Stallybrass, Peter, and Allon White. 1986. *The politics and poetics of transgression*. Ithaca, NY: Cornell University Press.

Steinberg, Stephen. 1989. *The ethnic myth: Race, ethnicity, and class in America*. Boston: Beacon Press.

Steinward, Jonathan. 1997. The future of nostalgia in Friedrich Schlegel's gender theory: Casting German aesthetics beyond ancient Greek and modern Europe. In *Narratives of nostalgia, gender, and nationalism*, ed. Suzanne Kehde and Jean Pickering, 9–29. New York: New York University Press.

Stephanson, Anders. 1989. Interview with Cornel West. In *Universal abandon? The politics of postmodernism*, ed. Andrew Ross, 269–84. Minneapolis: University of Minnesota Press.

Stoler, Ann. 1996. *Race and the education of desire: Foucault's history of sexuality and the colonial order of things*. Durham, NC: Duke University Press.

Stomajor, Sonia. 2002. A Latina judge's voice. *Berkeley La Raza Law Journal* 13 (1): 87–93.

Stonequest, Everett V. 1935. The problem of the marginal man. *American Journal of Sociology* 41 (1): 1–12.

Takagi, Dana Y. 1992. *The retreat from race: Asian-Americans admissions and racial politics*. New Brunswick, NJ: Rutgers University Press.

Takaki, Ronald. 1979. *Iron cages: Race and culture in nineteenth-century America*. New York: Knopf.

———. 1987. *From different shores: Perspectives on race and ethnicity in America*. New York: Oxford University Press.

———. 1993. *A different mirror: A history of multicultural America*. Boston: Little, Brown.

———. 1998. *A larger memory: A history of our diversity, with voices*. New York: Little, Brown.

Tatum, Beverly Daniel. 2004. Talking about race, learning about racism: The application of racial identity development theory in the classroom. In Bobo, Hudley, and Michel 2004, 389–410.

Taylor, Charles. 1992. *Multiculturalism and the politics of recognition: An essay*. Princeton, NJ. Princeton University Press.

———.1994. *Multiculturalism: Examining the politics of recognition*, with commentaries by K. Anthony Appiah, Jürgen Habermas, Steven C. Rockefeller, Michael Walzer, and Susan Wolf. Ed. Amy Gutmann. Princeton, NJ: Princeton University Press.

Tehranian, John. 2008. *Whitewashed: America's invisible middle eastern minority*. New York: New York University Press.

The New Republic. 1991. "Mr. Sobol's planet," July 15 & 22.

Thernstrom, Stephen, and Abigail Thernstrom. 1997. *America in black and white: One nation, indivisible*. New York: Touchstone Books.

Tingfang, Wu. 1914. *America through the spectacles of an oriental diplomat*. New York: Frederick A. Stokes Co.

Tocqueville, Alexis de. 1945. *Democracy in America*. Vol. 2. New York: Knopf.

———.1999. Democracy in America. In *Documents of American prejudice: An anthology of writings on race from Thomas Jefferson to David Duke*, ed. S. T. Joshi, 12–16. New York: Basic Books.

Tonry, Michael. 1995. *Malign neglect: Race, crime, and punishment in America*. New York: Oxford University Press.

Torres, Rodolfo D., Louis F. Mirón, and Jonathan Xavier Inda, eds. 1999. *Race, identity, and citizenship: A reader*. Malden, MA: Wiley-Blackwell.

Towers, Frank. 1998 Projecting whiteness: Race, and the state of labor history. *Journal of American Culture* 21 (2): 47–57.

Troyna, Barry. 1992. Can you see the join? An historical analysis of multicultural and anti-racist education policies. In *Racism and education: Structures and strategies* ed. Dawn Gill, Barbara Mayor, and Maud Blair, 63–91. London: Sage.

Tuan, Mia. 1998. *Forever foreigners or honorary whites? The Asian ethnic experience today.* New Brunswick, NJ: Rutgers University Press.

Turner, Richard B. 2004. Islam in the African-American experience. In Bobo, Hudley, and Michel, 2004, 445–71.

Twain, Mark. 1962. *The adventures of Huckleberry Finn.* New York: Macmillan.

van Dijk, Teun A. 1993. Principles of critical discourse analysis. *Discourse and Society* 4 (2): 249–83.

Van Evrie, John H. 1863. *Negroes and Negro "slavery": The first an inferior race: The latter its normal condition.* New York: Van Evrie, Horton & Co.

Vaughan, Alden T. 1989. The origins debate: Slavery and racism in seventeenth-century Virginia. *Virginia Magazine of History and Biography* 97 (3): 311–54.

Vickerman, Milton. 1998. *Crosscurrents: West Indian immigrants and race.* New York: Oxford University Press.

Wacquant, Loïc. 2002. From slavery to mass incarceration: Rethinking the "race question" in the US. *New Left Review*, no. 13:41–60.

Waldron, Jeremy. 1992. Minority cultures and the cosmopolitan alternative. *University of Michigan Journal of Law Reform* 25: 751–93.

Walzer, Michael. 1990. What does it means to be an "American"? *Social Research* 57 (3): 591–614.

———. 1997. *On toleration.* New Haven, CT: Yale University Press.

Waters, Mary C. 2000. *Black identities: West Indian immigrant dreams and American realities.* Cambridge, MA: Harvard University Press.

Wells-Barnett, Ida B. 1892. *Southern horrors. Lynch laws in all its phases.* New York: The New York Age Print.

———. 2005. *The red record.* Cirencester, UK: Echo Library.

Wendell, Barrett. 1968. *A literary history of America: New York, Scribner, 1900.* Detroit: Gale Research.

West, Cornel. 1992. Learning to talk of race. *New York Times Magazine*, August 2.

———. 2001. *Race matters.* New York: Vintage Press.

Westcott, Robyn. 2004 Witnessing whiteness: Articulating race and the politics of style. *Borderlines* 3 (2). http//www.borderlandsejournal.adelaide. edu.au/issues/vol3no2.html.

Wheeler, David L. 1995. A growing number of scientists reject the concept of race. In *Chronicle of Higher Education*, February 17.

White, James Boyd. 1994. *Justice as translation: An essay in cultural and legal criticism.* Chicago: University of Chicago Press.

Wickberg, Daniel. 2005. Heterosexual white male: Some recent inversions in American cultural history. *Journal of American History* 92 (1): 136–57.

Wiegman, Robyn. 1999 Whiteness studies and the paradox of particularity. *Boundary 2* 26 (2): 115–50.

Wieviorka, Michel. 1998. Is multiculturalism the solution? *Ethnic and Racial Studies* 21 (5): 881–910.

Wilkins, Roger. 2000. Racism has its privileges. In *The best of the nations*, ed. Victor Navasky and Katrina V. Heuvel 2000, 335–45. New York: Thunder's Month Press.

Williams, Eric. 1944. *Capitalism and slavery*. Chapel Hill: University of North Carolina Press.

Williams, George Washington. 1885. *History of the Negro race in America from 1619 to 1880*. New York: G. P. Putnam's Sons.

Wilson, Clint, and Felix Gutierrez. 1995. *Race, multiculturalism and the media: From mass to class communication*. Thousand Oaks, CA: Sage.

Wilson, William Julius. 1980. *The declining significance of race*. Chicago: University of Chicago Press.

Winant, Howard. 2001. White racial projects. In Rasmussen, Nexica, Klinenberg, and Wray 2001, 97–12.

Wray, Matt. 2006. *Not quite white: White trash and the boundaries of whiteness*. Durham, NC: Duke University Press.

Wright, Richard. 1937. *Black boy*. New York: Harper and Row.

Wright, Robert. 1994. *The moral animal: Evolutionary psychology and everyday life*. New York: Pantheon.

Wu, Frank H. 2002. *Yellow: Race in America beyond black and white*. New York: Basic Books.

Yamada, Mitsuye. 1992. *Camp notes and other writings*. New Brunswick, NJ: Rutgers University Press.

Yancy, George, ed. 2004a. *What white looks like: African-American philosophers on the whiteness question*. New York: Routledge.

———. 2004b. Introduction to Yancy 2004a.

———. 2004c. A Foucauldian (genealogical) reading of whiteness: The production of the black body/self and the racial deformation of Pecola Breedlove in Toni Morrison's *The Bluest Eye*. In Yancy 2004a, 107–42.

———. 2005. Whiteness and the return of the black body. *Journal of speculative philosophy* 19 (4): 215–41.

Young, Iris M. 1990. *Justice and the politics of difference*. Princeton, NJ: Princeton University Press.

Yuval-Davis, Nira. 1999. Ethnicity, gender relations and multiculturalism. In Torres, Mirón, and Inda 1999, 112–25.

Zangwell, Israel. 1909. *The melting pot, drama in four acts*. New York: Macmillan.

Žižek, Slavoj. 1993. *Tarrying with the negative: Kant, Hegel, and the critique of ideology*. Durham, NC: Duke University Press.

Index